Asian Values

An Encounter with Diversity

T0386365

Asian Values

An Encounter with Diversity

Edited by

Josiane Cauquelin
Paul Lim
Birgit Mayer-König

CURZON

A publication from *The European Institute for Asian Studies*

First Published in 1998
by Curzon Press
Richmond, Surrey
http://www.curzonpress.co.uk

Paperback edition 2000

Editorial matter © 1998 Josiane Cauquelin, Paul Lim and Birgit Mayer-König

Typeset in Stone Serif by LaserScript Ltd, Mitcham, Surrey
Printed and bound in Great Britain by
TJ International, Padstow, Cornwall

British Library Cataloguing in Publication Data
A catalogue record of this book is available from the British Library

ISBN 0-7007-1324-7

Contents

Preface

In recent years 'Asian values' have become a subject of discussion, particularly in Asia itself, and linked to the issue of human rights and a regard for ancient Asian cultures. Asian countries have grown in economic strength and have become world economic and political powers. The question is, how are ancient cultures and traditional values modified by modern developments, for example, under the impact of market forces, the consumer culture, and Westernization? Is there a conflict of values?

There is increasing awareness that a lack of understanding and acceptance of Asian values is an obstacle to closer relations between Asia and the West. Gaining a better understanding of Asian values will contribute to a deeper, more constructive and more beneficial relationship.

In this book we speak of 'Asia' in all its diversity, ranging from Pakistan to the Far East.[1] We are aware of a great variety of cultures and traditions. When some Asian governments speak of Asian values they mean the Confucian values which are relevant to them; they say that Western democracy is not an Asian value and is not appropriate for Asian countries. On the other hand, countries like the Philippines and India are proud of their democratic systems.

In *Asian Values: An Encounter with Diversity* we approach the subject in a multi-disciplinary way. In the first of nine chapters, the editors investigate the basic questions: what is meant by 'value' in Asia?; what are the origins of values?; what influence do different religions and philosophies have?; what is the distinction between religious and secular values?; what is the difference between values and codes of conduct?

ix

There is a need to understand the particular ways of thinking which determine values and codes of conduct. Three sections examine the Chinese way of thinking, in particular, the *yin* and *yang*, the way of thinking in South Asia and differences between the Western Cartesian and Eastern holistic philosophies. The influence of the values of Western education on Asian values since colonial times and the effects of the market economy are observed.

Chapter 2 discusses the debate on human rights, and the tendency to polarize the Western emphasis on individual rights and the Eastern focus on duties. Yash Ghai (Hong Kong) challenges this tendency by examining the meaning and implications of the notion of duty. He describes the different dimensions and values of a duty-based society, and argues that to understand its appeal, society must be placed in a historical and comparative context. He questions the contemporary assumptions that the notion of duty still pervades Asia; and asks how Asia's economic success can be attributed to Asian values when both Confucianism and Hinduism oppose the profit motive and the accumulation of wealth. Why do governments emphasize the notion of duty with regard to Confucianism and Hinduism? Surely it has much more to do with politics than culture, as can be seen from the various contradictions of policies and practices. Ghai gives three examples to illustrate this point: the communitarian argument, the conflation of the state with the community, and the market eroding the community.

Chapters 3, 4 5, and 6 discuss the philosophical and religious traditions of Buddhism, Confucianism, Islam and Hinduism. In Chapter 3 Thanh-Dam Truong (Den Haag) highlights in the first part two debates on Asian values, the Asian human rights debate and the 'inter-faith dialogue'. She argues that in the first debate, the process of re-traditionalization – reconstructing Asia and Europe as two separate and static entities – can be placed in binary opposition and mutual exclusion. She believes that this process is connected with attempts within Asia to forge a new economic and political entity. Discussing the second debate, Thanh-Dam Truong cites a statement by Pope John Paul II that 'Christ is absolutely original. He is the one mediator between God and humanity' and the observation by Thich Nhat Hanh that this stance 'excludes dialogue, fosters intolerance and discrimination between communities'. Thanh-Dam Truong shows how the terms of these two debates have changed over time, and outlines their implications for mutual understanding between Asia and Europe. In the second part of her chapter, she gives an account of the doctrine of the Four Noble Truths in Buddhism. A third part is dedicated to social justice as the main value in Buddhism which is 'not to be treated only within the parameter of law and order, but in the parameter of understanding and compassion'. Finally, the author offers the reader a panoramic description of the Socially Engaged Buddhist movement, which is spread throughout Asia including Sri Lanka and Thailand. She discusses the Tiep Hien Order of Vietnam in detail. In her conclusion she points out that the 'tolerance and openness of Buddhism which had been its political weakness has become its strength in its meeting with the West'.

In Chapter 4, Yang Baoyun (Beijing) interprets the value system of Chinese society from a holistic viewpoint. In the first section, he briefly recalls the decadent period in which this social morality developed and then introduces the scholars Mencius, Dong Zhonshu and Zhu Xi who presided over its evolution. In the second section, he distinguishes three value categories: ethical or moral, social and spiritual. These include among others the values relating to the rules of life in society and to reciprocity. He prescribes a set of values of which 'humanity' is the core. Yang Baoyun then deals with the negative influence of Confucianism. The moral, social and political order has, for him, kept Chinese technology in an experimental phase, preventing it from modernization. By citing the Master himself, 'when a man gets to the top, all his friends and relatives get there with him', the patrilineal/patrilocal system seems to have generated nepotism and corruption in China. In the last part, the author briefly describes the spreading of this doctrine to Vietnam, Korea and Japan and its impact on local thought. He cites, for example, the communist leader Ho Chi Minh who studied Confucius in his youth and maintained the precepts of the Master throughout his anti-colonialist struggle. Some Vietnamese intellectuals therefore assert that 'Ho's thoughts are the convergence of Confucius' theory and Marxism'. In his conclusion, Yang Baoyun establishes links between East and West and refers to the texts of the Chinese scholar Cai Yuanpei, who, at the turn of the century, compared the concepts of 'conscientiousness and altruism', 'humanity and benevolence', 'faithfulness and righteousness' in the cultural, ethical and moral Confucian tradition with the Western ideas of freedom, equality and universal fraternity.

In Chapter 5, Fateh M. Malik (Islamabad) investigates the twentieth-century's intellectual interpretation of Islam expressed by such eminent thinkers as M. Iqbal. He points out the prominent Muslim ideals of equality, tolerance and rationality. Equality does not acknowledge differences in race and status. It is directed towards universal brotherhood. Tolerance stresses respect for all scriptures and teachers of monotheism and advocates religious liberty. The Muslim doctrine that Muhammad is the final prophet is seen as an appeal to rationality. These ideals, according to Malik, show that democracy fits well with Islam, a fact which is exemplified by the modern Muslim republics of Pakistan and Bangladesh. In Islam, no distinction is made between sacred and secular. This gives rise to the demand for a Muslim nation which leaves no scope for a nationalism based on ethnic or territorial claims. In this non-distinction between the 'sacred' and the 'secular' , Malik observes that the roots of the prolonged conflict with the West are located in its 'dogma of secularism'. As Islam neither approves of a church institution nor of a privileged priesthood (with the exception of Iran: editors' note) it offers no basis for theocratic rule. Malik emphasizes the fact that Islam provides conditions very different from those of the Christian Church and he urges Westerners to notice this. The importance of the Prophet Muhammad is often underestimated in the West: he is venerated as the embodiment of all the Muslim values, he serves as a model to be imitated, and he binds the Muslim community together. Through Muhammad Islam becomes a distinct religion among other monotheistic teachings. Malik recognizes the 'wide gulf between the ideals of Islam and the realities of the present day Muslim world'. While he does not elaborate on the latter, he blames the unscrupulous striving for power on the 'self-serving ruling elite', beginning with *Umayyad* dynasty and their 'Arab imperialism'. The author also sees major problems because of the ignorance of Muslim values and continued prejudices in the West.

In Chapter 6, Debabrata Sen Sharma (Calcutta) gives an account of the values of Hinduism put forward in the vast corpus of ancient Sanskrit literature. He draws attention to the fact that the word 'Hindu' has been coined by outsiders, while the Indian tradition speaks of *sanatana dharma*, the 'eternal religion'. These teachings have a 'universal outlook' and are concerned with man irrespective of time and country. They arose from the intuitive vision of the seers and are directed towards overcoming misery and the attainment of the aims of life. These aims are living the good life in this world and discovering spiritual nature. In the course of time many currents of thought were incorporated into Hinduism, above all teachings from the tribes, the Buddhists and the Jains. Sen Sharma distinguishes three kinds of Hindu values: (1) moral or ethical, (2) spiritual, and (3) social values. These include among others (1) non-violence, truthfulness, non-stealing, self-control through redirection of thought, not through repression, (2) a renunciatory outlook on life, love; (3) unselfishness, respect for elders, hospitality, charity and mercy. According to Sen Sharma, self-purification gives way to deeper insight into the omnipresence of the Divine and from there to the experience of brotherhood and the oneness of all. No one set of values, however, is prescribed. Instead, the scriptures' advice is to observe the 'learned and wise people free from blemish' and follow the ways indicated by them. Without a codified dogma, Hinduism is tolerant and open-minded towards the views of others. Sen Sharma also explains the *Karma* doctrine. He discusses the caste system, its reference to different talents in ancient times, and its later misuse following Hindu law writers who replaced the old views with a 'rigid mode of class division'. The author observes a neglect of the old Hindu values by the modern urban elite, which favours consumerism.

Chapter 7 is written from a sociological point of view. Raul Pertierra (Manila) examines the effects of the market economy on society, and the extent of the changes it has caused. This case study of the Philippines as the only Catholic Asian country, describes contemporary Filipino culture as 'bricolage'. The author examines the role and implications of highly developed personal networks. Pertierra attributes the importance of the private domain to the ineffectualness of a weak state. He contrasts the personal network with the impersonal, anonymous and autonomous structure of relations exemplified by impersonal public institutions, with structures of communication enabling the rational basis for resource allocation' attributed to a strong and dominating state. This opposition between the so-called old and the new is applied to different fields throughout the chapter, for example, Pertierra examines the role of the middle class in the modern capitalist state. One might wonder whether it is the market which has brought the modern capitalist state apparatus and changes to societal mores to the Philippine. Pertierra speaks of the process of rejection, adaptation and cultural invention.

In the concluding chapters we ask whether – and for what reasons – there is greater interest in Asian cultures today in Europe. Is it only for economic ends? In Chapter 8, Karin Bogart (Brussels), discusses this question in 'Asian Values and their Impact on Business Practices in Asia'. The author concentrates on three areas: Japan, China and South-East Asia. Although history, geography and philosophies differ, these areas share a number of similarities. Bogart studies the origins of two cultures: the first is the rice-cultivating culture which brought collectivism and inter-group responsibilities; the second is Confucianism, the philosophy on which most of the value systems were founded. Bogart provides a brief summary of Japanese and Chinese history, and describes business customs and practice in both countries. Although Japan and China seem different in their methods of decision-making and negotiation, both rely on family and/or geographical networks. Bogart then turns to South-East Asia, and looks briefly at Malaysia and Thailand. She chose to study Malaysia, as an example of a multi-racial society of Malays, Chinese and Indians; and Thailand, as a Buddhist country where the Chinese have integrated into society and business and is dominated by the Sino-Thai community. The author recalls that Thailand has never fallen under colonial rule. Bogart's study allows comparison between two sets of countries, first China and Japan and second Thailand and Malaysia, and between the countries themselves.

In Chapter 9, Willy Vande Walle (Leuven) examines the historical background of the relations between Europe and Asia from antiquity to pre-colonial times. This was the period when the relationship between Europe and Asia was held in a balance making it 'more attractive as a framework for finding prefigurations of the present-day relationship'. To illustrate this balanced relationship, the author tries to show how Asia influenced Europe in the Enlightenment. Vande Walle refers to the work of authors like Joseph Needham and his colleagues showing Western civilization's indebtedness to the Asian heritage. He illustrates this balanced relationship in terms of intellectual exchange by studying the Jesuits' venture into Asia particularly India, Japan and China. He does not avoid the negative side of Europe's relations with Asia: he speaks of Asians wanting 'to be left to mind their own business' while 'the Westerners tried to convert the Asians to their own tenets and beliefs or to lure them into commercial dealings that were beneficial to themselves'. Concepts like 'brotherhood of men', or even less far-flung notions like 'mutual cultural enrichment', 'exchange of ideas' or 'communication' were not the main motives of the relationship; 'Securing trading privileges from local kings and potentates involved much conflict and possession and administration of territory frictional'. In pre-colonial times, this relationship can only be described in terms of power, competition and conflict. Nevertheless, it was held in balance until the beginning of the nineteenth century. It is only by improving our understanding of the past that we can develop useful perspectives for the future.

In *Asian Values* we look at the roots of values and traditions, as well as developments in Asia. The contributions from authors of different Asian countries on a variety of topics, attempt to give justice to this demanding subject. The editors are fully aware that these investigations need to be continued, enlarged, and deepened in all respects. The arguments put forward in this book may indicate the lines along which further studies of Asian values could be conducted in a fruitful way.

Josiane Cauquelin, Paul Lim and Birgit Mayer-König
Brussels

Note

1 Specifically this study focuses on the dominant cultures, religions, philosophies, and developments of the countries in these areas with the exception of Central Asia.

# Notes on the Contributors

Prof. Karin Bogart is Associate Professor in the Intercultural Management Masters programme at the Institut Catholique des Hautes Etudes Commerciales (ICHEC), Brussels, Belgium. She is also a Lecturer in Japanese Business at the Economische Hogeschool Sint-Aloysius (EHSAL), Brussels. Her field of interest is Japanese labour, employment, social affairs and management issues.

Dr Josiane Cauquelin (co-editor) is Chargé de Cours at the Ecoles Supérieures de Commerce and Researcher at CNRS/LASEMA France. She was a member of the task force for the Asian Values project at EIAS. Dr Cauquelin collaborated on a Franco-Chinese project on the Zhuang People of China. Her published works include books and articles on the indigenous Buyi and Puyuma people of South West China and Taiwan.

Prof. Yash Ghai is Chair of the Faculty of Law, University of Hong Kong. He has published extensively on public law. He has advised various governments on constitutional matters, including the Commonwealth Human Rights Initiative (CHRI). He is currently writing on human rights in Hong Kong.

Dr Paul Lim (co-editor) is a Senior Research Fellow of the European Institute for Asian Studies. He was Maître de Conférence invité at the Institut d'etudes du Développement at the Université Catholique de Louvain de la Neuve. He works on Asia in the European Parliament. While he specializes in South-East Asia, his present interest is Euro-Asian relations.

Prof. Fateh Mohammad Malik was formerly with the National Institute of Pakistan Studies at the Quaid-I-Azam

University, Islamabad, Pakistan. He was a Senior Research Fellow at Colombia University and Visiting Professor holding the Iqbal Chair at Heidelberg University. He has written on questions of Islam, identity and nationality, as well as 'Iqbaliat' and literary criticism.

Dr Birgit Mayer-König (co-editor) is an Assistant Professor at the Institute of Indology at the University of Halle. She was a temporary lecturer at the South Asia Institute, University of Heidelberg. Her published works include a book on Shaivism and several articles in the field of Indian Philosophy and Religion.

Prof. Raul Pertierra is an Associate Professor at the University of New South Wales, Australia. He is also Visiting Professor at the Department of Sociology, Asia Centre, University of the Philippines. Specializing in Philippines studies, his published works include essays and articles on social theory, ethnography, culture and identity.

Prof. Debabrata Sen Sharma, Senior Research Professor of the Asiatic Society, Calcutta, India, is now retired. He specialised in Indian philosophy and religion. He was formerly Professor of Sanskrit at Kurukshetra University, and continues to publish regularly and lecture widely.

Dr Thanh-Dam Truong is Senior Lecturer in Women and Development Studies at the Institute of Social Sciences, The Hague, Netherlands. She is also involved in the Institute's Advisory Service. She has published on prostitution and tourism in South-East Asia, and on issues of gender and development.

Prof. Willy Vande Walle is Chair of the Department of Oriental Studies, University of Leuven, Belgium and was Visiting Professor at the International Research Centre for Japanese Studies. He has published on oriental history and culture and Buddhism.

Prof. Yang Baoyun is Director of South-East Asian Studies and a Deputy Director of the Institute of Afro-Asian Studies, Peking University, Peking, China. Professor Yang is a specialist of South-East Asian history in general and Vietnamese history (1600–1700) in particular.

Acknowledgements

This volume is the result of a study undertaken by the European Institute for Asian Studies which was commissioned to contribute to the understanding of Asian Values as an input into the Venice Forum on Culture, Values and Technology, an event leading up to the first Asia Europe Meeting (ASEM) in 1996 in Bangkok. The Institute and the editors are particuarly grateful to Mr Emiliano Fossati, Director for South and South-East Asia of the European Commission, who encouraged us to take on the challenge of this study.

We would also like to thank Dr Willem van der Geest, Researcher Director of the Institute for his intellectual advice in the final stages of completing the manuscript. Ms Anindita Sen Gupta, the Institute's Publications Officer was extremely helpful in producing the final version of the manuscript.

Ms Hilary Hodgson offered linguistic and editorial advice which was much appreciated.

Our thanks also go to Mr Jonathan Price of Curzon Press who showed keen interest in the publication of this book and greatly encouraged us.

As editors we are very much indebted to the authors for their contributions during the two workshops and for their cooperation in revising their chapters.

The Editors

Chapter 1

Understanding Asian Values

Josiane Cauquelin, Paul Lim and Birgit Mayer-König

1.1 Introduction

Globalization is changing activities in all spheres. On the economic, political, professional and private levels, Europeans meet Asians, Asians travel to Europe, and Europeans travel to Asia. We have the chance to find out how the people in other parts of our globe really live and work. What are their customs, and what are the ideas at the root of these customs? What are the ideals which they strive to follow in their lives? What are the values which give them orientation, inspiration and direction? In all human contact, we know that there can be misunderstandings, these can sometimes be amusing but at other times they cause unintended problems. With the aim of peace and mutual understanding in mind, we ask whether Europe and Asia share common values, or are their values indeed different? Can a line be drawn between European and Asian values? And what about the differences between Asians and Europeans?

Europeans look at Asian values with Western eyes, while Asians view Western values with Asian eyes. Being an outsider is partly an advantage, partly a disadvantage, when investigating the values of others. As Lévi-Strauss rightly stated, 'It is from inside that we can apprehend the ruptures but from outside that some effects of coherence appear.' While the insider has access to the details, the outsider has to rely on limited first-hand experience and secondary sources. However, the horizon can be wider with a more distant view, as in the Chinese proverb: 'The frog lying at the bottom of the well cannot speak of the sea.'

1

Although we aim for an objective, not a subjective view we are aware that our own history and experiences influence our choice and treatment of the subjects of study.[1]

In section 1.2 we look at the definition of values and search for corresponding notions in the languages of Europe and Asia. Values are distinguished from codes of conduct. In tracing the origins of values, we return to the sources of religions and philosophies and recognise the importance of the ways of thinking. In section 1.3, we investigate the structure of thought in depth and find practical examples which point to values. In 1.3.1, we study the way of thinking in China, in 1.3.2, in South Asia and in 1.3.3, we distinguish the Western Cartesian and Eastern holistic ways of thinking.

1.2 What are values and where do they come from?

As a first step towards a definition of values, we consulted a standard English dictionary. Values are there defined as 'the moral principles and beliefs or accepted standards of a person or social group'.[2] This definition is very wide, encompassing not only virtues and ideals, but also convictions and models followed individually or collectively.

The concept of values exists in all the regional varieties of Western culture; there are synonymous terms in all European languages. Western values are united by common roots in Christianity and by historical events. This is not necessarily the same in Asian cultures. Indeed, it becomes evident in translation that Asia values are expressed in terms which hold connotations different from those in European languages.

The word 'value' in four main Asian languages is as follows:

● In Hindi and Sanskrit: *dharman, artha, vishvâsa, guna* (all singular)
● In Urdu: *qaderê* (plural)
● In Chinese: *jia zhi guan*[3]
● In Japanese: *kachi ka*

In South Asia, with the imprint of Hinduism, Islam, and the historical influence of Buddhism, the people are very aware

2

of values. But efforts to translate the word 'value' show that the main languages do not provide a single equivalent word. Words cover different interpretations of 'value'. There is no distinction between value, religion, way of thinking, belief, purpose, or custom as in Western languages. For example, *dharman* refers to a person's religious, moral and social principles and customs; *artha* refers to the aims, goals and aspirations; *vishvâsa* to beliefs and attitudes in general; *guna* to the qualities or virtues which excel. The meanings of these words are partly distinct, partly overlapping. In Chinese, it must be noted that *jia zhi guan* is not really used in the European sense (see below). Chinese people have values, although these may be different from those elsewhere.

After the terminology, the nature and content of values are investigated. Values may be distinguished according to different categories: religious, moral, social, political and aesthetic. While the specific values which are cherished by an individual or society may vary, in general, the following may be considered: truth, honesty, harmony, order, liberty, democracy, justice, mercy, compassion, forgiveness, patience, love, respect, children, family and kinship, friendship, politeness, charity, beauty, simplicity, poverty, chastity and obedience (the monastic values), education, wisdom, good health, common weal.

It should be noted that none of the religions or philosophies particular to Asia (Confucianism, Hinduism, Buddhism, Islam, Jainism, Sikhism, Animism) draws a distinction between religious and secular values. The religious scriptures contain guidelines not only for worship, but also for correct conduct in everyday life, even including politics, economy and the arts. There is also a tendency to trace modern developments back to the ancient religious sources, with the aim of conferring importance on the ancient texts or of providing support to modern issues, as in the case of democracy and Islam.

Some values are easily identifiable, while doubts remain about others: it is difficult to draw a clear line between values and codes of conduct. Take, for example, shaking hands. Does this code of conduct express the value of politeness or is it a

3

value in itself? We tend to deny that such conventions are values. Codes of conduct can be seen as the practice or expression of values such as harmony and respect in everyday life.

Values as such are abstract. Harmony, respect, justice are approved by many: which religion or society would not preach them? They are probably common values. However, when they are put into practice, we observe a variety of outcomes. It is not enough to know which values are cherished in Asia if we want to understand Asians and communicate, share, and build bridges. We need to know what determines the selection of the values and endows them with specific characteristics when they are put into practice. Often the problems that occur in communications between East and West reveal a lack of understanding of behaviour. What does it mean when the partner smiles, offers a gift, or speaks of 'tomorrow'? It is not enough to enumerate the values from the religious and philosophical sources: we need to know also what marks the Asian ways of thinking as well.

The origins of Asian values can be traced in religious and philosophical texts and traditions. But other factors too have an impact. What about historical experiences, developments in society, the rise of the market economy with the phenomena of urbanization and industrialization, geographical and climatic conditions, experiences of wars and ecological disasters?

Societies and their values change; habits are adopted from colonizers and world powers. The present changes are often described as an erosion of values in East and West. Instead of honesty, corruption is widespread. The special importance of the family is not favoured by separate housing, increasing divorces and economic divisions. During this process, values are rediscovered and reconsidered.

When we look at Asian societies today we find a great diversity of life styles. Traditional Asian ways and Western and modern trends exist side by side. However, a Japanese in a Western suit does not mean that his way of thinking has become Western. Basic attitudes remain the same. They are investigated in the following sections.

4

1.3 Ways of thinking as the determinants of values and codes of conduct

1.3.1 The Chinese way of thinking

China differs from Europe but how and in what way? Two concepts will be explored in this section which may bring us nearer to an understanding. Chinese thinking is monist and morphological, which means it emphasizes the study of the forms of things.

A general idea of the yin/yang concept

The concept of *yin/yang* appeared in *Kouei Tsang,* the book of divination, which according to tradition, was written during the Yin dynasty (eighteenth–twelfth centuries BC). The text refers to the son of Hi Ho, the mother of the suns: 'look at him climbing up to the sky, one light, one dark'. This concept is based on alternate and complementary dyads. The *yin/yang* principle of going and coming movements, of expansion and contraction, is the root of the cosmic harmony. For Chinese thinking, harmony was the origin of the world.

'At the beginning there was an alternation', says the Confucian classic, *The Analects*. The basis of Confucius' teachings is harmony. Chinese thinking considers the alternating opposites, for example autumn–winter/spring–summer, rest–activity, night–day; and complementary opposites, sky–earth, left–right, and so on. Day and night alternate. When the sun sets, the moon rises: moon and sun push and pull each other for the benefit of life, as the Chinese remember that there were once eight suns and life on earth was miserable. The cycle of seasons follows the same interdependent action, for spring and summer are the times for the blossoming of nature, autumn and winter are the times for its withdrawal. But it is during the dark seasons that nature is nourishing its energy, waiting under the earth to emerge at springtime. These images illustrate the regular cosmological flow.

The *yin/yang* concept leads to a monist way of thinking

Chinese thinking is monist, and works in terms of and/and, while Europeans are dualists, and think in terms of or/or and either/or. One notion cannot be considered without the other, both exist only in their relationship to the other; one is implicit in the other. Chinese writing reflects this duality, as many basic characters are composed of opposites, for example landscape is seen as 'mountain+water'. 'One *yin*–one *yang*, here is the Tao: at the same time yin – at the same time *yang*, here is the Tao', says the *Zhouyi Xici*, annexed to the Book of Changes. But having a translation is already an interpretation, because *yin* and *yang* are melting into the Tao, and then Tao alone persists.[4] *Yin* and *yang* continuously alternate and this alternation gives the Tao.

Since Chinese thinking refers to a natural order which creates harmony, there is no absolute goodness or badness, no immortal soul, no creator, no absolute otherness. No creator, because this coherent system leaves no room for a transcendental creator. No immortal soul, as life is like day, the time for activity, and night is like death, the time for rest. We can just say one is visible and the other one is invisible. There is no absolute otherness. In China all non-Chinese people are 'barbarians'. In texts one can read the expression 'raw and cooked barbarians', whether Chinese or not.

The yin/yang as visible/invisible

The grammatical category 'gender' does not exist in China but Chinese thinking is dominated by the male and female categories of *yin/yang*. Everything, every notion, is organized under the *yin/yang* concept, even the visible and invisible world. The first is *yang* and the second is *yin*. From ancient times, the two worlds have communicated. Anything, good and/or bad, happening within the visible world on earth is due to the invisible world of the spirits. The spirit world is not impersonal, two worlds have always communicated with mediums or shamans (both categories exist in China).[5] The supernatural world of the spirits gives to human beings who in turn give back their due to the spirits, then the spirits will

6

give again, and so on. This is a world of the 'give and counter-give' interconnected system.[6] Even today, some Chinese and Japanese agree that the practice has strong impact on their lives. Many Japanese businessmen would not undertake any business without first consulting the medium.[7]

Another expression of this dyadic concept is the culture of the 'indirect' where it becomes an aesthetic value in poetry and painting.[8] The art in painting is to paint the visible to reveal the invisible. The emptiness of the sky animates the landscape, just as wind animates nature. The un-said, which belongs to the invisible notion, is *yin*. From the Book of Poetry (compiled between the ninth to sixth centuries BC), the Chinese have expressed themselves through poetry. Whenever a mandarin wanted to bring something to the notice of his superiors, or to criticize the Imperial Court, he wrote a poem describing landscape, birds, or butterflies for instance. But the allegorical message was always understood by the one(s) to whom it was dedicated. For a contemporary reader, it is always difficult to discover the real meaning of a poem, as he has not only to understand the poet's style, but also his biography. Confucius used metaphors and allegories.[9] All civil servants in China are poets! The Official Chronicles tells that when welcoming diplomats from neighbouring countries, Chinese princes and their ministers recited poems from the Book of Poetry and used allegories in conversation with their guests. This roundabout way of expressing one's thoughts is still in favour today. For example Vice-President Zhou Enlai died in January 1976; then in April, the Chinese worshipped All Souls' day. Nobody knows how it happened, but within a few hours Tian An Men square was white, it was covered with flowers and anonymous poems with no poetic value, but full of puns and metaphors hostile to the government. The government understood: the square was cleaned, spick and span, in one night. Poems hold a social, moral and political message – not merely for the writer, but for all.

For the Chinese, the un-said or the use of other words does not hide the meaning but expresses it more deeply, a cultural trait which may have prevented the democratic process in China. This contrasts with the European approach. From the fifth century in Greece, Europeans have learned that there are

7

two sides to every argument, they have learned the art of rhetoric and oratory, the culture of 'face-to-face', which seems to have contributed to the tradition of democracy in the West.

Examining the use of poetry for expression may be esoteric, so let us take a more prosaic approach and look at contemporary newspapers. It is not enough to understand the Chinese language to read a daily newspapers; one has to catch the subtlety. After Mao's death, at the beginning of 1978, a marxist slogan no longer appeared in bold characters on the first page of the *People's Daily*. But a few days later it reappeared. Later still, it was printed on an inside page of the paper. From this inclusion and exclusion the people understood that de-maoization was in progress.

The mural newspapers, or *dazibao,* are another way for people to express their criticisms. You will not see two politicians debating on television as you see in Europe. The youth in Tian An Men in 1989 asked for democracy, but admitted they had to invent their own democratic system according to their own way of thinking. Some of them think that the *dazibao* may lead to further democracy. Nowadays, most intellectuals, are still protecting themselves behind the curtain of clouds and wind; open dissidence is still impossible.

Saving face

The process of creation is continuous and organic, devoid of teleological interpretation. There are no external causes: nature is a force of its own, with its own alternations. Images are the keys to understanding Chinese writing. Think of the notion of *li*, which in translation means reason, in the same terms of the *Greek logos*. The French sinologist Démieville points out, that the literal meaning of *li* is 'the veins of a jade stone', that is, the profound structure.[10] The Chinese mandarin does not express himself directly, not for want of courage but on principle. If he reveals his thoughts, his *li*, the mandarin is exposed and vulnerable to his interlocutor who may take advantage and attack. The civil servant can both criticize and respect the hierarchy at the same time, thanks to this roundabout way of thinking.

8

This understanding may explain why Chinese people pay such attention to external forms, observance to which a moral value is attached. The principle of saving face or losing face is very deep, nothing can hurt a Chinese person more than to feel 'naked'.[11] To avoid such situations, Chinese use subterfuges which do not fool anyone but which can solve the problem. There is an old Chinese story that there was a master and his domestic servant. The former complained to the latter that the sugar was rapidly diminishing, he thought there must be a thief at night. The servant suggested putting a lock on the door, which the master did. The sugar no longer disappeared. Both men knew that there had never been any thief, but both saved face.

A Chinese person will talk of different things before making a request. An intellectual will answer using a poetic metaphor as in times past when a prince gave an audience to a foreign diplomat. The Chinese link patience to sensitivity. Europeans should keep in mind that it is easy to hurt a Chinese: in order to avoid misunderstandings consultants and interpreters interpret the Chinese point of view and are prepared to lose face themselves in order to save the face of the two parties.The principle of saving face may explain why Chinese like compromises and need intermediaries even in their own daily lives.

Values in China are part of the harmony of nature, not external to it. Confucius said, 'At the beginning, there was an alternation.' All his teachings come from or go towards harmony.[12] Whatever is done, whoever does it, wherever and whenever it is done, there has to be harmony. This explains the culture of the 'indirect', of no direct attacks. For a Chinese strategist in warfare, to have frontal attacks destroying one of the two belligerents is perceived as stupid. By using poetry and *dazibao* the Chinese people leave the way open for consensus, and give those who govern a chance to use the Middle Way; as said below 'the waves comes into shore and goes out'. Confucian values seek harmony in all circumstances: the community, the family, authority, decision-making, and in moral and aesthetic judgements. Chinese and Japanese doing business with another Asian know from the very beginning that they will reach a consensus, but they

9

are defensive whenever they have to negotiate a contract with Westerners for they fear the 'wave will go so far away in discussion that it will not come back'. The code of conduct should be the practice of a set of values: politeness, honesty, patience, wisdom, and so on, which all aim at harmony.[13] In the hierarchy of values harmony stands highest.

1.3.2 The way of thinking in South Asia

In South Asian culture, the way of thinking can be described as dialectical, circular and holistic, taking a relative rather than absolute standpoint. This applies not only to Hindus, but also to Buddhists and Jains, and to some extent to Christians, Sikhs and Muslims in this part of the world. There are some common features of the South Asian culture and ways of thinking which are shared by the people irrespective of the differences in theologies. For this reason, an outsider will find it difficult to identify the religious adherence of a South Asian person on the basis of his or her way of thinking and behaviour.

Before going into detail, attention should be drawn to the fact that Hinduism is a term given to the religious teachings of the Indians by outsiders.[14] Looking more closely, one finds a great variety of religious and philosophical teachings and practices in India: some have remained separate traditions, and some have blended into common teachings. All possible reciprocal influences exist side-by-side. What is of religious importance to one Hindu may not be so for his neighbour. Take pilgrimages as an example: while millions of Hindus from all over the country gather to bathe in the holy river near Allahabad at an auspicious time, others who live nearby stay at home because that pilgrimage is not the religious path they have chosen to follow. There are also different ways for Hindus to worship: one makes fire offerings every morning at home; another worships certain idols; and a third finds peace seeing his or her spiritual teacher. Hindu religious scriptures are also varied, different Hindus prefer different texts.[15] The spread of different Hindu religious schools is to some extent regionally determined and historically connected with eminent teachers, for example the Vaishnava school of Caitanya (*ca.*1485–1533) is widespread in Bengal or among Bengalis who live elsewhere. However, Hindus choose their practices individually and there is a saying that there are multiple paths in order to suit the different characters. Some indologists, for example, Heinrich von Stietencron (Tübingen) suggested that instead of speaking of one Hinduism we should preferably speak of many Hindu religions.[16] When we continue to use the term 'Hinduism', we should be aware that it refers to multiple religious schools and practices.

Islam, the second largest religion on the subcontinent, has neither a church nor a priesthood (except in Iran). It largely relies on the individual Muslim, the study centres of Muslim law (*ulamâ*), and the *Sufi* orders. The *Sufis* were influential in the conversion of the people; and Sufi teachers took part in discussions and exchanges with the religious and cultural world around them. The Brahmanical stream of Hinduism and orthodox Islam emphasize rituals and clearly differ from each other. The popular practices of Hindus and Muslims, however, are devotional. It is in this domain that Hindus and Muslims have abundant similarities and even substantial overlappings. For example, Kabir, a Muslim by birth, was a teacher whose poems are still ceremoniously recited by Hindus, Sikhs and Muslims alike. In short, South Asia presents a picture of diverse religious traditions but with many shared cultural traits.

The ancient Hindu philosophical school of Samkhya and Tantrism, a religious tradition which arose in Buddhism and in the Vaishnava, Shaiva and Shakta traditions contributed to Hinduism as we know it today.[17] Based on a dialectical form, it argues that the static male and the dynamic female are aspects of complementary nature and always exist in combination. The male is seen as the unchanging essence and the female as the power of transformation and change present in subtle and material forms of the world. This principle is reflected in the Hindu pantheon where every male deity has a female partner. In everyday life it is evident in many religious and secular customs. Above all, marriage is seen as essential in order to be complete, the roles traditionally attributed to husband and wife as complementary.

Tantrism is also holistic; according to its cosmology all manifestations (beings, things) are expressions of the divine

11

power (*shakti*). The microcosm contains the essence of the macrocosm.[18] This teaching is elaborated in philosophical theories, for example by Abhinavagupta of Kashmir at the end of the tenth century AD. It is also expressed in the widespread use of symbols and symbolic practices.

Hindus, Buddhists, Jains and Sikhs are aware of symbolic meanings of geometrical figures, numbers, colours, sounds, gestures and food. The symbols which are seen as auspicious, like the *svâstika* figure or the sounds of *OM* and *Shree*, must be present at the beginning of an enterprise, as at the entrance of the house. A married Hindu woman is not seen without some auspicious red colour on her forehead, nowadays supplemented by red lipstick and nail enamel. If some inauspicious sound is heard, some will postpone their action and wait for a better time. An auspicious or inauspicious sign revealed at the time of a business meeting is taken much more seriously than a Westerner would suspect.

In Islam, the holistic view is evident in the lack of distinction between secular and profane life – a feature of all the religions and philosophies of the East – and also in the concept of the omnipresence of God. God can take any form in order to observe or teach a person. In popular Muslim practice, belief in blessings is widespread. People pray at the tombs of the Sufi teachers. The orthodox scholars of Islam reject any belief in magic and revelation, as well as astrology.

The circular feature is probably the most universal feature of the South Asian way of thinking. All things are seen as connected and changing while remaining essentially the same. The ancient vedic seers taught that there is a cosmic harmony. In it every manifestation has its particular place. Every person and every thing contributes to this cosmic harmony. The actions of anyone, any part, have an effect on the whole. For this reason, duties are emphasized.

With the rise of Buddhism the moral aspects of acts became important and the concept of *karma* developed in the form in which it is still recognized today. According to this doctrine every action has certain effects, nothing happens by chance. Buddha and other teachers used this idea to encourage good behaviour, non-violence and religious observance. It is thought that people should take responsibility for themselves and improve their lives by their good deeds.

While the concept of *karma* describes every action as a cause, it also points out every state of affairs as an effect. In this way it is used to explain inequality and serves as a theoretical support for the caste system by attributing an individual's social position at birth to his or her virtue in a previous life.

The doctrine of cause and effect together with the idea of regeneration unites human lives. The circularity of causes and effects is linked to the idea of multiple births. It gives rise to the idea that persons who are related now also had relationships in previous lives. Belief in reincarnation supports the idea of close relationships in previous or future lives.

Further moral and sociological consequences of the circular thinking, based on the doctrine of *karma*, result in the attitudes towards the value of mercy. Non-mercy is often seen as a behaviour of those persons who do not feel any connection with the other persons who may belong to a different community. They are left to receive 'fruits of their own deeds'.[19] Mercy is extended to people with whom a connection is established through family, village, caste, religion, profession, teachers, friends, or language. Forgiveness is another recognized value, mostly in devotional traditions.

The idea of cosmic harmony is reflected in the view of time. In the linear way of thinking time is limited, in the circular way of thinking time is fluid, nothing is really lost or gained. Time exists in abundance. What cannot be achieved in this life, may be achieved in the next. Yesterday and tomorrow are expressed in the Hindi language by the same word *kal*. Restlessness, though not unknown in the modern towns, is not appreciated in South Asia. Patience is a highly praised quality. Control of the passions is described as indifference to any occurrence whether pleasant or unpleasant. Losing one's temper is a sign of immaturity, they say.

The circular thinking advocates that there is no one standard or set advice which is applicable to all people. What is a good and useful action for one person, may not be so for another. In South Asia this concept is not always purely individualistic as individualism is seen in the West, instead it is individualistic in reference to certain social groups and to certain stages of life. For example, while it is good for a student to live chastely and to study, a householder is expected to have children and to take care of his or her family. While it is thought brave of a soldier to fight, for a religious person it is advised that he endure. A soldier may even be encouraged to kill, while in general – and especially for religious people – non-killing, non-violence, and non-hurting are the foremost virtues or values.

Western visitors may often experience an attitude of generosity towards their beliefs, and tolerance if they fail to respect the local customs. This is connected with the attitude of relativity; hence what is necessary or good for a Westerner is not automatically good for an Indian, and vice versa. The same thing is not appropriate for all. There is no big step to the opinion that Western political and economic concepts cannot and should not be blindly transferred to the East.

Truthfulness is one of the foremost values of Hindus, Muslims and Buddhists alike. However, there are some differences in comparison to the Western concepts. In the West, we have an absolute concept of truth presuming objectivity. In South Asia, this is not the case. In Asia 'truth without love' is not understood as truth because it can hurt somebody. It is common practice to refrain from criticizing even when justified, and to try to say something pleasant instead, especially to outsiders. Similarly, a polite question should not be answered in the negative. Even if a person in the street is asked for direction they are unlikely to be offensive by answering that they do not know the way; they will attempt to be helpful and indicate something.

The relativity of statements and the capability to grasp the whole is often described by the allegory of the elephant and the blind. A number of blind persons encountered an elephant and described it according to the parts they touched. one side is smooth, another is covered with hair, and so on. They began to argue about it when a person with clear sight came and explained to them how they all were right to some extent, as one had truly described the belly, another the tail etc. This story illustrates the commonness of the ways of

14

thinking or attitudes as it is taught by Buddhists, Jains, Hindus and Muslims alike, and cherished by Christians.

1.3.3 Two ways of thinking

This section deals with the aspect of holism which marks the Asian ways of thinking. Although Western ideas have left an impression on Asian ways of thinking, the Asian mind has not lost its holistic approach. To help the holistic approach we will contrast it with the Cartesian view which still shapes European thinking.

Oskar Weggel, in his book *Die Asiaten*[20], points out that the holistic approach (*Ganzheitlichkeit*) is traditional in Asia, and that it is a very different philosophy from that of the West. According to Weggel, this holistic attitude is expressed both in ways of thinking and behaving, and in the structure of the society; thus it shows a remarkable contrast to the Western tendency to differentiate and divide. Weggel sees holism as the key to understanding Asians. He believes that where holism had disappeared as a philosophy, many people felt uneasiness and irritation. In the following we investigate this problem.

The Cartesian way of thinking of the West is to look at a part, or an aspect of the reality separated from the whole assuming that it is the whole and the reality. A holistic approach or mind, however, would never look at an aspect, or part, separate from the whole. It sees everything as interconnected, overlapping, inseparable, every part as held together by every other part or aspect. They are one. In the holistic, we do not separate, we do not even make distinctions. We take in the whole reality as one. We do not attempt to analyse because analysing takes the reality apart. In the Cartesian approach, we take the reality, the object of study, apart or isolate a part of it in order to analyse and define it. In Asia, on the other hand, there is no distinction between value, religion, way of thinking, belief, purpose or custom as in Western languages and no distinction between religious and secular values.

Now, in day-to-day politics, we can find examples of a Cartesian approach. If one pushes the market economy, privatization and liberalization as a panacea in the post-Cold War period regardless of psychological, social and enviromental ill-effects, that is Cartesian. To consider the economic as the centre of gravity, as the only and total reality, is Cartesian. A holistic approach will never prefer the economic; it will put the social, the environmental, on equal footing with the economic. However, the reality is that the economic occupies the predominant and decisive place in any decision-making process.

To define development as economic as if it were unconnected to the social, to the ecological, to the environmental, to the psychological, is a Cartesian construction of the reality. The same applies to seeing development policy as an instrument of foreign policy and to judging the funding of development projects with economic eyes. A holistic approach will take everything into consideration, it will put everything into the construction of reality. The holistic approach will never take a purely economistic approach. It seems that narrow economic self-interest stand in the way of a holistic approach.

The danger of the destruction of the environment has pushed the holistic approach to the fore. The World Bank/IMF today take into consideration the environmental cost in measuring economic growth. There is a realization in certain circles of the need to imprint on the mind a holistic approach. University education is becoming more and more interdisciplinary while, at the same time, the market economy dictates that university education must produce specialists tailored to the needs of the economy.

This holistic approach or world view is Tao, and is not static. It is in the continuous process of flow, transformation, and change which are the essential features of nature. It is dynamic. The one Western philosopher who is close to this way of thinking is Heraclitus who said that everything flows and that all changes are cyclic and not linear. Cyclic as in waves coming into shore and then going out. You cannot pinpoint a place in this motion; this coming in and going out is repeated continuously on a cyclical pattern. The climaxing of *yang* gives way to *yin*, when *yin* reaches its climax, it in turn gives way to *yang* in a repetitive manner.

16

There are some important implications. In the Western mind, good is good, bad is bad. It is an 'either or'. You must make your choice. The good must win over the bad. In fact, it is an absolutist position. In the Chinese mind, there is a dynamic balance between good and bad. Although they are conflictual, each is relatively good and relatively bad. There is no such thing as a victory of good over bad for otherwise there would not be a dynamic interplay of opposites. In political terms, capitalism is neither absolutely good, nor absolutely bad. Similarly, communism is neither absolutely good, nor absolutely bad. The Cold War propaganda of bad communism and good capitalism is contrary to *yin* and *yang*, and reflects the Cartesian mind.

It is probably difficult for the Western mind to accept a balance, a harmony between good and bad which are contrary to one another, to accept that they are aspects of the same thing. Does the Western mind accept that love and hate are two sides of the same coin, that war and peace are a paired unity? That conflictual opposites are one reality, are part and parcel of the same reality? The Chinese mind would say war will bring peace, hate will bring love and perceive it as a unity, a harmony.

It should be pointed out that this *yin* and *yang* approach is intuitive. There is mysticism in it expressed at the deepest level of meditation where the distinction between the observer and observed, the subject and object fuse into an undifferentiated whole. This is the Tao where everything is one, where there is no dualism.

Notes

1 The difficulty of objectivity in perception has been pointed out by philosophers like Kant and also by psychologists.
2 *Collins English Dictionary*, Third edition, 1991, Glasgow: HarperCollins, 1991, p. 1694, point (5).
3 Definition from *Xin hua ze dian* (Peking, Commercial Press, 1990) p. 202.
4 Here we refer to the Tao as the one expression of *ying:yang* and not of Taoism as a religion.
5 The medium (mainly female in China) is chosen by one or several spirits who speak through her mouth. The medium's body becomes a vehicle for the spirits. A shaman however is chosen by the spirits and speak with

them on an equal level, she knows the spirits' language. Both categories are the intermediaries between the people and the spirits.

6 Honesty is a common value but the Chinese practice of giving presents is interpreted by the Westerner as corruption. It is not denied that the act could be intended to corrupt but it is also the system of 'give-and-counter give'. Give and counter-give exists in ancestor worship where the living family has to give to their dead ancestors who will return protection. There is an element of obligation, of sealing a relationship, of trust, of confidence in this exchange. It is not always easy to see whether these exchanges are corrupt. This can lead to a troubled relationship between a Westerner and a Chinese.

7 Bouchy, A, Les oracles de Shirataka, 1991, Paris, Picquier.

8 cf. Jullien, F. 1989, Procès ou création, Une introduction à la pensée chinoise, Paris, Des Travaux/Seuil. 1995, Le détour et l'accès, Stratégies du sens en Chine, en Grèce. Paris, Le Collège de philosophie, Grasset.

9 When Hegel read this text, he was very disappointed: 'One only finds good and honest moral, no more. No philosophical research and no speculation' (Leçons sur l'histoire de la philosophie, III, E.1).

10 Li is the profound structure, the personality of one being like the inner veins of jade making the quality of the stone.

11 Zheng Li-Hua, Les Chinois de Paris et leurs jeux de face, Logiques Sociales, (Paris, L'Harmattan 1995.)

12 Confucius was born during a decadent, chaotic period of the Zhou Dynasty, in the sixth century. BC

13 Those Japanese who still respect Confucian values feel a sense of obligation and are compelled to help foreigners who lose their way. If they do not help the foreigner, they suffer a sense of disharmony.

14 The ancient Persians called the people living near the river Hindu (the Indus in English) the 'Hindus'. The Muslims who came later to the subcontinent called those there who were neither Buddhists nor Muslims 'Hindus'. The Europeans adopted this term and introduced the word 'Indian' for secular purposes; without realizing the diversity of beliefs they called the religion of the Hindus 'Hinduism'.

15 Individual Hindus may prefer Vedic hymns, the Bhagavadgîtâ, the Devîmâhâtmya, the Hanumân Châlîsâ, the poems of saints such as Dâdû, Mîrâbâi, or the Alvâr saints, or some orally transmitted stories and songs. These texts may be in Sanskrit, or in Tamil, or in one of the many regional languages and dialects.

16 Heinrich von Stietencron, in Theologische Realenzyklopädie, 1986, Vol. XV, p.54 and Hinduism: On the Proper Use of a Deceptive Term in Sontheimer, Günther-Dietz, and Kulke, Hinduism Reconsidered, (New Delhi, Manohar, 1986) pp. 11–27.

17 For a correct understanding of Tantrism see André Padoux's article 'Tantrism' in Mircea Eliade, (ed.), The Encyclopedia of Religion, vol. 14, (New York: Macmillan, 1993) p. 272–280 or Sanjukta Gupta, Dirk Jan Hoens, and Teun Goudriaan, Hindu Tantrism, (Leiden: E.J. Brill 1979).

18 This is expressed by the saying 'all is in all' (sarvam sarvâtmakam). For more information, see Raffaele, Torella, Examples of the influence of

Sanskrit Grammar on Indian Philosophy, in *East and West*, (Rome 1987) vol xxxvii, p. 151–64.

19 Further, in Mahâyâna Buddhism which is only liminally present in modern South Asia, compassion or mercy is the ideal exemplified by the Bodhisattva who serves as the model for the behaviour of the people.

20 Weggel, Oskar, *Die Asiaten*, München, C. H. Beck, 1989, Part 1.2.1, pg 38. 'Der eigentliche Unterschied: Ganzheitlichkeit. (..) Gleichwohl lässt sich auch heute noch ein panasiatisches Durchschnittsverhalten und -denken ausmachen,das sich vom westlichen beträchtlich unterscheidet. Gemeint ist hier die zumindest in der Tradition so selbstverständliche Ganzheitlichkeit, wie sie sich sowohl im Denken als auch im Einzelverhalten und im Gesellschaftsaufbau ausdrückt und wie sie in so bemerkenswertem Gegensatz zur westlichen Differenzierungs- und Aufspaltungstendenz steht. Diese Ganzheitlichkeit liefert, wo sie sich gehalten hat, den Schlüssel für das Verständnis, wo sie aber verlorengegangen ist, die Erklärung für das Unbehagen und die Reizbarkeit vieler Asiaten in der modernen Welt.'

Chapter 2

Rights, Duties and Responsibilities

Yash Ghai

> The rich man in his castle,
> The poor man at his gate,
> God made them high or lowly,
> And ordered their estate.
>
> Christian hymn 'All Things Bright and Beautiful'

> Duke Ching of Ch'i asked Master K'ung about government. Master K'ung replied saying, let the prince be a prince, the minister a minister, the father a father and the son a son.
>
> Confucius, *Analects* 12.11

> The system of caste insists that the law of social life should not be cold and cruel competition, but harmony and cooperation . . . A man born in a particular group is trained to its manner, and will find it extremely hard to adjust himself to a new way . . . The worker has the fulfilment of his being through and in his work. According to the Bhagavad Gita, one obtains perfection if one does one's duty in the proper spirit of non-attachment.
>
> S. Radhakrishnan, *The Hindu View of Life*, p. 112

2.1 Introduction

In this chapter, I discuss notions of rights, duties and responsibilities in the context of contemporary debates about Asian values. The rise of 'Asian values' as a political doctrine can be traced to the end of the Cold War. Its most active proponents were Singapore and Malaysia. It came into prominence to challenge what was claimed to be the attempts of the West to establish its global intellectual and cultural hegemony by imposing Western notions of rights under the guise of their universalism. Before the collapse of Western communist regimes, the discourse of rights was dominated by the great ideological differences between liberal-capitalism and socialism, and in which the contest was seen to lie in the competing claims of primacy of civil and political rights on the one hand and economic and social rights on the other. The West was deemed to conceive of rights largely as political, while the socialist states provided the impetus for social and economic rights. At the heart of the controversy was the role of the market in the organization of the economy and the distribution of resources. Socialist states not only deployed the well-known critique by Marx of what he called bourgeois rights, but also claimed to have established a better framework for rights in which economic and social rights were ensured to all people, enabling them to live a life of dignity. Socialist states therefore analysed rights in class terms. The leaders of developing states hovered uneasily between these opposed views, reluctant to disengage from the rhetoric of rights which had been invoked extensively in the colonial period, but also conscious of the difficulties of establishing political authority, especially in multi-ethnic societies, and increasingly driven to restrictions of rights. 'Developmentalism' became an ideology of sorts, for both socialist regimes and those which operated market economies under the hegemony of the West, with its undertones of control and authority.

The collapse of communist regimes in Europe and the end of the Cold War changed dramatically the context for the discourse of human rights. The discourse achieved a high salience. The collapse of communism was widely represented as the victory of human rights and democracy. The West defined its mission in the extension of rights and democracy to other parts of the world. It was no longer encumbered by the need to placate and boost its former authoritarian allies as part of its strategy to fight communism worldwide and was able to respond to their own publics who had begun to question the assumptions and practice of foreign aid. Human rights and democracy-based conditionalities began to be imposed on foreign aid and trade relations, resulting in massive structural adjustments and the opening up of third

21

world economies to world investments and markets. Human rights and democracy seemed to provide the framework for the reconstitution of the former Soviet Union and other states in Eastern Europe, including Yugoslavia (despite, or perhaps because of, all the carnage), evident in the rules enunciated by the European Union for the recognition of its breakaway republics. Earlier a similar framework had justified international intervention in Cambodia for its reconstruction (even if it did not facilitate the reconstruction); and today UN interventions, whether in Somalia, Rwanda or Zaire, are routinely justified on human rights/humanitarian grounds.

The emphasis on rights was not welcomed by all states. Those states which had felt safe in the immunity from international scrutiny of their authoritarian political systems (which in East and South-East Asia had been justified on the basis of the menace of communism) found themselves a little like the emperor without clothes. They were anxious about what were considered to be the likely consequences of human rights for their political systems. They were resentful also of conditionalities, which derogated from their political and economic sovereignty. The universalization of rights was seen as the imposition of Western cultural norms. They were anxious because of the effects of the emphasis on rights on their competitiveness in the framework for international trade ushered in by globalization, and claimed to detect in this emphasis a Western conspiracy to undermine newly growing economies.

The challenge to the new emphasis on rights and democracy was, paradoxically, led by states in East and South-East Asia, which by many standards were unlikely candidates. They were unlikely candidates because they shared a wide set of interests with the West, especially the US. They were well integrated in the global economy and there was a large consensus on the market mechanism; they needed Western capital and technology; they had close common interests in the security of the region, under the umbrella of the US; they were heavy purchasers of Western weaponry; and they were not directly affected by earlier phases of conditionality and structural adjustment. There were two factors which prompted them to lead the resistance to attempts at the universalization of human rights. First, their special clientist relationship with the West was in jeopardy in the new post-Cold War geopolitics, and the consequent vulnerability of their regimes to human rights-based criticism. Second, while they were integrated into the global economic system, their versions of the market were less than liberal, there being a complex (if not necessarily subtle) set of connections between the state and the market which gave governments considerable leverage over economic (and consequently political) processes. Implicit in the concept of governance was a different version of the market and a new framework for international economic competition, likely to have relatively greater effect on states already well integrated into the global economy. But above all, these states were well placed to challenge what they saw as Western pretensions. They had achieved remarkable economic development in the preceding decades, and a measure of social and political stability. Moreover, if they were dependent on the West, they also offered attractive conditions for Western capital and markets, ruling out significant Western retaliation.

The wide consensus on the market and global economic processes the countries of East and South-East Asia shared with the West determined the specific nature of their challenge to the rights regime – the claim of cultural specificity of rights. There was also a subsidiary riposte based on that old-fashioned artefact of Western statecraft and international relations – sovereignty. In the positioning preceding the Vienna Conference on Human Rights (orchestrated largely by Singapore and Malaysia), China was ambivalent about the cultural response, having denounced Confucianism only a few years earlier. China's opposition (as in the White Paper of 1991, *Human Rights in China*, issued by the Information Office of the State Council of the PRC) was based on materialist rather than cultural grounds: it said that 'the evolution of the situation in regard to human rights is circumscribed by the historical, social, economic and cultural conditions of various nations, and involves a process of historical development'. Due to these reasons, 'countries differ in their understanding and practice of human rights' (both quotations are from page 2 of the document). The same

23

position is stated in an update of that paper issued in December 1995 (despite some attempts at the revival of Confucian thought in China). Although in one sense China argues for the primacy of rights related to basic, physical needs, it asserts that it has protected civil and political rights just as effectively. China's principal position is that rights are essentially domestic matters within state sovereignty, and not subject to international interference. Only with strong sovereignty can a state protect the rights of its citizens (for which the predations against China by the West in the nineteenth century might be seen to provide enough justification).

Although some other East and South-East Asian states subscribe to this theory of sovereignty (and thus deny the responsibility of the international community for the protection of human rights), their principal response has been cultural. This response was a direct attack on the claim of universalism of human rights: it opposed 'Western' rights with 'Asian values'. What is more, it claimed that the economic and social success of Asia was based on these values, and the economic crisis and moral decadence of the West was the result of its pre-occupation with rights. There were antecedents for this cultural perspective. An early challenge to universalism came from certain members of Islamic societies, especially in the Middle East in the wake of Arab defeat in the Arab-Israeli war. The defeat was ascribed by some to the creeping Westernization of their states and societies; a return to Islamic values was the prescription (see Nasr 1987; Mayer 1995). The rise of the Islamic movement put a stop in many countries to the reform (i.e. modernization) of the law as the new laws, especially in the area of family, were seen as contrary to the *Sharia*.

Western pre-occupation with Asian economic success and the distinctiveness of its culture, was given an impetus by the well-known article by Samuel Huntington in which he states that the next major global conflict would be between civilizations and/or cultures, not ideologies (Huntington 1993). Although the article is weak both theoretically and empirically, it has been highly influential, and has moulded US foreign policy and given rise to the notion that cultures are

24

both different and antagonistic. As with 'Asian values' it seeks to fill the void left by the Cold War, to sharpen differences with others, to 'enjoy' them as enemies.

There is no particular coherence in the doctrine of Asian values. Its intellectual roots are weak, and it shifts its ground as expediency demands. Although perceived and intended to be an attack on human rights, it is in fact concerned with ethics and the organization of society, and does not engage directly with the nature of human rights. It sets up false polarities and has a dubious theory of causation with which it seeks to attack the notion of rights. The doctrine of Asian values seeks to achieve various objectives. It seeks to differentiate Asia from the West, and indeed to show the superiority of the former over the latter. Through this differentiation, it seeks to disapply norms of rights and democracy. It aims to fight the gospel of governance by 'demonstrating' the distinct cultural foundations of Asian capitalism and markets, which unlike the West, are not dependent on legal norms and independent judiciaries, but the ties of family and kinship and the trust they generate (Redding 1990; Hamilton 1991; Wong 1991). It aims to strengthen Asian solidarity by positing (a false) unity.[1]

An argument which seeks to establish the essential difference between East and West is the relative importance of rights and duties in the two cultures. In brief the argument is that the West emphasizes rights, and the East duties. Various consequences are then drawn from the distinction, as regards the atomization of society (when rights based) or its solidarity (when duty based). Rights-based regimes are said to promote confrontation and conflict, while duty-based regimes harmony and consensus. In a duty-based regime a person relates to the family and the community in a different way than in a rights-based regime; the former linking the individual to society in a more organic manner than in the other. In the contemporary discourse of some Asian governments, the decadence and the moral decay in the West is due to its obsession with rights, while the social and political stability in Asia (more precisely East Asia) is due to its cultivation of a sense of duty. These views are expressed not only by government leaders who have a political axe to grind,

25

but also by thoughtful Asians. For example, Professor Onuma has argued that the abuse of power by the ruler and the violation of values and interests of the people have been checked not by judicial mechanisms but by virtue of the rules and the wisdom and prudence of the elite in securing humane and good governance (1996: 3).

I propose to take up this debate by examining questions on the moral or material basis of duties and the rights; the consequences of a duty-based regime; and contemporary circumstances which bear on them.

2.2 The virtues of duties

Duties are frequently understood as correlatives of rights. My right to privacy becomes your duty to respect it. In that sense the notion of duty serves no additional purpose, except to give precision to the notion of right (right to what? right against whom? with what redress? a concern essentially of lawyers, who find it conceptually difficult to think of rights without duties). As White (1984) says, 'Bentham and other . . . argued that since, in their view, rights and duties are correlative, the idea of a right could be regarded as superfluous and all the necessary work done by the idea of duty.' Historically White argues that the notion of duty, encapsulated in the term 'officium', is much older than the notion of right.

It is unnecessary for our purposes to enter a philosophical inquiry into the relations between right and duty, which are complex and ever changing as new forms of entitlements are established. What I seek to examine are duties in a more abstract sense as in claims that while the West emphasises rights, the East emphasizes duties and that duties provide a better way to organize society than rights. In this sense duties are not merely correlatives of rights. An Indian scholar has put the matter in this way, 'Indians . . . base their social structure on duties and obligations rather than on rights. Persons are seen not first and by nature as bearers of rights but rather as bearers of duties' (Saksena 1967: 372).When invited by UNESCO to contribute to a symposium on human rights, Mahatma Gandhi wrote back that 'all rights to be deserved and preserved come from duty well done' (1947).

26

The essence of the claim is illustrated by the following quotation from Soedjatmoko:

> We should not forget that many of the traditional cultures have not felt the need to make individuation and human freedom explicit values in their own perception of their culture. The viability and cohesiveness of these societies derived from a closely knit texture of mutual obligations rather from the human individual and his rights. Thus, there are many societies where individual rights are not likely to be the focal point in the value of configuration. Many of the more primitive societies are collective societies, whereas part of the modernisation process rests on individualisation and greater awareness of the rights of the person. Still, collective societies have not precluded the possibility of self-realization of the individual. Rather, this self-realization takes place in the context of the moral fabric of the society and in the web of obligations towards the community rather than primarily in the context of rights. Moreover, all these societies do recognize and value the dignity of the human person and they all have developed sensitivity and forms of social intercourse for careful preservation and observance of it.
>
> Soedjatmoko, 1985: 76–7

A vivid illustration of the same point is presented in that minor classic, *The Hindu View of Life* by the eminent philosopher and former president of India, Radhakrishnan in his defence of the caste system in Hinduism. Referring to the stratification involved in caste, he wrote,

> Caste on its social side is a product of human organisation and not a mystery of divine appointment. It is an attempt to regulate society with a view to actual differences and ideal unity. The first reference to it is in the Purusa Sukta, where the different sections of society are regarded as the limbs of the great self. Human society is an organic whole, the parts of which are naturally dependent in such a way that each part in fulfilling its distinctive functions conditions the fulfilment of functions by the rest, and is in turn conditioned by the fulfilment of its function by the rest. In this sense the whole is presented in each part, while each part is indispensable to the

27

whole. Every society consists of groups working for the fulfilment of the wants of the society. As the different groups work for a common end they are bound by a sense of unity and social brotherhood. The cultural and the spiritual, the military and the political, the economic classes and the unskilled workers constitute the four-fold caste organisation. The different functions of the human life were clearly separated and their specific and complementary character was recognised. Each caste had its social purpose and function, its own code and tradition. It is a close corporation equipped with a certain traditional and independent organisation, observing certain usages regarding food and marriage. Each group is free to pursue its own aims free from interference by others. The functions of different castes were regarded as equally important to the well-being of the whole. The serenity of the teacher, the heroism of the warrior, the honesty of the business man, and the patience and energy of the worker all contribute to the social growth. *'Each has its own perfection.'*

Radhakrishnan, 1927, 107–8, italics added

Although Confucianism is less bound by rigid caste distinctions which prevent mobility, a similar reasoning underlies the five key relationships in its thought: ruler–subject; father–son; husband–wife; elder brother–younger brother; and friend-friend, as well as the four social classes: the scholars; farmers; soldiers; and merchants (the first not much different from the Brahmin, although the last are not quite outcastes).[2] Accordingly, the role of each person was defined precisely and the rites appropriate to that role were carefully set out. There is a similar sense that social harmony and personal satisfaction derive from the perfect performance of one's role (as in the quotation from the *Analects* at the top of this paper). Hsieh Yu Wei, while acknowledging the presence of the notion of rights in Confucianism, summarizes the position as follows, 'But it was the rights of the individual that were considered most important. Of most importance were the duties or obligations of the individual. According to Confucian ethics, in order to be a man or to be a sage, it is necessary, first, to perform one's duties, not to claim one's rights' (1967: 314).

28

2.3 The nature of a duty-based society

It is time to draw out the implications of the notion of duty. The concept is not used in this context to show that duty is a correlative of right, although some duties may indeed be a response to the rights of another. It is more like a case of duty without right. In that sense it is more like responsibilities, the sense of right and proper conduct. Many duties mentioned in Confucian and Hindu thought are rooted in morality, not legal obligations. Nor are duties a method of prescription of a subject's relationship with the state alone; they are deeply embedded in social and familial relationships also, providing a structure for all society. The ambit of duties is therefore wider than that of rights.[3] There are several dimensions of such a notion.

First, that the members of a society based on duties may be said to be less selfish than a society which is rights based.

Second (related to the preceding point), it is sometimes claimed that a society based on duties is communitarian while a rights-based society is individualistic; in the former the individual is subordinate to and subsumed under the family and society.[4]

Third, it may be said that a duty-based society is more oriented towards harmony and stability than conflict, for while assertions of rights are adversarial and confrontational, the performance of duty is based on cooperation and the acceptance of obligations, and thus it may be claimed that a duty-based society is civil and values courteous behaviour. The key duties are loyalty, obedience, filial piety, respect and protection.

Fourth, it is argued that the tendency in a rights-based society is towards formalism, the transformation of values as legal rights. Based on a theory of competition and suspicion of authority, this leads to demands rather than concessions, to confrontation rather than reciprocity and accommodation. An emphasis on duties on the other hand leads to honour and peace, as well as stability. It is argued that the rights-based emphasis leads to the impoverishment of society, so that in the search for the protection of the citizen against the state, the community collapses and non-state actors become the principal source of oppression and insecurity. There is also the danger in formalization of values as 'rights' that the form may elude substance (so that the satisfaction of formal criteria hides realities that deny the values; as Professor Mazrui once said, the West may have abolished child marriages, but the number of teenage pregnancies has vastly increased). From this perspective, the role of duty is particularly important in civil society, and indeed the notion of duty finds its strongest application in the family, particularly in the Confucian tradition.

Fifth, it is assumed that true happiness lies in the fulfilment of duty. I have already referred to assertions to the effect that 'perfection lies in duty'. Seen in this way, duty is infinitely superior to rights.

Sixth, it is said that the real protection of subjects lies in the duties that are imposed on rulers. Confucianism is particularly strong on this point. The ruler must act benevolently. One of the clearest examples of this appears in *Analects* (2.20). 'Chi K'ang-tzu asked about inducing the people to be respectful and loyal so that they might be encouraged to support him. The Master said, 'If you approach them with dignity, they will respect you. If you are dutiful towards your parents and kind to your children, then they will be loyal. If you promote the good and instruct the incompetent, then they will be encouraged.'[5] The state is to be patterned on the family, with the monarch acting as the kind father to his subjects who reciprocate with filial piety and loyalty. In Confucian society leaders were expected to lead by example, by virtue and morality. Unless they do that, they are likely to forfeit the Mandate of Heaven, which is their authority to rule, and the people then may overthrow the regime. It has been said that the fear of the loss of the Mandate has through centuries acted as a powerful deterrent against despotic rule.

Stated in this way a duty-based society is particularly attractive. However, to provide a balanced picture of a duty-based society and to clarify the nature of the arguments, it is necessary to set it in a historical and comparative context.

First, it is necessary to dispel the notion that a duty- and right-based distinction can serve as a useful basis for distinguishing Eastern from Western societies. Societies in most continents have passed through a duty-based, communitarian period; some of the most sophisticated disquisitions on the virtue of duty come from the West. The change from the primacy of duty to the primacy of right comes about as the political relationship between the rulers and the ruled change. In a despotic regime, the duties of the subject are emphasized; in a democratic society, the rights of citizens are emphasized (Bobbio 1996: 38–43). Rights are therefore concerned with political relationships; they have been intimately connected with the rise of centralized states (for an essay delineating the subtle and varied connections between rights, duties and powers, and the changing political configurations for their juxtaposition in China, see Wang 1980). Before the advent of colonialism in Asia, the structures of political authority were fluid; boundaries of the domain of a ruler fluctuated with the rise and ebb of his power; and the state had little pretence of regulating the life of its subjects (Tambiah 1992; Nissan and Stirrat 1990). Colonialism produced highly centralized and authoritarian state systems, which became the legacy of nationalist leaders at independence. In most cases independence settlement was based on a balance between the rulers and the ruled, mediated principally through the medium of human rights.

Second, the fact that the West has formalized rights and strengthened the legal machinery for their enforcement does not make it either adversarial or individualistic. An attempt to assert a right is not a challenge to society; the person asserting a right does not set her or himself in opposition to the society; instead she or he seeks a confirmation of community and/or national values. The fact that public challenges to the administration are allowed in the courts and other forums is merely evidence of the cohesiveness, strength and stability of the community and the nation. The occasions when it is necessary to resort to courts to enforce rights are relatively few. This is because there are relatively few serious violations of rights; and when there are, their redress is achieved in non-judicial ways. For the most part, political processes in the West are far more consensual than in the East where there is considerable reliance on coercion and the suppression of free speech. It is particularly ironic that despotic leaders should accuse democracies where the governments are elected by the people and are responsive to them of being adversarial, with people pitted against the government.

Third, duty-based societies have historically been status-based and hierarchical. Several consequences follow.

1 Duties are not equally distributed but depend on status. So the duties of the father are different from the son, those of the wife different from the husband, of a Brahmin different from a sudra. There is no concept of equal duties. In most such systems, the position of the women is particularly inferior. Manu reminds us in his Laws:

> 'By a girl, by a young woman, or even by an aged one, nothing must be done independently, even in her own house. In childhood a female must be subject to her father, in youth to her husband, when her lord is dead to her sons; a woman must never be independent'.
>
> Doniger and Smith, 1991, verse: 147, 115[6]

2 Duties are to preserve hierarchies and ensure obedience for the purposes of stability. The emphasis on the family itself serves to protect the state. When asked why he was not in the public service, Confucius replied, 'Be filial, only be filial and friendly towards your brothers, and you will be contributing to government. There are other sorts of service quite different from what you mean by service' (*Analects*. 2.21). This has been interpreted to mean a virtuous private life makes a real contribution towards public welfare or the stability of government (Waley 1989: 93). Master Yu is quoted as having said that 'Those who in private life behave well towards their parents and elder brothers, in public life seldom show a disposition to resist the authority of their superiors. And as for such men starting a revolution, no instance of it has ever occurred' (*Analects*. 1.2). For the same reason, the behaviour of groups and individuals is *prescribed* in great detail, often connected with rituals to impart to them a sense of the sacred. Confucius, emphasizing the extreme importance of rites, sets out in elaborate detail the ritual appropriate to different occasions and persons. Dr Radhakrishnan reminds

us how Hinduism regulates the most intimate details of daily life (1927: 80). The careful ascription of duties to specific persons reinforces status, office and hierarchy as is evident from the well-known Confucian story about the emperor who, fatigued by his journey or drink, fell asleep while resting. The minister of hats, passing by, took the emperor's robe which was lying nearby and covered the emperor with it. On waking up, the emperor was touched to see the robe over him and enquired as to who had been so kind as to place it there. However, on being told that it was the minister of hats, he was extremely angry with him for exceeding *his* duty, which had little to do with robes, and equally angry with the minister of robes for neglecting his duty!

3 The constant emphasis on the imperative of duty, on its glorification, on how true fulfilment lies in the perfect discharge of duty, and so on, serve to enhance the ideology of obedience and subservience. Indeed, it is the force of this ideological indoctrination that continues to cause unease among the people about a challenge to the system that oppresses them. The purveyors of this ideology are, not surprisingly, the scholar-bureaucrats (in Confucianism) and the high caste (in Hinduism), the principal beneficiaries and intellectuals of the respective systems.

2.4 The contemporary relevance of the notion of duties

Some contemporary presentations of 'Asian values' assume that the notion of duties outlined above still pervades Asia. Quite apart from the fact that even in ancient times 'duties', particularly those laid on rulers, did not operate in the idealized versions of Confucius and Manu, it would be surprising if they were to be the defining characteristics of Asian societies today, transformed as they have been by new forms of economic and political organization. It is seldom clear whether government leaders are making normative or empirical statements when they talk about Asian values, although one assumes that they are making empirical statements as they ascribe their political stability and

33

economic success to them. On the other hand, the vigour with which Confucianism is presented today as the specificity which distinguishes East from the West itself suggests that it may not be well or even alive. Certainly the social foundations of Confucianism, structured around agrarian relations, have altered beyond recognition. Nor are the values that it extolled consistent with the style of governance or economy. Asian values are used to explain economic success, yet Confucianism and Hinduism are alike opposed to the profit motive and the accumulation of wealth. Persons most revered in China, Hong Kong, Taiwan and Singapore today tend to be those with wealth and business empires.[7] If the social foundations of the old system have disappeared, why do the governments of these countries harp upon the notion of duties that were connected to it?

There would appear to be several reasons for this preoccupation with duties (for a detailed exposition, see Ghai 1994). One is to provide a counterpoint to the West, to ward off real or imagined pressures for democratization and human rights, providing an intellectual justification for different moral standards. The second is connected with the original ideological purpose of the concept of duty, that of obedience and subservience. It serves to down-grade rights, which are the vehicles of protest and the justification for equality and justice. Nowhere is this more evident than in Singapore where the government is cultivating an ideology with remarkable resemblance to Confucianism – minus the exemplary behaviour of the leaders. That the contemporary celebration of the concept of duty has little to do with culture and much to do with politics is evident from various contradictions of policies and practices of governments most heavily engaged in its exhortation. I will take three examples to illustrate my point.

As already noted, these governments claim that their societies place a higher value on the community than in the West, that individuals find fulfilment in their participation in communal life and community tasks, and that this factor constitutes a primary distinction in the approach to human rights. The Western preoccupation with individualism is explained by the alienation resulting from its economic system which has sapped the vitality of the community, and forced introspection on individuals as a means of finding their identity. This argument is advanced as an instance of the general proposition that rights are culture specific.

The 'communitarian' argument is Janus-faced. It is often used against the claim of universal human rights to distinguish the allegedly Western, individual-oriented approaches to rights from the community-centred values of the East. Yet it is also used to deny the claims and assertions of communities in the name of 'national unity and stability'. It suffers from at least two further weaknesses. First, it overstates the 'individualism' of Western society and traditions of thought. Even within Western liberalism, there are strands of analysis which assert claims of the community (for example, Rousseau); and most Western human rights instruments allow limitations on and derogations from human rights in the public interest. Western courts regularly engage in the task of balancing the respective interests of the individual and the community. Within liberal societies there are nuances in the approach to and the primacy of human rights, as becomes evident when one examines the differences among the US, Canada, France and the UK. Furthermore, liberalism does not exhaust Western political thought or practice. Social democracy, which emphasizes collective and economic rights, and Marxism, which elevates the community to a high moral order, are also reflective of important schools of Western thought. There is much celebration in Western political thought of 'civil society', a personification of the community, standing between the state and the individual and family (Cohen and Arato 1992).

Second, Asian governments (notwithstanding the attempt in the Singapore Paper *Eastern Express* to distinguish the 'nation' and the community) fall into the easy but wrong assumption that they or the state constitute the 'community'.[8] Nothing can be more destructive of the community than this conflation. The community and state are different institutions, and to some extent in a contrary juxtaposition. The community, for the most part, depends on popular norms developed through forms of consensus and enforced through mediation and persuasion. The state is an imposition on society, and unless humanized and democratized (as it has not been in most of Asia), it relies on edicts, the military, coercion and sanctions. It is the tension between them which has elsewhere underpinned human rights. In the name of the community, most Asian governments have stifled social and political initiatives of private groups. Most of them have repressive legislation like the British colonially inspired Societies Act[9] which gives the government pervasive control over civil society. Similarly rights to assemble and march peacefully have been mortgaged to the government. Governments have destroyed many communities in the name of development or state stability, and the consistent refusal of most of them to recognize that there are indigenous peoples among their population (who have a right to preserve their traditional culture, economy and beliefs) is but a demonstration of their lack of commitment to the real community. The vitality of the community comes from the exercise of the rights to organize, meet, debate and protest, dismissed as 'liberal' rights by these governments. Nor is the tight regulation of society as in China and Singapore particularly Confucian. Confucius argued against reliance on law or coercion, and advocated a government of limited powers and functions.[10]

Another attack on the community comes from the economic, market-oriented policies of the governments. Although Asian capitalism appears to rely on the family and clan associations, there is little doubt that it weakens the community and its cohesion. The organizing matrix of the market is not the same as that of the community. Nor are its values or methods particularly communitarian. The moving frontier of the market, seeking new resources, has been particularly disruptive of communities which have managed to preserve intact a great deal of their culture and organization during the colonial and post-colonial periods. The emphasis on the market and with it individual rights of property is also at odds with communal organization and enjoyment of property. (A further irony is that Asian leaders who vow their allegiance to communal supremacy and values are among the most ardent opponents of a Marxism that espouses the moral worth and authority of the community.) Market policies have relied greatly on multinational capital and corporations, which have brought new values and tastes, and are increasingly integrating their economies and elites into a global economy and culture. Indeed, it is these very considerations which prompted the Singapore government to undertake the propagation of an official ideology, patently based on Confucianism (even if that required the assistance of foreign experts! See Kuo 1996), but the contradictions of official policies largely escaped its authors. It totally ignored the impact, indeed the onslaught, of modern technologies on traditional communities. Capitalism in Asia (and Asia capitalism overseas) tends to be extremely predatory, often disregarding industrial safety standards, and marked by a high degree of the exploitation of both labour and the environment – and certainly not driven by any sense of duty.

A final point is the contradiction between claims of a consensus and harmonious society and the extensive arming of the state apparatus. The pervasive use of draconian measures like administrative detention, disestablishment of societies, press censorship, charges of sedition, etc., belies claims to respect alternative views, promote a dialogue, and seek consensus. The contemporary state intolerance of opposition is inconsistent with traditional communal values and processes. Contemporary states' processes in Asia are less hospitable to community politics than the much derided adversarial processes of the West, which at least ensure a hearing for all parties.

2.5 Conclusion

I have argued in this chapter that a duty-based society has traditionally been status oriented and hierarchical. I do not wish to oppose a broader notion of duty in the sense of responsibilities or civic virtue. There is clearly much that is attractive in persons who are mindful of the concerns of others, who wish to contribute to the welfare of the community, who place society above their own personal interests. No civilized society is possible without such persons. There is also much that is attractive in societies that seek a balance between rights and responsibilities and emphasize harmony. Nor do I wish to underestimate the potential of the

37

concept of duty as a safeguard against the abuse of power or office. I am much attracted to the notion of the withdrawal of the Mandate of Heaven from rulers who transgress upon their duties as rulers (although I am also aware that this was largely impotent as a device of responsiveness or accountability or discipline on rulers).

My arguments have been addressed here to the pretensions of some governments which have advanced claims of the moral superiority of their societies and assertions of Asian values. It will be obvious that I am unimpressed by these claims and wish to expose their dissembling strategies. However, it would be unfortunate if the disquiet with these strategies were to obscure the interesting new explorations of the notion of duty and self-cultivation in Confucian studies. These studies seek to demonstrate that the balance between the individual and the community is not what it has often presented to be – a subordination of the individual in and to the community – but a recognition of the importance of the individual (Hsieh 1967; Tu Wei-Ming 1985) nor that Confucianism – with its emphasis on the family-failed to develop a proper civic sense (de Bary 1991), the results of which are too obvious in the corruption of public life in so many Asian states, where the notion of duty barely extends beyond the family and the clan. It would be equally unfortunate if rights were seen as antagonist to a well-functioning and caring society in which there is a strong sense of responsibility and obligation (as appears to be sometimes the perception in the West today). With rights we deal essentially with the state, with obligations we deal with fellow human beings and the society they constitute. There are, of course, many points of interaction between the state and society when rights and duties in the senses used here may conflict, but the regime of rights provides the machinery to strike appropriate balances.

Notes

1 For two clear but extreme versions of this approach, see B. Kausikan, 'Asia's Different Standard', *Foreign Policy*, 29 (1993) 24–41 and F. Zakaria, 'Culture is Destiny-A Conversation with Lee Kuan Yew' *Foreign Affairs* 73 (2) (1994) 109–26.

2 For an interesting (but to my mind unsuccessful) attempt to defend the obviously confining circumstances of filial piety in terms of humanity, self-cultivation, reciprocity and example, see Tu Wei-ming (1985).

3 These points are well illustrated by the following cable from Mahatma Gandhi to H. G. Wells who sent him draft articles on human rights. 'Received your cable. Have carefully read your five articles. You will permit me to say you are on the wrong track. I feel sure that I can draw up a better Charter of Rights than you have drawn up. But of what good will it be? Who will become its guardian? If you mean propaganda or popular education you have begun at the wrong end. I suggest the right way. Begin with a Charter of Duties of Man (Both D and M capitals: emphasis added) and I promise the rights will follow as spring follows winter. I write from experience. As a young man I began life by seeking to assert my rights and I soon discovered that I had none not even over my wife. So I began by discovering and performing my duty as by my wife, my children, friends, companions and society and I find today that I have greater rights, perhaps than any living man I know. If this is too tall a claim then I do not know anyone who possesses greater rights than I.' (Reprinted in Iyer (1987: 492).

4 The idea of surrender of individual desires in the wider interests of the family and society so dominant in Confucian thought is somewhat qualified in Hinduism which has deeper spiritual roots. Radhakrishnan quotes a Sanskrit verse, 'For the family sacrifice the individual; for the community the family; for the country the community, and for the soul the whole world.' (1927: 90).

5 Confucius also said, 'Govern the people by regulations, keep order among them by chastisement, and they will flee from you, and lose all self-respect. Govern them by moral force, keep order by ritual and they will keep their self-respect and come to you of their own accord.' (*Analects* 2.3).

6 Manu goes onto say, 'A woman should not try to separate herself from her father, her husband, or her sons, for her separation from them would make both (her and her husband's) families contemptible. She should be always cheerful, and clever at household affairs; she should keep her utensils well polished and not have too free a hand in spending. When her father, or her brother with her father's permission, gives her to someone, she should obey that man while he is alive and not violate her vow to him when he is dead . . .

'A virtuous wife should constantly serve her husband like a god, even if he behaves badly, freely indulges his lust, and is devoid of any good qualities . . . it is because a woman obeys her husband that she is exalted in heaven..She should be long suffering until death, self-restrained, and chaste, striving (to fulfil) the unsurpassed duty of women who have one husband.' (p. 115).

7 There is no time to go into the debate as to how far the economic success of South and East Asia is due to Asian values or other economic and policy factors. Redding (1990; 1996) and Hamilton (1991; 1996) have argued that Confucianism has been fundamental to the development of 'Chinese' capitalism, both in terms of motivation and social structure – a viewpoint which has been challenged by, *inter alia* John Wong (1996). The

assumption that, the answer to the question is not straightforward is provoked by the following considerations: Why is it that Confucianism, which has been around for millennia, should only now be promoting economic growth? Why should it, with its traditional contempt for merchants and profits, become the incubator of capitalism? What about the Catholic Philippines which is now showing signs of rapid economic advancement? How is that un-Confucian Europe gave birth to capitalism?

8 Although, as I argue, that lip service to the 'community' is hypocritical, the real 'community' which motivates politicians is parochial and clannish, pursuing its selfish interest at the expense of other communities, and is the basis of public corruption and graft – and therefore nothing to be proud of. An interesting light on 'community' occurred in Hong Kong in April 1994, when two shoppers beat up a shop assistant, while her colleagues watched but did nothing to defend her. However, she bore no grudge against them, saying, 'Even though I have known them for a long time what difference does it make? You cannot expect some one to help you. I am not their relative.' (*Eastern Express*, 11–12 June. 1994). For the role of Confucianism in family and business, see Lau 1981 and King 1996.

9 Typically such legislation provides that a society has to be registered before it can operate. The government has the discretion to refuse to register a society and to de-register it. It has the power to seek information from the society about its membership, finances and other affairs, and to control or prohibit political links with outside bodies.

10 As with religion, Confucianism has been used for political purposes so that its essence has become somewhat obscure. It is undisputed, however, that Confucius was against tough laws and strong punishments, believing in the virtue of rulers and their sense of duty. See Rubin 1976; van der Sprenkel 1962; Tu Wei-Ming 1985a.

References

Cohen, Jean and Arato, Andrew, (1992) *Civil Society and Political Theory* (Cambridge, Mass: MIT Press).

de Bary, William Theodore, (1991) *The Trouble with Confucianism* (Cambridge, Mass.: Harvard University Press).

Doniger W and Smith B, (1991) *The Laws of Manu* (Harmondsworth: Penguin Books).

Ghai Yash, (1994) *Human Rights and Governance: The Asia Debate* (San Francisco: The Asia Foundation).

Hamilton, Gary G., (1991) 'The Organisational Foundations of Western and Chinese Commerce: A Historical and Comparative Economic Development in East and Southeast Asia' in Hamilton (ed.),

—— *Business Networks and Economic Development in East and Southeast Asia.* (Hong Kong: Centre of Asian Studies, University of Hong Kong).

—— (1996) 'Overseas Chinese Capitalism' in Tu, Wei-Ming (ed.), Confucian Traditions in East Asian Modernity. (Cambridge, Mass.: Harvard University Press).

Hsieh, Yu-Wei, (1967) 'The Status of the Individual in Chinese Ethics' in Charles A O Moore (ed.), *The Chinese Mind: Essentials of Chinese Philosophy and Culture*. (Honolulu: University of Hawaii Press).

Iyer, Raghavan, (1987) *The Moral and Political Writings of Mahatma.Gandhi Vol. 3 Non-Violent Resistance and Social Transformation*. (Oxford: Clarendon Press).

King, Ambrose Y.C., (1996) 'The Transformation of Confucianism in the Post-Confucian Era: The Emergence of Rationalistic Traditionalism in Hong Kong' in Tu, Wei-Ming (ed.), *Confucian Traditions in East Asian Modernity*. (Cambridge, Mass.: Harvard University Press).

Kuo, Eddie C.Y., (1996) 'Confucianism as Political Discourse in Singapore: The Case of an Incomplete Revitalization Movement' in Tu, Wei-Ming (ed.), *Confucian Traditions in East Asian Modernity*. (Cambridge, Mass: Harvard University Press).

Lau, Siu-kai, (1981) 'Utilitarianistic Familism: The Basis of Political Stability' in Ambrose King and Rance Lee (eds.), *Social Life and Development in Hong Kong*. (Hong Kong: The Chinese University Press).

Mayer, Ann E. (1995) *Islam and Human Rights*. (Boulder: Westview).

Nars, Seyyed Hossain, (1987) *Traditional Islam in the Modern World* (London: Kegan Paul International).

Nissan, Elizabeth and Sirrat, R.L. (1990) 'The generation of communal identities' in Jonathan Spencer, (ed.), *Sri Lanka: History and the Roots of Conflict*. (London: Routledge).

Onuma, Yasuaki, (1996) *In Quest of Intercivilisational Human Rights*. (San Francisco: Asia Foundation).

Radhakrishnan, S., (1927) *The Hindu View of Life*. (London: George and Unwin).

Redding, Gordon, (1990) *The Spirit of Chinese Capitalism*. (Berlin: Walter de Gruyter).

—— (1996) 'Societal Transformation and the Contribution of Authority Relations and Cooperation Norms in Overseas Chinese Business' in Tu, Wei-Ming (ed.), *Confucian Traditions in East Asian Modernity* (Cambridge, Mass: Harvard University Press).

Rubin, V., (1976) *Individual and State in Ancient China* (New York: Columbia Univ. Press).

Said, Edward, (1978) *Orientalism*. (Harmondsworth: Penguin Books).

Saksena, S. (1967) 'The individual un Social Thought and Practice' in Moore, Charles (ed), *The Indian Mind: Essentials of Indian Philosophy and Culture* (Honolulu: University oh.Hawai Press).

Soedjatmoko (1984) *The Primacy of Freedom in Development*. (Lanham: University Press of America).

Tambiah, Stanley (1992) *Buddhism Betrayed?: religion, politics, and violence in Sri Lanka*. (Chicago: University of Chicago Press).

Tu Wei-Ming (1985) *Confucian Thought: Self-hood as Creative Transformation* (Albany: State University of New York Press).

Van der Sprenkel, S. (1962) *Legal Institutions in Manchu China*. (London: The Althlone Press).

Waley, Arthur (1989) *The Analects of Confucius*. (New York: Vintage Books).

Wang, Gungwu (1980) 'Power, Rights, and Duties in Chinese History' *Australian Journal of Chinese Affairs* 1–26.

White, Alan (1984) *Rights*. (Oxford: Clarendon Press).

Wong, John (1996) 'Promoting Confucianism for Socio-economic Development: The Singapore Experience' in Tu, Wei-Ming (ed.), *Confucian Traditions in East Asian Modernity*. (Cambridge, Mass: Harvard University Press).

Chapter 3

'Asian' Values and the Heart of Understanding: A Buddhist View

Thanh-Dam Truong

3.1 Introduction

We are living in a period of vertiginous change marked by greater anxiety and tension manifested in many different ways and levels of our societies. Giddens (1991), an authority on Western political science and philosophy, locates this anxiety and tension in the threat to the notion of the self and the questioning of self-identity, which he called ontological security. He describes three main processes which affect this security both as an abstract system and a psychic process. These include globalization, de-traditionalization and re-traditionalization (1995). He defines globalization as shifts in space and time, and as a transformation in the way we relate our experiences to larger systems. He sees the effects of globalization as de-traditionalization and re-traditionalization: processes whereby local customs and traditions are being attacked and reconstituted in different forms. The process of reconstituting new values and traditions is only emerging, it is therefore bound to be experimental and uncertain. This uncertainty is the source of new forms of anxiety (ethnic, cultural, religious, political and economic), which give rise to current waves of violence and cruelty.

To Giddens, the search for alternatives must be based on two main principles, recognition and accommodation founded on the method of 'dialogic democracy,' which he regards as the struggle for the early part of the twenty-first century. Giddens writes that democracy must be understood in two dimensions: first, recognition of diversity of interests (so that one can form political parties and associations); and second, dialogue and the possibility to replace violence with discussion, or dialogic democracy. Dialogic democracy must not be limited government, must run through from personal and family life to large institutional systems to create positive lines of communication between individuals and social groups.

A comparison of Giddens' perception of violence as a manifestation of globalization and his concept of dialogic democracy, and the ancient Buddhist perspective of the self not as an unchanging substance but an outcome of social interaction, indicates that there may be a meeting-point between modern and ancient, the Western and Oriental.[1] A Buddhist view would see social tension as a crisis of disharmony, the tendency in human beings to cling to false notions of the self and the other, a condition that favours individuality to the exclusion of the common good. The search for harmony requires an abnegation of the self and a shift of interest to others. Buddhist epistemology emphasizes the need to learn to be part of whatever one seeks to understand, to generate a process of dialogue within oneself and with others, eliminating the barriers which separate human lives.[2]

Buddhism cannot provide insights on 'modern' political institutions for reasons related to its history and emphasis. Through the concept of compassion, Buddhist teachings focus on compassion, the civil and not the political. Buddhism emerged some 2500 years ago in what is now known as Nepal and spread through the Indian subcontinent. It expanded in Asia some 300 years after Buddha's death through a missionary movement initiated by King Asoka of India, the patron of the Third Buddhist Council. This movement sought to make local customs and social organiza-tion more compassionate through Buddhist principles. Cul-tural diversity and the absence of a claim to a universal rationality have been two central characteristics of Buddhism.

The current debate on Asian values and ways of thinking, needs to be re-examined for many reasons. First, this debate must be recognized as a cultural and political discourse with implications for cross-cultural practices, relations between governments, and ways of cooperating between the peoples of

44

two continents. Thus, it is important to identify the actors engaged in this debate, and their motives. Second, contrary to claims about the specificities of Asian and Western cultures, it is simplistic to see Asia and Europe as two separate and homogeneous cultural poles.

Following Bohm and Edwards (1991), this chapter argues for the need to bridge cultural barriers rather than create them. We will discuss two debates on Asian values, namely the Asian human rights debate and the inter-faith dialogue to show how and why these two debates have changed over time, and their implications on the understanding between Asia and Europe. We will then discuss Buddhism and human nature, and relate these to Buddhist principles of social justice. Finally, the chapter will examine the emergence of Socially Engaged Buddhism, as a movement seeking to discover ancient wisdom and to show its relevance to the contemporary world. We will emphasize the positive aspects of the Asia–Europe dialogue to show that people can move across cultural and political barriers to forge an alliance of hope for the future.

3.2 Conflict cooperation and the need for understanding

Asia and Europe have a long history of cultural exchange: the two continents have not always been in conflict. Cooperative exchange dates back to Hellenic times when philosophers from the two continents shared ideas.[3] Violent conflicts date back to pre-Hellenic time, and continued with the Crusades, colonial expansion and the post-colonial development. More recently globalization has brought new dimensions to this exchange in what Giddens calls the process of re-traditionalization which creates opposing forces as well as opportunities for cooperation unknown before.

There is a process of evaluation taking place in Europe and Asia, to assess the effects of 'modernity' (Nandy 1988; Banuri 1990), and to restore cultural visions which have been silenced by war, environmental degradation, and social injustice. The crisis of 'modernity' and its accompanied violence, is seen as the outcome of eighteenth-century Enlightenment thinking as a particular mode of thought initially generated in the European, which emphasized the function of rationality at the expenses of other human qualities (Haraway 1989, 1991; Toulmin 1990; Smart, 1992; Plumwood 1993).

The objective of this evaluation is to re-appropriate the legacy of humanism to balance the effects of technocracy originated in the Enlightenment era. Attempts are being made to: a) connect and weave together different perspectives on the process of learning and understanding of the self and the world of form, and b) discover unity between human beings irrespective of the technological and cultural age to which they belong (Gardet *et al.* 1976; Weber 1986; Hayward 1987; Edwards 1991; Eck 1993; and Bohm). Ancient and alternative philosophies from Asia and elsewhere, have been seen as a positive source of wisdom.

This return to ancient wisdom is less concerned with the labels assigned to different modes of thought, than with the wisdom generated from them. However, the purposes of many epistemological journeys may differ and become conflictive, as manifested in the different positions expressed by Deep Ecology, Eco-feminism, and Feminist environment-alism (Asian NGO Coalition for Agrarian Reform and Rural Development 1993; Mies and Shiva 1993; Argawal 1994; Braidotti et al. 1994). An uncritical return to ancient wisdom can reinforce the 'idolization' of traditional values and pave the way for various forms of cultural fundamentalism. That epistemological journeys cannot be liberated from vested interests may reflect the nature of power inherent in the process of knowledge construction, and the failure to distinguish between wisdom as a holistic body of values that connects the spiritual with the moral and social, and knowl-edge as a social field with competing legitimacy. In spite of this conflictive trend, epistemological re-traditionalization as a process still represents a positive force that can stimulate a dialogue between different epistemic communities and potentially open new paths of understanding to find the necessary solutions to the crisis of human kind.

In contrast, the process of re-traditionalization can be divisive: it can portray Asia and Europe as two separate entities, placed in binary opposition and mutual exclusion.

46

Two sources of this view may be identified. Among economists and the business community, the social construction of 'Asia' connects Asian values with the continuing economic growth in many countries on the Asian side of the Pacific Rim. This economic success is ascribed to the potency of Asian cultures founded on a unique value system which combines social cohesion with firm communal and familial foundations (Hofstede and Bond, 1988; Fukuyama, 1995). The notion of universality inherent in the current framework of human rights and social justice is contested, and claims are being made that there is an Asian view on human rights, based on the primacy of the community rather than the individual (Ghai 1994).

It is clear that the later process of re-traditionalization is connected with attempts within Asia to forge a new economic and political entity, a new counterpoint of Western power. In many ways, Asian resistance today is an echo of the past when Christianity and Western secular thought were seen as a threat to the feudal order. Some countries turned to total isolationism, others opted for a return to fundamentalism. Others opened up only to absorb Western science and technology without allowing Western secular thought to undermine the prevailing sociocultural and political order. This resistance continues on much the same lines, that is, resistance to the claim to universality of human rights as defined in the West, combined with an openness to Western science and technology and market forces.

However, a deeper look at this debate shows that there has been an important shift of terms around which the debate was initiated. In the debate between civic organizations in Asia in the mid-1970s, discussions on human rights in Asia initially established a link between human rights violation and development policies. The policies sought to broaden the interpretation of the human rights framework which was then limited only to civil and political rights. In 1981, the debate proposed a package called the 'right to development' which provides equal legitimacy to socioeconomic and cultural rights with civil and political rights (International Commission of Jurists and Consumers' Association of Penang 1981).

47

Thus contemporary critique of the West began not as a rejection of the Western-defined human rights framework, but as a selective application and a critique of development policies adopted by Asian governments which ignored the broad range of issues concerning social justice. The objective was to change the development terms and to broaden the human rights framework rather than rejecting it. Asian cultural values have entered the debate in the search for development alternatives with social injustice (Asian Regional Fellowship, 4th Assembly 1987). First, it has been argued that the development process has destroyed both the cultural values and identities of communities, and that they feel marginalized and dispossessed in consequence. Second, Asian religious values and traditional practices of sharing were considered as a resource base for community development. They were revived in the spirit of resource redistribution and diversification of methods to raise capital for the poor (Bangprapha, 1985).

However, in the late 1980s this debate changed from a critique of development policies to the defence of the Asian style of governance, democracy and human right practices. Ironically, the leaders of many Asian countries endorse the development process criticized by civic groups, and stress the right of Asian governments to determine for themselves the relationship between development and social justice. From an opposition between civic groups and governments, we now see an opposition between the governments in the West and Asia. Challenging the West becomes an objective in itself, and in this process the issues behind the Asian Debate on human rights, such as the effects of development on women, the peasantry, tribal communities and the environment, have been pushed aside.

In this new opposition, the techniques of the Asian debate reflect those of the opponent that it seeks to challenge, the homogenization of Asian-ness and European-ness as cultural categories, and the fragmentation of social life into different compartments such as science/technology, economy and politics. It is not surprising that so far the outcome of this debate is a reversal of the so-called 'European' hierarchy of values, i.e. community over individual versus individual over community, rather than offering a sounder alternative. The Asian Debate on human rights has yet to come up with a model of science and technology and economy that does not violate the rights of communities to life. Moreover, while the need to reclaim Asia's own identity and the significance Asians attached to their communities are recognized, Asian debate on human rights seems to negate the hierarchical character of social relations within communities, and hence endorses internal relations of domination. Thus, intra-cultural domination is being overlooked for the sake of inter-cultural opposition.[4]

Another case of confrontation is the inter-faith dialogue initiated some time ago to facilitate understanding between different religions, and religious experiences, and to find a sense of inter-religious unity (Eck 1993). Despite continuous calls for humility and respect for each other's religious experience, the spirit of this dialogue has recently been blessed by Pope John Paul II in his recent book, Crossing the Threshold of Hope, which re-asserts the originality of Christ above founding members of other religions. He states:

> Christ is absolutely original. If He were only a wise man like Socrates, if He were a 'prophet' like Mohammed, if He were 'enlightened' like the Buddha, without any doubt He would not be what He is. He is the one mediator between God and humanity.
>
> cited by Thich Nhat Hanh 1995

Thich Nhat Hanh (1995), points out that this statement reveals the assumption which is the notion that Christianity provides the only way to salvation. This position excludes dialogue, and fosters intolerance and discrimination between communities. Ultimately it re-enforces the spirit of inter-cultural domination painfully pervasive for the last five hundred years under the name of Christ.

The current claims to originality in both East and West re-enforce Foucault's insights on the power of discourse, and bring to the fore the pressing need to bridge differences in order to re-discover common bonds between humans rather than to continue to re-enforce differences. Each cultural entity must recognize its own logic of domination, and see

49

that no logic of domination can be contained internally without an eventual process of externalization, or without a process of exacerbation by external forces. Rather than a confrontational strategy, we need a two-way process of understanding that seeks to overcome the Self–Other dichotomy and the simultaneous claims to originality. The main objective of understanding should be the mutual enhancement of each other's space to be and to relate to one another. Hence, it cannot be based on the separation and insulation of the Self from the Others. Claims to originality does precisely this.

A genuine process of understanding between East and West would need an initiative from both sides to reflect on their own internal values, and thus recognize each other's cultures in non-dominant terms. No culture is free from domination or devoid of human creativity. Just as the seeds of domination can be consciously removed, so too can the potential for human creativity be consciously stimulated. A dialogue between East and West with a common objective to enhance human creativity and minimize violence would bear more fruits for future generations than a conversation in which each side seeks to promote its own legitimacy and ascendence, and to insulate one from the other.

3.3 Buddhism and the process of understanding

Like other religions, Buddhism is not free from sectarianism. Nor are Buddhist societies free from violence and internal domination. It is a Buddhist contention that social division, violence and domination are reflections of a deep-seated anxiety in the human being. Buddhism seeks to remove the causes of anxiety in order to free humans from suffering; for this reason it is referred to as the science of man rather than the revelation of God. Humans are central to Buddhism, both as the cause of social division, suffering and violence, and as the followers of a path which respects virtuousness and non-violence.

The main body of Buddhist teachings can be summed up in the doctrine of the Four Noble Truths which locate the causes of suffering, and the Eightfold Path which prescribes ways to alleviate suffering. Buddhist doctrines are called Dhammas, often translated as universal law. Rather than representing universal 'truth', Buddhist doctrines must be seen as ways of leading human development from spiritual confusion or false perception, desire and suffering, to 'perfect understanding' or penetrating insight as the basis of emancipation. The doctrine of Four Noble Truths describes four causes of suffering:

1 The First Noble Truth refers to the objective forms of suffering, of the human condition, such as birth, old age, illness, and death, and the subjective form such as separation from the pleasant, union with the unpleasant, unfulfilled desire.
2 The Second Noble Truth refers to the causes of suffering, stemming from the transient nature of all beings. The human being is made up of five skandhas, aggregates:
 • *rupa* (form, matter, corporeality)
 • *vedana* (feeling, sensation derived from the activities of the six organs: sight, hearing, smell, touch, taste, mind)
 • *sanna* (perception, the faculty that receives impressions of objects whether physical or mental)
 • *samkhara* (mental activities, impulsion and violation)[5]
 • *vinnana* (awareness, acts of consciousness defined as responses to the six sense organs: such as being aware of a feeling or a taste, an interaction of spirit and matter. Spirit or mind (*nama*) and matter (*rupa*) are two aspects of the same reality called *nama-rupa* because they are interdependent and integral to each other.

de Silva, 1979; Hayward, 1987, Trungpa, 1987

None of the five *skandhas* are unchanging or have a separate identity of their own. Rather, they arise through an infinite process of co-dependent conditioning. Because each Skandha is integral to the others, none of them can exist independently but is integral to all others. Each human being is subject to a continuous process of change which conditions human will to action (*karma*). *Karma* is the embodiment of physical, verbal and cognitive actions, and has the capacity to reproduce itself.[6] *Karma* is closely linked with the notion of self. The self which is self-centred produces selfish actions and reinforces craving, clinging and affliction; but *karma* can be changed by unselfish behaviour that awakens the relational nature of the self, and hence minimizes suffering.

From a Buddhist point of view, human suffering (*dukkha*) stems from the human tendency to cling to an unchanging notion of self and its craving (*tanha*). *Tanha* is created simultaneously by bodily instincts and the formation of ego. The ego (*Samkhara*) is a swamp that drowns the human subject because of its conceptual errors, mistaking non-self for self, the subjective for the objective, matter for mind and vice versa. This swamp is the cult of the ego as 'self'. These conceptual errors act like a veil (*maya*) which prevents humans from understanding 'suchness' (*Tathagata*), or things as they are; because of these errors, humans live in ignorance (*avidya*). *Avidya* is not a lack of intelligence but an optical illusion – the ego as an entity of essence and substance.

According to Trungpa (1973), the first level of *avidya* is the birth of the duality between the notion of self and the world of form (*rupaloka*) from where the notion of other arises. Through conditioning, this duality nourishes instincts to-wards protecting and enhancing the notion of self. With perception, imagination and awareness, the ego or self is driven by impulses and emotions such as anger, greed, desire and hatred. Action driven by impulses and emotions is self-destructive because it functions at the expense of the other.

3 The Third Noble Truth deals with the ending of suffering, based on understanding the transient and empty nature of the self. Emptiness does not mean the annihilation of the self, it means coming to terms with the relationship to others, and the needs of others.

4 The Fourth Noble Truth deals with the path to the ending of suffering which is eightfold: right views, right aspira-tions, right speech, right conduct, right mode of living, right effort, right minded, right concentration.

Right views and right aspirations are connected with *prajna* or 'perfect understanding or wisdom' (i.e. viewing the world according to the five skandhas and the law of consideration for others, and wholesome thoughts and feelings.

Right speech, conduct and mode of living are connected with *sila* or virtue (speaking the truth without resorting to slander, hard words, and lies: conducting oneself correctly without harming others, for example, by stealing, killing and disloyalty; earning a living without harming the lives of others).

Right effort, right mindfulness and right concentration are connected with *samadhi* or meditation. Right effort refers to the constant struggle to free the mind from harmful thoughts and consider ways that overcome duality and fragmentation. Right mindfulness refers to the constant state of consciousness. Right concentration is a higher stage of mindfulness.

Buddhism stresses the universality of the Four Noble Truths. The Eightfold Path must be adapted to the infinitely varying circumstances of actual life. Buddhism respects the moral autonomy of the individual as he/she is the central figure in freeing him/herself from confusion and the chain of causation. In his last sermon, the Buddha taught his disciple: 'Be a lamp to yourself' Be a refuge to yourself. Betake yourself to no external refuge. Don't look for refuge to anyone besides yourself'. (Nakamura 1976). Individual moral autonomy is encouraged, through inner reflection and penetrating insight (*prajna*). Out of respect for the individual moral autonomy, Buddhism has always chosen the Middle Path, or avoidance of extremes (extreme views, extreme speech and extreme actions).

This approach to individual moral autonomy is closely connected with the notion of compassion (*karuna*). Since the notion of individuality in Buddhism is indivisible from the totality of the universe, to be moral means to develop this insight. Compassion is a consequence of penetrating insight.[7] It is only through penetrating insight into the law of the five skandhas, its origins and chain of causation, that compassion can emerge. The Buddhist notion of compassion as an outcome Prajna is more than a moral value: the common bonds between humans must be discovered, rather than imposed as moral obligations. Compassion for fellow humans and the world of form (animals, nature) is part and parcel of the Buddhist outlook on mind-matter: social action and the awakening of the mind are intimately related.

Compassion in Buddhism begins with the care for the self, as the self is a microcosmic form of the larger world.

Understanding the world through the eye of Prajna produces a state of awareness called equanimity or mindfulness (*upekkha*). Mindfulness transforms compassion as a value exterior to the individual into a value that emerges from within the individual. Buddha-nature, or the capacity to be awakened and the mindful,[8] to cut through all sources of conceptual errors, is believed to be inherent in all human beings, but it must be found through self-reflection. Self-reflection does not imply ego-centricity, it implies freeing the mind from the ego before perceiving the world of others.

To recapitulate, in Buddhist thinking there can be no compassion without understanding, and there can be no understanding without self-reflection, self-discovery and the discovery of the relations binding the self to others, and allowing the self to be transformed by the awareness of the others. There can be no social harmony without compassion and understanding. Inner peace generates outer peace: meditation is central to the awakening of the mind to this reality and to the emergence of compassion.

3.4 Buddhism and social justice

Buddhist principles of social justice are derived from the principles governing the *sangha* (community of monks). Any discussion of these principles must take into account the character of Buddhist history and the two standards for veracity in Buddhism, namely scriptures and logical reasoning. Buddhist history, as histories of other religions, is shaped by economic, political, and cultural forces. In some countries, Buddhist principles were woven into state practices, in others Buddhism remained the religion of the masses. The diversity of Buddhist history does not allow for an over-generalization of its principles of social justice as applied in Buddhist states. It is possible, however, to read such principles as an extension of Buddhist ontology and epistemology.

Thich Nhat Hanh (1991) notes that in many dialogues with his disciples the Buddha stressed that his teachings were to be considered as vehicles for knowledge and not knowledge itself. Furthermore, knowledge must be subjected to the scrutiny of logic (van Bijlert, 1989), and should not be dogmatic. Many precepts were produced, to meet particular needs at the time to enable the Buddhist community of monks and the secular society to exist. Authoritarian applications of the precepts produced contradictions, even in the Buddha's lifetime, owing to the difficulty of prescribing for different situations. For this reason, the Buddha advised his disciples to record only those precepts that were essential to advance Prajna. After his death his disciples could not agree on which were the essential precepts and, fearing the loss of important messages, they decided to record everything they could remember, hence, the overwhelming number of precepts.

Attempts to institutionalize Buddhist ethics through formal education and state practice have led to a disengagement from society, and created a reverse trend, using Buddhist thought to legitimize a ruling order (Suksamran 1982; Tambia 1992). As pointed out by Phra Debvedi, Buddhist education began in monasteries; Buddhists teaching in universities tended to emphasize morality, philosophy and epistemology removed from social contact. This shift in emphasis coincided with the decline of Buddhism in its place of origin, India. Buddhist education which developed later elsewhere in the Asian continent sought to establish contact with society through popular education (Phra Debvedi 1990). But such education was limited to scriptural teachings, history, cosmology and medicine, or the care of mind and body. The health of society based on healthy social institutions was left as an assumed outcome of mental health.

Lafitte (1990) has pointed out, that historical analysis of Buddhism tends to emphasize material factors, and pays little attention to subjective factors such as clarity of mind, depth of awareness of reality, intuitive ability to know others, and their potential to transform individual lives. Buddhist practices adopted by kings and rulers as a way of legitimizing their rule in Buddhist states in South Asia and in South-East Asia have not been analysed in relation to evidence of social justice and harmony at the time.[9] They have been seen mainly as a practice of rulers to gain acceptance and political legitimacy (Truong 1990).

Buddhist principles of social organization based on the principles governing the Sangha show the importance of meditation. Reflection and mediation is central to the recognition of the individual's role as one part of an entity. Decisions are based on consensus of views; no particular interest is allowed to take a commanding role, except to resolve conflict, or to promote the spirit of peace and to preserve human dignity.[10] The metaphor used for decision-making is that the people who come together, like the four streams, merge together (Chakrawarti 1992: 16). The individual may judge what is right or wrong for himself or herself, but always in relation to others. Correct behaviour requires a constant self-repositioning of the individual until perfect understanding is reached and social harmony achieved.

Social responsibility lies not only with those who rule, but with each individual through whom the promotion of the value of inter-connectedness rather than selfishness makes a difference in a given ruling system. Claims to justice must be accompanied by awareness of responsibility towards one another. Conflicts between individuals are settled by negotiation through deep reflection: resorting to the judicial system to claim one's rights signifies the failure of each party to reflect and understand, a breakdown of trust in social relations, and most important of all a breakdown of individual moral autonomy. Conflicts are not to be solved through confrontation but through dialogues.

McConnell (1990: 200) notes that avoidance of confrontation on principle is based on the view that 'once escalation has taken place, threats made, and violence[11] employed, the space for thoughtful consideration of new directions narrows down.[12] Buddhism opposes threefold clinging: (1) clinging to view points; (2) clinging to personal belief; (3) clinging to rituals. Only through freeing oneself from threefold clinging, can a dialogue be used to solve tension. Open confrontation signifies that threefold clinging still prevails, still insulates the self from the other and generates conflict rather than peaceful settlement.

Pasanathamo (1987) lists five main principles of social justice articulated in early social formation in Thailand:

1 Respect for the right of animals and other transient beings.[13]

2 Respect for the rights of other people's husbands, wives, loved ones.[14]
3 Respect for the rights of other peoples' property.
4 Respect for the right of access to true information.
5 Respect for the right to obtain mindful communication.

These principles were relevant to an agrarian society where the state was less complex than it is today. Buddhist principles of social justice also respect ecological harmony, personal rights, economic rights, the right to information, reflection and meaningful debate. Rights to true information may include political rights (to being heard and being informed). The right to mindful communication means the right to seek advice and the right to discuss. Social justice is not an absolute set of legal claims, but is sought through reasoning, reflection and mutual understanding. It is not to be treated only within the parameter of law and order, but in the spirit of understanding and compassion.

3.5 Buddhism and economic justice

Principles of economic justice in Buddhism may be extrapolated from the principle of right living from the Eight Fold Path. Right living means living in a way that is not exploitative of others but which is governed by the principle of diligent work, sharing and mutual help. Buddhism sees exploitation as the effect of greed. Avoiding exploitation does not mean banning wealth, for that would contradict the principle of respect for other people's property. Material wealth has value only if it helps improve social justice through redistribution: it is not in itself a value. Wealth for its own sake is considered to be a disruptive force. The following extract from the Pali canon by Pasanathamo illustrates this point:

> Wealth can belong to a private ownership when its owner serves the basic necessity to the society. If not so, wealth is of no value, and the wealthy are worthless. The accumulation of wealth becomes unrighteous . . . if private wealth does not become the wealth of the society, and does not bring goodness,

the society should attempt to manage or reorganize the ownership system of that wealth and distribute it to make it thoroughly reach all members. This is the basis for the development and individual moral attainment of all members in societies . . .

Pasanathamo, 1987: 96

Modernist thinking claims that traditional values may be instrumental to economic performance, Buddhist thinking insists that economic development must respect the harmony between the social and natural world. Economic development and wealth are instrumental to compassion as a central value in Buddhist thought and not the other way around. The Buddhist model of socioeconomic development may be termed 'mindful development' or a model of development that is sensitive to different life forms and which treats people in compassionate rather than instrumental terms.

A similar logic is applied to work: Buddhism advocates diligent work believing that work is a medium through which compassion can be realized. Work and meditation should be two sides of the same coin. Meditation is seen as a non-physical activity, but it should be integrated in every activity, including work, thus joining mind and matter. Work must consist of moral and social values, in addition to economic values. Buddhism when seen in this light is not anti-capitalist and does not oppose private production, but it opposes capitalism which is destructive of social relations or the environment.

3.6 Socially engaged buddhism: a new meeting of East and West

Buddhism has a long history of interaction with the West; King Asoka is known to have sent Buddhist missionaries to Macedonia, Asia Minor and Egypt. According to Benz (1976: 309), traces of Buddhist influence can be seen in the asceticism of Eastern Christian mystics, the life of Buddha is transformed into the life of a Christian saint in the legends of Barlaam and Joasaph by John of Darmacus. Records of Buddhist teachings in Persian were translated into German by Arthur Schopenhauer in 1819 (Conze 1971: 242), and paved the way for more exchanges between Buddhism and the Western world. This influence can be traced in the work of many intellectuals such as Carl Jung, Friedrich Nietzsche, Henry David Thoreau and many others. In 1893, Buddhism first penetrated the religious consciousness of the people of the USA at the World's Parliament of Religions in Chicago where a representative of Zen Buddhism spoke in English to a Western audience. His name was Soyen Shaku from Kamakura, Japan. His sermon was translated by D.T. Suzuki and contributed to the spread of Buddhism in the West (Benz 1976). At the Sixth Great Buddhist Council between 1954 and 1956, U Nu, the Prime Minister of Burma organized a fundraising drive to build an educational institution for Buddhist missionaries in Europe. The seminary was built in Hamburg in 1957 (Benz 1976).

> Efforts to institutionalize Buddhism through formal education channels have produced a new Buddhist scholarship in the West, primarily attracted by its teachings. Buddhism has made a significant impact in the process of reflection in 'Western' civilization. In 1929, the philosopher Max Scheler wrote an essay entitled 'Man in the Age of Compensation' in which he wrote, 'We must learn anew to envisage the great, invisible solidarity of all living beings in universal life, of all minds in the eternal spirit – and at the same time the mutual solidarity of the world process and the destiny of its supreme principle. And we must not just accept this world unity as a mere doctrine, but practice and promote it in our inner and outer lives.'
>
> Benz, 1976: 321

Socially engaged Buddhism is a movement which emerged in Asia as a pragmatic response to specific acts of violence and social injustice. There are many socially engaged Buddhist movements such as the Sarvodaya movement in Sri Lanka active since 1958, the movement of Youth for Social Service in Thailand, Coordinating Group for Religion in Society in Thailand, the network of NGOs under the umbrella of the Asian Cultural Forum on Development in the 1970s. One form of socially engaged Buddhism that reached Western countries and provided a meeting point between social activism in the West and Asia has its roots in the Vietnam war and the invasion of Tibet.

During the 1960s, in response to the escalation of the war in Vietnam and the massive destruction and human suffering, a group of Vietnamese Buddhist monks and nuns began to work on a non-partisan, non-violent way to help their countrymen. The idea was to form two lines of monks and nuns in yellow robes, symbolizing the respect for life, to lead the civilians out of the war zone. Soldiers on both sides of the conflict showed their respect for life by not shooting at the people, although several nuns and monks were seriously hurt by stray bullets and this led to the realization that an active involvement by Buddhists in society could compel compassion in the midst of violent conflict (Kraft 1985).

The Tiep Hien Order is a form of engaged Buddhism in Vietnam established in response to the conflict which killed millions of people and caused major socioeconomic and political upheavals. The order reformulated ancient Buddhist precepts into fourteen new commands to that meet the conditions of the time. These may be summarized as follows (Thich Nhat Hanh 1987):

1 Do not be idolatrous about or bound to doctrine, theory or ideology, even Buddhist ones. All systems of thoughts are guiding means; they are not absolute truths.

2 Do not think the knowledge you presently possess is changeless, absolute truth. Learn and practise detachment in order to be receptive to other points of view. Truth is found in life and not merely in conceptual knowledge.

3 Do not force others, including children, by any means, to adopt your views, whether by authority, threat, money, propaganda, or even education. Through compassionate dialogue, help others to renounce fanaticism and narrowness.

4 Do not avoid contact with suffering or close your eyes to suffering. Find ways to be with those who are suffering by any means and, awaken yourself and others to the reality of suffering.

5 Do not accumulate wealth while millions are hungry.

6 Do not hold on to anger or hatred. Practice meditation on compassion in order to understand those who have caused anger and hatred.

7 Do not lose yourself in your surroundings. Learn to practise breathing in order to regain composure of body and mind, to practise mindfulness, and to develop concentration and understanding.

8 Do not use words that can create discord and divide the community. Make every effort to reconcile and resolve all conflicts, however small.

9 Do not say untruthful things for the sake of personal interest or to impress people. Do not utter words that cause division and hatred. Do not spread news that you do not know to be certain. Do not criticize or condemn things that you are not sure of. Always speak truthfully and constructively. Have the courage to speak out about situations of injustice, even when doing so may threaten your own safety.

10 Do not use the Buddhist community for personal gains or profit, or to transform your community into a political party.

11 Do not live with a vocation that is harmful to humans and nature. Do not invest in companies that deprive others of their chance to live.

12 Do not kill and do not let others kill. Find whatever means possible to protect life and prevent war.

13 Possess nothing that should belong to others. Respect the property of others, but prevent others from enriching themselves by human suffering or the suffering of other beings.

14 Do not mistreat your body. Learn to handle it with respect. Do not look at your body as an instrument. Be fully aware of the responsibility of bringing new life into the world. Meditate on the world into which you are bringing new beings.

As Thich Nhat Hanh (1987: 89) explains, the meaning of the first precept deals with the destructive function of thought, 'if you have a gun, you can shoot one, two, three, five people; but if you have an ideology and stick to it, thinking it is the absolute truth, you can kill millions. This precept includes the precept of not killing in its deepest sense. Human kind suffers very much from attachment to views'. The second precept addresses the creative function of thought and urges a receptive mind to different ideas and viewpoints. The third stimulates the spirit of inquiry. The fourth and fifth urge an engagement with society and redistributive justice without political manipulation. The sixth, seventh, eighth, and ninth precepts stimulate the re-positioning of the self for social harmony. In these precepts, meditation emerges as a crucial element in achieving peace. As Eppsteiner (1985: 152) explains 'the fourteen precepts of the Tiep Hien order are a unique expression of traditional Buddhist morality coming to terms with contemporary issues . . . they were not developed by secluded monks attempting to update the traditional Buddhist precepts. Rather, they were forged in the crucible of war and devastation that was the daily experience of many South-East Asians countries'.

The Tiep Hien order and its peace workers became engaged in helping the population as well as in non-violent appeals for a cease-fire, appeals which were widespread across the country as well as abroad. Several founding members of the Tiep Hien order travelled abroad to persuade civic groups in the USA and elsewhere to influence the US government to stop the war in their country. The contact between the exiled Tiep Hien community and civic groups such as the Quakers, the Civil Rights movements, the Anti-nuclear movement and ecological movement in the West led to the rediscovery of Buddhist values in social activism in the West. Tiep Hien became known in the West as the Order of Inter-Being. Thich Nhat Hanh became a leading inspirational figure for members of the Buddhist Peace Fellowship, a national organization composed of independent local groups in the USA, each working on its own projects. The Buddhist Peace Fellowship now has chapters in the United Kingdom and Australia.

Two important issues emerged from the interaction between Buddhist and Western activism. First, the South Vietnamese government accused the Tiep Hien order in the 1960s of having communist links. The communist government today also accuses members of affiliation with a US based antigovernment group, reflecting the legacy of the Cold War as an ideological conflict. Second, notwithstanding the social and political complexity behind the US government's decision to withdraw from Vietnam and to put an end to the war, the fact that civic groups in Western Europe and the USA could put pressure on the government to make this decision demonstrates the importance of democratic institutions.

Cooperation between Buddhist organizations and peace research institutes may be regarded as the realization that Buddhist values and existing institutions can potentially bring about more compassionate action towards attaining global peace. The Fourth International Seminar on Buddhism and Leadership for Peace held in Ulan Bator, Mongolia in 1989 represents a major step in this cooperation. It was sponsored by the Asian Buddhist Conference for Peace in cooperation with the Centre for Global Nonviolence Planning Project at the Institute for Peace, University of Hawaii, and the Dae Won Sa Buddhist temple of Hawaii. Contributors to the seminar included religious leaders and scientists from Asia, Western Europe, the former Soviet Union and the USA. The objective was to seek ways in which Buddhism can contribute to the major problems that confront humankind at the end of the twentieth century (peace, disarmament, economic justice, human rights, ecological viability and universal cooperation).

According to Paige (1990), three key aspects of Buddhism were identified at this conference as positive forces. First, for an international network of engaged Buddhists who can cooperate meaningfully in a common struggle against oppressive social forces was stressed. Second, the global crisis of human survival was seen as a result of the convergence of military, political, economic, social, cultural, ecological and spiritual factors, for which Buddhist tolerance had an essential role in helping to solve this crisis. 'Mutual tolerance among different ideologies must be guaranteed by the pluralism of the Middle Path. The sustainability of the coming global civilization can only build on *ahimsa*, non-violence and care for all living beings' (Mushakoji, cited in Paige 1990: 140). Third, ways of realizing peace were presented in two dimensions, i.e. negative peace (absence of war) and positive peace (presence of peace factors).

63

Following this conference, two international Non-Governmental Organisations were set up, namely the International Network of Engaged Buddhists (INEB), and the Unrepresented Nations and Peoples Organization (UNPO). INEB has chapters in Europe, North America, Asia and Australia, and includes scientists and activists who share a common goal in bringing Buddhist values into their everyday lives. Apart from different activities directed at minimizing conflict and violence in countries such as Burma, Cambodia, India and Sri Lanka, INEB seeks to encourage a stronger link between the academic/theoretical community and the activist community (*see Seeds of Peace*, Vol. 7, No. 2, 1991: 10) which resulted in new associations of scientists seeking to create alternative economic and political analytical frameworks to respond to the socially unjust and ecologically destructive international economic and political system.[15] The UNPO, supported by the Dalai Lama of Tibet, seeks to enhance the voice and representation of nations, peoples and minorities who do not have a recognized state or government of their own, and hence cannot be represented at the United Nations. UNPO adopts five main principles which reflect an integration of international legal standards with the Buddhist spirit of non-violence and tolerance.[16] UNPO acts as an international forum for the voiceless peoples. In assisting its members in bringing change by effective, democratic, and non-violent means, UNPO tries to develop preventive diplomacy by promoting mindful dialogues between governments, international organizations and its members.

Socially engaged Buddhism under the form of INEP and UNPO, represents an alliance of hope which cuts across national and ethnic boundaries, and reflects the 'homelessness' nature of Buddhism.[17] It re-connects the ancient with the modern, and the Eastern with the Western, and through this re-connection the disjunction of thought caused by preoccupation with the self may be solved. Buddhism has maintained its traditional approach in its meetings with the West: it links its values with existing systems and allows for transformation. In that sense, it may be argued that Buddhism is transforming itself through an engagement with global issues.

3.7 Conclusion

The international climate of trust today leaves much to be desired. Violence in society has many physical causes; but the mental causes are equally, if not more, important. In many societies today, people's material needs have been satisfied, but anxiety and violence persist. Violence is an expression of the poor quality of human relations which can only be changed through changing the ways in which we look at each other. The Buddhists claim that dualistic thinking is a universal phenomenon and lies at the root of violence and affliction which is relevant today.

The Buddhist definition of individuality as being indivisible from the totality of the universe contains many theories which are relevant to reflections on the relationship between science and scientists, social and ecological forms of violence. Buddhism can make a significant contribution to a new world view of science that is less destructive. Buddhist teachings emphasize on the notion of civility, but do not take account of civil society and the struggle for power. Yet, the tolerance and openness of Buddhism which had been its political weakness has become its strength in its meeting with the West.

Just as thinkers in the West have responded to Buddhist teachings so Buddhist thinkers, too, have discovered the significance of an organized civil society. A continued and constructive dialogue between thinkers of the two traditions may eventually lead to a new morality, a morality which can change the character of science and governance. An alternative framework of science and politics based on compassion can still be proposed with joint efforts from East and West.

Notes

1 This meeting-point may also be found in other authors, such as Carl Jung, Claude Lévi-Strauss, Michel Foucault, and David Bohm.
2 Professor Kinhide Mushakolji is gratefully acknowledged for his succinct formulation.
3 For example, on reincarnation, Head and Cranston (1961) dispel the myth that it is an Oriental concept incompatible with Western thinking and belief. Pre-existence of the soul was taught by Pythagoras, and many other religious teachers.

4 Civic organizations in Asia are responding to the reframing of their issues through closer alliances in order to prepare a People's Charter for the 21st century, a process initiated since 1988 and expected to be completed in 1996/7.

5 According to de Silva (1979), the Buddhist cannon listed some fifty mental activities.

6 The notion of *karma* is often interpreted as a collection of good or bad actions which determine the reincarnation of the human being in his/her next life. It is often interpreted as 'fate'. However, *karma* as human action also concerns the here and now. It is possible to change one's action and fate at every moment of one's life.

7 Sometimes *Prajna* is translated as 'penetrating insight', 'perfect understanding' or 'perfect wisdom'.

8 The term is often translated as the Enlightened. To avoid confusion with the European Age of Enlightenment in the eighteenth century, the term mindful is preferred.

9 Meditation has often been stereotyped as a composed sitting position to obtain calmness of the mind. However, meditation must also be practised as an integral aspect of everyday life activity. A calm mind must rule over every gesture, word and act.

10 Thich Nhat Hanh (1991) explains that Buddhism should not be seen as the preservation of the Buddhist hierarchy, the pagodas and monasteries, the scriptures, rituals and traditions, but as the defence of human dignity and freedom which must be led towards peace and compassion (Sivaraksa 1994:100).

11 Violence is recognized in Buddhism in many forms (thought, word, look, body).

12 An example of the destructiveness of confrontational thought may be found in the Tonkin Gulf incidents which led the US government to escalate the war in Vietnam in 1964. According to Shapley (1993: 302–308), in August 1964 Washington was informed that Hanoi's navy attacked a US destroyer in the Tonkin Gulf. Two days later Hanoi *seemed* to strike again. Although there was little proof for these events, the reported incident provoked anxious feelings in Washington that led to the bombing of North Vietnam and the eventual escalation of the war.

13 Respect for the rights of animals originated from the prohibition on the use of animals in religious sacrifice. According to Buddhist teachings it makes no sense to show one's devotion by causing pain to another.

14 This precept was based on the case of the admission of a child into the Buddhist order at his own request which lead to parents suffering at the loss of their child (Thich Nhat Hanh 1991). This precept was applied later to reinforce rules regulating the 'private' (see Truong 1990, ch. 4).

15 The New Economics Foundation based in London.

16 These include: (1) the equal right to self-determination of all nations and peoples; (2) adherence to internationally accepted human rights standards; (3) adherence to the principle of democracy and rejection of totalitarianism and intolerance; (4) promotion of non-violence and the

rejection of terrorism as an instrument of policy; (5) protection of the natural environment.

17 Buddhism is a vehicle for the promotion of human dignity. As such it needs no identity, or in Sirivaksa's term buddhism with a lower case b.

References

Agarwal, B. (1992) 'The Gender and Environment Debate: Lessons from India', *Feminist Studies*.

Asian NGO Coalition for Agrarian Reform and Rural Development (1993) *Economy, Ecology and Spirituality: Towards a Theory and Practice of Sustainability*, ANGOC, Manila.

Bangprapha, W. (1985) 'The Work of the Co-ordinating Group for Religion in Society in Developing People's Resources', in *Access to Justice: The Struggle for Human Rights in South East Asia*, H.M. Scoble and L.S. Wiseberg (eds.), (London: Zed Press).

Banuri, T. (1990) 'Modernization and its Discontents: A Cultural Perspective on the Theories of Development' in F. A Marglin,. and S.A. Marglin, *Dominating Knowledge* (Oxford: Clarendon Press).

Benz, E. (1976) 'Buddhism in the Western World', in *The Cultural, Political and Religious Significance of Buddhism in the Modern World*. (eds.) by H. Moulin and J.C. Maraldo (London:Collier MacMillan).

Bohn, D. and M. Edwards (1991) *Changing Consciousness: Exploring the Hidden Source of the Social, Political and Environmental Crises Facing Our World* (San: Francisco Harper).

Braidotti, R. (1991) *Patterns of Dissonance*. (Cambridge: Polity Press).

—— et al (1994) *Women, The Environment and Sustainable Development*, (London: Zed Press).

Bylert van, V. (1989) *Epistemology and Spiritual Authority: The development of epistemology and logic in old Nyaya and the Buddhist School of Epistemology*. (Vienna; University of Vienna).

Callinicos, A. (1989) *Against Post-Modernism: A Marxist Critique* (Oxford: Basil Blackwell).

Chakrawati, U. 'Buddhism as a Discourse or Dissent: Class and Gender', *Pravada*. 1:5 (1992) 12–18.

Connolly, W.E. (1993) 'Beyond Good and Evil: The Ethical Sensibility of Michel Foucault', *Political Theory*. 4:3.

Conze, E. (1971) *Le Bouddhisme dans son essence et son développement* (Paris: Payot).

Eck, D. (1993) *Encountering God: A Spiritual Journey From Bozeman to Banaras*. (London: Penguin Books).

Eppsteiner, F. (ed) (1985) *The Path of Compassion: Writings on Socially Engaged Buddhism*. (Berkeley: Parallax Press).

Fukuyama, F. (1995) *Trust: Social Virtues and the Creation of Prosperity*. (New York:The Free Press).

Gardet. L. et al (1976) *Cultures and Time: At the Crossroads of Cultures*. (Paris: UNESCO Press).

Ghai, Y. (1994) *Human Rights and Governance: The Asia Debate,* Occasional Paper Series, Asia Foundation.

Giddens, A. (1991) *Modernity and Self-Identity: The Self and Society in the Late Modern Age.* (Stanford: Stanford University Press).

—— (1995) 'The New Context of Politics' in *Democratic Dialogue,* 1.

Haraway, D. (1989) *Primate Visions: Gender, Race and Nature in the World of Modern Science.* (London: Routledge).

—— (1991) *Simians, Cyborgs, and Women: The Reinvention of Nature,* (London: Free Association Books).

Hayward, S. (1987) *Shifting World Changing Minds: Where the Sciences and Buddhism meet,* Shambala (Boston New: Science Library).

Head, J. and Cranston, S.L. (eds) (1970) *Reincarnation: An East West Anthology* (Wheaton Illinois: Quest Books).

Horowitz, G. (1992) 'Groundless Democracy' in *The Shadow of Spirit: Post-Modernism and Religion.* (London: Routledge).

Hofstede, G. and Bond, M. (1988) 'The Confucius Connection: From Cultural Roots to Economic Growth' *Organizational Dynamics*

Kraft, K. (1985) 'Engaged Buddhism: An Introduction' in *The Path of Compassion* (eds.) Eppsteiner.

International Commission of Jurists and Consumers' Association of Penang (1981) *Rural Development and Human Rights in South East Asia,* seminar, report Penang.

Lafitte, G. (1990) 'A Meditation on Buddhist History and its Lessons for Today' in *Radical Conservatism,* (ed.) by S. Sivaraksa Bangkok: INEB.

Mathur, G.B. (1989) 'The Current Impasses of Development Thinking: The Metaphysics of Power' in *Alternatives,*. 14:2.

McConnell, J.A. (1990) 'The Rohini Conflict and the Buddhist Intervention' in *Radical Conservatism,* (ed.) S. Sivaraksa, Bangkok: INEB.

Mies, M. and Shiva V. (1992) *EcoFeminism.* (London: Zed Press).

Nandy, A. (ed) (1988) *Science, Hegemony and Violence: A Requiem for Modernity* (Oxford University Press: United Nations University).

Pasanathamo, P. (1987) 'Buddhism and Social Justice', in *Religions and Ideologies in the Asian Struggle,* Asia Regional Fellowship, 4th Assembly, Chiang-mai Thailand, May 19–24.

Phra Debvedi (1990) 'Buddhist Education', in *Radical Conservatism,* (ed.) by S. Sivaraksa,. Bangkok: INEB.

Plumwood, V. (1993) *Feminism and the Mastery of Nature.* (London: Routledge).

Schumacher, E.F. (1987) 'Buddhist Economics', *Resurgence,* 1, N. 11, Jan–Feb.

Sen, A. (1987) *On Ethics and Economics* (Oxford: Basil Blackwell).

Shapley, D. (1993) *Promise and Power: The Life and Times of Robert McNamara,* (Boston: Little, Brown and Company).

Silva de, L. (1979) *The Problem of the Self in Buddhism and Christianity.* (London: MacMillan).

Sivaraksa, S. (1988) *A Socially Engaged Buddhism,* Thai Inter-Religious Commission for Development, Bangkok.

—— (1993) *Buddhist Perception for Desirable Societies in the Future,* Thai Inter-Religious Commission for Development Bangkok.

—— (1994) *A Buddhist Vision for Renewing Society,* Thai Inter-Religious Commission for Development, Bangkok.

Smart, B. (1992) *Modern Conditions, Postmodern Controversies* (London: Routledge).

Smart N. (1990) 'Western Society and Buddhism' in *Radical Conservatism* (ed.) S. Sivaraksa Bangkok: INEB.

Suksamran, S. (1983) *Buddhism and Politics in Thailand,* Institute of South East Asian Studies, Singapore.

Tambiah, S.J. (1992) *Buddhism Betrayed? Religion, Politics and Violence in Sri Lanka.* (Chicago; Chicago University Press).

Thich Nhat Hanh (1988) *The Heart of Understanding: Commentaries on the Prajnaparamita Heart Sutra.*(Berkeley: Parallax Press).

—— (1987) *Being Peace.*(Berkeley: Parallax Press).

—— (1991) *Old Path White Clouds: The Life Story of the Buddha.* (London: Rider).

—— *Living Buddha, Living Christ* (1995) (New York: A Riverhead Book).

Toulmin, S. (1990) *Cosmopolis: The Hidden Agenda of Modernity* (Chicago: University of Chicago Press).

Trungpa, C. (1987) *Cutting Through Spiritual Materialism.* (Boston: Shambala).

Truong, T.D. (1990) 'Gender Relations and Prostitution in Thailand' in *Sex, Money and Morality: Prostitution and Tourism in South East Asia* (London: Zed Press).

Weber, R. (1986) *Dialogues with Scientists and Sages: The Search for Unity* (London: Routledge and Kegan Paul).

Chapter 4

The Relevance of Confucianism Today

Yang Baoyun

4.1 Introduction

In the West, people associate Confucius and Confucianism with traditional Chinese culture. Confucianism has held a paramount position in the development of traditional Chinese culture for more than two thousand years, and has cast a wide and far-reaching influence on some of China's neighbours. Even today when China has a campaign of modernization on a large scale and has maintained its world-renowned high economic growth rates, Confucianism still remains, to a certain degree, influential on the minds and behaviour of the Chinese people.

With China's economic reform deepening and China becoming increasingly open to the outer world, more and more Western countries and peoples are engaged actively in trade and cultural communications with China. Due to the cultural differences between China and the West, however, many Westerners do not have much knowledge, let alone profound understanding, of China and its traditional culture. Confucianism is at the core: it blocks the successful exchange and communication between the two sides. For this reason, many Westerners have tried to obtain a comprehensive understanding of Chinese cultural tradition and values affected by its cultural tradition. Based on the research achievements of Chinese scholars, this chapter summarizes the fundamental ideas of Confucianism and their influence on Western readers.

4.2 Moral-ethical, social and spiritual values in Confucianism

Confucius who lived in the Spring and Autumn Era (770 BC–476 BC), founded Confucianism. His family name was *Kong*, his first name was *Qiu,* and his nick name was *Zhongni*; he was born in Zhouyi, Lu State (now Qufu county, Shangdong Province) in 551 BC and died in 479 BC. He is known in every household as a pre-eminent thinker, statesman and educator in Chinese history.

Confucius came from a declining aristocratic slaveholder family. He was once appointed in charge of the storehouses and domestic animals for public use when he was young. Later, he was engaged in private education as a professional teacher for a long time. It is said that all his life he had a total of three thousand pupils among whom over seventy were outstanding. He often travelled around the vassals' territories at that time accompanied by some of his pupils. He had been courteously received and consulted by potentates, but never got a chance to put his political ideals into practice by himself. In his fifties he was appointed Minister of Justice in Lu State but resigned after only three months. During his old age he collated some ancient books and records in Lu State. It is said that the *Book of Historical Documents* (*Shang Shu*) and the *Book of Odes* (*Shi Jing*) were collated by him; The *Book of Changes* (*Yi Jing*) has his annotations; and the *Spring and Autumn Annals* (*Chun Qiu*) was compiled by him. He also examined and revised the *Book of Rites* (*Li Ji*) and the *Book of Music* (*Yue Jing*). The books, with the exception the *Book of Music*, which had been lost, became the classics of the Confucian School. Among the 'Five Classics', *Spring and Autumn Annals* was the oldest and most complete to survive: it made an enormous impact on Chinese historical works.

It was because Confucius lived in an era during which significant social changes took place that he studied various issues concerning human life and state affairs, thus developing his own theoretical system. The school of thought founded by Confucius is called Confucianism. His speeches were compiled after his death by his disciples in a book named *The Analects,* which mirrored Confucius' theory and thoughts, and laid the principal theoretical foundation of Confucianism.

71

The theory of Confucianism has undergone a long process of development, but it has evolved according to the fundamental thoughts of Confucius. It pays special attention to the relationship among people and concentrates on developing social ethical thinking. The principal values in Confucius' theory are represented by three fields: moral-ethical, social and spiritual.

In the moral-ethical field, the core category of Confucius' thought is 'Humanity', from which two basic propositions are stated: 'Be benevolent to others' and 'To master oneself and return to propriety is humanity'.

Confucius attaches great importance to the role of human beings. His idea of 'Be benevolent to others', on the one hand, means that compared with spiritual things or other objects, man is the most important. Take the tenth chapter of The *Analects* of Confucius, for instance, 'A certain stable was burned down. On returning from court, Confucius asked: Anyone hurt? He did not ask about the horses.' The story fully exemplified Confucius' positive attitude towards man's social value as a human being. Confucius takes moral cultivation as the criterion for measuring the value of human life, which is shown in his words such as 'the superior man cherishes virtues', 'the superior man understands righteousness', 'the superior man considers the righteousness as the most important', 'the superior man regards righteousness as the substance of everything'. Confucius also thinks that the purpose of cultivating morality lies in 'pacifying people', 'pacifying the populace'.

The Confucian proposition 'To master oneself and return to propriety is humanity', mainly concerns the relationship between 'propriety' and 'humanity'. 'Humanity' forms the kernel of Confucius' thoughts, while 'propriety' is also a very important concept of Confucius' theoretical system; 'propriety' includes political institutions and ethical codes. 'To master oneself and return to propriety is humanity' means to restrain one's desire and observe 'propriety' in one's speeches, behaviour, and in what one sees and hears, so that 'humanity' can be accomplished. In other words, with the external coercion of institutions and codes and with the perfect internal moral cultivation and realm of lofty spirit, one can consummate 'humanity'.

In the social world, Confucius holds that rulers should 'keep frugality and cherish his subjects, employ the labour of the populace only in the right seasons', and strongly opposes the extortion and excessive imposition by monarchs, and monarchs ruling with an iron hand. On the contrary, Confucius advocates that a ruler should 'govern his state by virtue'. He also initiated the idea that those who administer a state or a family 'do not worry about poverty, but worry about unequal distribution of wealth; do not worry about there being too few people, but worry about the lack of security and peace'.

On the other hand, Confucius' idea of 'Be benevolent to others' also means that people should get along with each other and love each other, live together peacefully. For example, between family members, the father should be lenient and the son should be filial, the older brother should be friendly to the younger, while the younger should be respectful to the older. One should keep one's promise to friends. A ruler should treat his subjects with propriety and ministers serve their ruler with loyalty. Between the ruler and his people, rules should 'seek benefits for his people', 'make use of the populace for righteous reasons' and 'keep being frugal and benevolent to the populace', while the populace should 'be ready to serve their rulers'. In short, 'A man of humanity, wishing to establish his own character, also establishes the character of others, and wishing to be prominent himself, also helps others to be prominent'. 'Do not do to others what you do not want them to do to you.' Should all these precepts be realized, there would be peace and tranquillity in the whole world. Confucius' thought 'be benevolent to others' had obvious influence upon later generations. Mencius, for example, based his idea of 'benevolent government' on Confucius' teachings.

Confucius devoted his whole life to education and fostered many talented students, thus making significant contributions to the development of ancient Chinese scholarship. He himself often learned from others as he thought with modesty, 'when walking in the company of three men, there must be one I can learn something from', and assumed a 'untiring learning' attitude. He 'teaches others without being wearied': he recommended 'seeking truth from facts', which

73

he described as 'to say that you know when you do know and say that you do not know when you do not know'. He offered many humble disciples the chance to acquire knowledge, according to the principle of 'In education there should be no class distinction.' Confucius initiated a new style of education, which was reflected in the unprecedented prosperity of Chinese academic culture and education in the Warring States Period (475–221 BC).

In the spiritual field, on the aspect of the view of Heaven (*tian*) and its Way (*dao*), Confucius believed in deity and stood in awe of the Mandate of Heaven. But Confucius was sceptical about the existence of gods and ghosts. He held that one should 'respect spiritual beings but stand afar' and once said, 'If we are not yet able to serve man, how can we serve spiritual beings?' He gave priority to solving mundane problems, and established the Confucian tradition of valuing human affairs.

4.3 The Development of Confucianism

4.3.1 Warring states period (475–221 BC): Mencius

Confucianism was divided into several sub-schools after Confucius' death, of which the sub-school of Mencius was the most influential. This is the reason why Confucianism is usually called 'The doctrines of Confucius and Mencius'.

The name of Mencius is Meng, his given name is Ke and his style name is Ziyu. He was born in Zhou State (now in Zhou County, Shandong Province) in the Warring States Period. He lived from about 372 BC to 289 BC and was a pupil of Confucius' grandson Zisi. His career was similar to that of Confucius. He devoted most of his life to private education as a professional teacher, and also travelled around several states. According to historical records, 'There are scores of chariots following his, while the number of his followers are hundreds' at a time when Mencius had most pupils. Although, like Confucius, he was courteously received by potentates in those states, his political opinions were never accepted by them. His speeches were later compiled in a book titled *Mencius*.

Mencius inherited and developed Confucius' idea of 'humanity'. He believed that man had an innate feeling of 'commiseration', 'the feeling of shame and dislike', 'the feeling of deference and compliance', 'the feeling of right and wrong', which did not mean everyone was born a saint. He pointed out that at birth a human being was only the embryo of 'good', which needed cultivation and growth, and that, if one developed the embryo of 'good' to the utmost, one could be a 'saint'. Otherwise, 'good' might be lost. Once the 'good' in one's mind disappeared, he could not be called 'human'. For that reason, Mencius urged people repeatedly to pay attention to preserving and cultivating the character of 'good'.

Mencius' famous theory of 'humane government' is based on his philosophy that human nature is originally good. The tenet of his theory of 'humane government' is 'valuing the populace', Mencius is against despotic rule, which he describes as 'leading beasts to devour people'. He holds that: 'Dukes have three precious properties. They are land, populace, and state affairs', and advocates that the 'populace are more important than the monarch', and 'in a state the people are the most important; the state is the next; the ruler is of slight importance'. He points out that to unify the states and govern the nation, it is paramount to handle the populace's affairs well. In fact, Mencius' thoughts are the simple democratic precepts in ancient Chinese history.

Mencius drew the conclusion from historical experience that the decisive factor of a ruler's political success was the degree of the people's support. Only one who wins the support of his subjects can be a successful monarch, and one who loses the hearts of his subjects is a 'mere fellow' who should be killed by all of the people. A monarch who is harmful to his country should be replaced. Mencius even gives an example to illustrate this point. He once said, if the despots like King Zhou (1066 BC) of the Shang Dynasty (c1600–1066 BC) were killed by their subjects, the action could not be called murdering the ruler. A monarch can win the support of his subjects only by carrying on 'humane government'. The prime measurement of 'humane government' is to 'let people have their properties', in other words, to guarantee people that their goods, possessions, or properties are safe and not subject to expropriation. Mencius

75

believes that 'one who has his possessions guaranteed safe has the good mind', he said that the ruler should let a family of eight mouths have a farm of one hundred *mu* in order to have sufficient food and suffer no hunger, to raise domestic animals for meat, to plant mulberry trees and raise silkworms for clothing; the ruler should also set up schools teaching the principles of filial piety and brotherly respect in order to make people friendly and helpful to each other, to take good care of the sick, and never leave their home towns. Only in this way, Mencius said, can a country become strong and powerful, and people keep constant moral order and codes of behaviour. Therefore, Mencius requires the rulers to 'reduce punishments and fines, lower taxes and levies', 'take benefits from the populace according to their position', so that people are able to take care of their 'constant properties'.

Mencius' idea of 'constant property' means the individual small-scale peasant economy which combines farming and weaving together in a family and ties labour to farmlands. During the era in which Mencius lived, Chinese society was undergoing a transition towards feudalism. It was progressive for Mencius to advocate the state's use of administrative measures to adopt a new style of production.

During the Warring States Period several states waged endless wars upon each other and inflicted great suffering upon the people. Mencius vigorously opposed the wars of annexation at that time, bearing in mind his thoughts on 'humane government'. He thought those who encouraged wars should be severely punished. However, he was also aware that unification of the warring states was inevitable, so he put forward the idea that only those opposed to massacre could achieve unification, only those who practised 'humane government' could unify states, and those who relied on violence would never achieve unification.

Mencius also advanced his view on 'righteousness' and 'profit'. He raised righteousness to the highest level of moral values and he advocated the spirit of self-sacrifice in the cause of righteousness. He pointed out that people pursued both life and humanity with righteousness: he declared that people should 'lay down their life for a just cause' when conflict existed between these two. Mencius valued 'righteousness' much more than 'profits'. For example, when King Hui of Liang State asked him 'What do you have which is profitable to my country?', Mencius answered, 'Why must your Majesty use the term profit? What I have to offer are nothing but humanity and righteousness and that's enough.' Mencius' philosophy of valuing righteousness and despising profit influenced Chinese feudal society for a long time.

4.3.2 West Han Dynasty (206 BC–AD 23): Dong Zhongshu

Confucianism has not followed a rigid course of development. It has constantly changed and reformed while retaining the core of Confucius' basic theoretical system.

During the West Han Dynasty owing to the vigorous advocacy of the Emperor Wu (139–87 BC), Confucianism acquired a supreme position among various theories. Confucianism in this period was characterized by the idea of 'reciprocal responsiveness between Heaven and Mankind' and the 'divine right of kings', with Dong Zhongshu as its chief representative.

Dong Zhongshu (c179–104 BC) preached his political theory of 'Great Unification'. He said that 'the principles of great unification exemplified in Spring and Autumn Annals is immortal and would be handed down from generation to generation forever'. What he called great unification meant the restriction of the vassals' power so that they had to submit to the reign of the emperor, and people all over the world would show their obedience. However, the emperor would never achieve unification if 'people learned different theories and had different opinions; different schools of thought upheld different doctrines which had different tenets'. Based on this belief, Dong demanded Emperor Wu to ban all other schools of thought and honour Confucianism only. His proposal was adopted by Emperor Wu, and relevant measures were soon carried out all over China.

Dong believed that since Heaven conferred on the emperor the right to rule, 'the common people should be diminished while emperor be raised, emperors should be diminished while Heaven be raised'. If the emperor did not rule in a proper way, Heaven would send disasters of condemnation and warning. If the emperor did not rectify his way of ruling after disasters had occurred, his country would go to the dogs. So in Dong's opinion, an emperor should 'endeavour to rule according to the Way of Heaven': that is the basis of his theory that 'Man and Heaven are reciprocally responsive' and the 'emperor has the divine right to rule'.

Dong believed that the creation and change of everything in the universe embodied the will and virtue of Heaven. Politically, he taught that only by example of its moral responsibility could feudal powers educate and persuade people, and that penalties would inevitably follow its failure to do so. This kind of ruling principle with moral education as the target and the penalty to be paid for failing to achieve this was basically consistent with the thoughts of Confucianism before the Qin Dynasty, except that Dong connected that principle with the will of Heaven to show its rationality and inevitability.

Dong preached the 'Three Cardinal Guides' (*san gang*) and the 'Five Constant Virtues' (*wu chang*). The Three Cardinal Guides, namely, 'the ruler guides his subjects, the father guides his son, the husband guides his wife' was the code of distinguishing superiority and inferiority between rulers and subjects, father and son, husband and wife. He also declared that these Three Cardinal Guides of ruling could be inferred from the Way of Heaven. The 'Five Constant Virtues' are humanity, righteousness, propriety, wisdom and faithfulness, which the emperor should cultivate by himself. In other words, the Five Constant Virtues were the requirements and moral standards of the emperor's self-cultivation. Confucian scholars also encouraged 'Five Standards' and pointed out that 'Five Constant Virtues' mean the same as Five Standards, that is, father be righteous, mother be lenient, elder brother be friendly, younger brother be respectful, and son be filial. These five are the constant virtues of mankind. They set these Five Standards (*wu dian*) as five codes of behaviour in feudal society. A complete system of social codes was established by advancing 'Five Constant Virtues' to cooperate with 'Three Cardinal Guides' and combining 'Three Cardinal Guides' with 'Five Constant Virtues', for emperors to follow. All of the above specified, standardized, and unified people's goals of

78

behaviour; this system of control played a significant role in alleviating social conflicts, stabilizing the social order, and consolidating feudal rule.

4.3.3 Southern Song Period (AD 1127–1279): Zhu Xi

Confucianism experienced its second important transformation in the Song Dynasty (AD 960–1279). Its representative then was Zhu Xi (AD 1130–1200) living in Southern Song Period (AD 1127–1279). Its characteristic was the establishment of an idealistic noumenon, whose kernel is 'Principle' (*li*), in Confucianism. This kind of theory believes that 'everything has its principle', and explains the ethical morality of feudal society as the embodiment of 'principle' or 'the principle of Heaven'. Zhu Xi believed that 'human relations are like the principle of Heaven', 'propriety is the principle'. He argued the case for feudal hierarchy and moral codes according to these points. Zhu Xi said, 'Everything has this principle, and this principle originates from the same source. However, the role of the principle differs as people's status is different. For example, as an emperor he should be humanitarian, as a subject he should be respectful, as a son he should be filial, and as a father he should be lenient.' Thus the feudal hierarchy and ethical codes in relationships become innately reasonable and perpetually existing forms.

Confucianism's development, with the support of rulers of successive dynasties and propagation by Confucian scholars, has been continually sanctified and deified, even deemed as a kind of religion with Confucius as its founder. Confucianism had been mixed gradually with other religions, Buddhism, and the native Chinese religion, Taoism, and formed 'an unity of three religions', which influenced Chinese traditional culture.

4.4 The influence of Confucianism on Chinese society

For thousands of years, vigorously promoted by successive feudal dynasties, Confucianism had been regarded as the only orthodox system of thought. It has infused the multitude's minds, thereby exerting significant and far-reaching influ-

79

ences on the philosophy of life, the values, and behaviour of Chinese people.

4.4.1 Moral-ethical values

Under Confucianism's influence, Chinese people value highly the position and role of human beings. They emphasize especially the will, humanity and moral quality which men should have, and attach great importance to the harmony between men and nature, individual and society.

Confucianism holds that a human being possesses an independent will. Confucius once said, 'The commander of three armies may be taken away, but the will of even a common man may not be taken away from him.' This inalienable 'will' means the independent will. One who keeps his independent will maintains his independent moral quality at the same time. Confucianism puts forward its model about ideal human character on the basis of affirming the independent personality. Confucianism's model of ideal human character is embodied in the unity of 'wisdom, humanity and courage'. The criterion given by Mencius for judging whether a man is what he called a 'Great Man' is that: 'He is not extravagant when he is noble and rich, he does not change his will when he is humble and poor, and he does not bend under the pressure of threat or violence.' This concept of Confucianism's ideal personality has played an exhortative role in Chinese history for both the intellectuals and the populace. These thoughts of Confucius have had an extremely profound and far-reaching influence in Chinese history. In Chinese culture, the tradition of valuing a human being's affairs while ignoring spiritual being, valuing moral cultivation while ignoring religious belief, and ideas such as 'Every man has a share of responsibility for the fate of his country', etc. have all been influenced by the thoughts of Confucius.

Chinese traditional culture influenced by Confucianism, lays stress on human nature in the relationship between individual and society, and on the social codes of handling social relationships between people, one of which is to pursue the lofty goal of ameliorating moral quality constantly by

80

means of self-cultivation. For example, seeking wealth and power has never been regarded as the prime goal in the theory of Confucianism. Moreover, Chinese traditional culture advocates that one should be 'sanctified' instead of 'deified' in the process of self-cultivation. Pursuing sanctification means making great efforts to realize a kind of perfect moral quality and become a paragon, which plays an exemplary role to everyone pursuing self-realization. In China, the reason why a person can be called great always lies in his profound thoughts and broad mind, never in his wealth and power.

Confucianism emphasizes that people should regard the whole of nature, society and mankind itself as a systematic object of knowledge and should practice and clearly recognize that, as man coexists with nature and society, man should comply with them first, understand them later, then trans- form them in order to utilize them. Such ideas impel people, especially intellectuals, to adopt an active attitude of 'invol- ving the world', namely an attitude of taking care of social reality, getting to know and understand things happening in the world in an active way. As a result, Chinese intellectuals of past decades seldom isolated themselves from the world and viewed the world as outsiders. On the contrary, they never forgot the respective relations among multifarious things, and took an attitude best described in a Chinese couplet: 'Family things, country affairs and all the things concern me', toward the society and the world. This idea of regarding nature, society and human beings in a harmonious unity is one of the most important features of Chinese human tradition.

Just because Confucianism emphasizes the importance of the harmonious relationship between man and nature, man and society, man and himself, it puts man's self-cultivation to the paramount position from the beginning to the end. Such kind of thinking has affected Chinese tradition profoundly.

Confucius consistently takes 'moral cultivation' as a start- ing-point to ruling a country and pacifying the whole world, thus attaching great importance to adopting values which use morality as the basis. Confucius teaches that 'the superior man considers righteousness as the most important', here 'righteousness' refers to moral codes, and 'the most impor- tant' means the value orientation a superior man should have.

Although the emperor's power is superior in Chinese tradition, according to Confucianism, the nation's wealth should
be spent on the multitude as it is obtained from them, and the
rulers should pursue sufficiency and abundance for the
people's sake instead of exploitation and accumulation for
their own.

As to self-cultivation, Confucianism demands that one
should 'cultivate his morality first, then participate in
external affairs', and value the qualities of 'self-affirmation',
'self-esteem', and 'self-improvement'. One of the purposes of
improving self-cultivation is to deal well with relationships
among people. Confucianism stresses harmony between man
and man, and man and his external world. The core of
Confucian principles is 'harmony'. Among the propositions
advocated are 'harmony is precious', 'stand in the middle
instead of leaning towards any direction', 'there is nothing
more important in the world than harmony', 'because of
harmony, everything develops naturally', 'no virtue is more
precious than keeping harmony', and 'enmity must be melted
by harmony'. Stressing harmonious relationships among
people and avoiding conflict of interest in order to make
people live together harmoniously, is what Chinese call 'the
Golden Mean' in Chinese social culture.

The ways of thinking and ethical ideas of 'the mean' lay
stress on *zhong he*, which means literally 'Mean and
Harmony', and is one important characteristic of Confucianism. Two sayings by Confucius in the Doctrine of the Mean, a
chapter in the *Book of Rites*, 'Synthesize all different opinion
but don't support any one of them', 'Hold and adopt the
opinion which is not extreme', sum up what *Zhong he* means.
Zhong he highlights two aspects: one is *zhong*, which means
the accuracy of managing things, the other is *he*, which is the
reasonable combination of different factors and different
parts. The spirit of 'the mean' reflects the basic attitude
towards the relationships of four aspects between man and
nature, man and society, man and man, man and himself. As
far as the relationship between man and nature is concerned,
man is taken as *zhong* (central) in the three parts of Heaven,
Earth and Mankind, and there is such a saying that 'Heaven is
set up for man, as the earth is formed for man.'

82

The fact that the spirit of 'the mean' has been infused into the Chinese people's character makes the Chinese scrupulously abide by the creed 'All things develop together without jeopardizing each other. All codes function together without conflicting with each other'. They obey the principle of 'harmony is precious'. The Chinese not only value harmony in families, but also seek for the good relations among countries. The view 'coordinate all countries to coexist peacefully' means to maintain the independence of countries and nations without incursion on each other for the sake of keeping world peace. In short, Chinese people have many meritorious characters under the influence of 'the mean', such as being sagacious and brave, seeking efficacy with flexibility, seeking common ground and leaving differences behind, being hard-working, persevering, simple and plain in style of living style, loving peace, observing civilized and polite manners.

The two aspects of pursuing self-cultivation and realizing the Mean have together formed the relatively stable cultural ethical ideas in Chinese tradition, and become the fundamental principles for disciplining people's lives and safeguarding the social order. Since individual behaviour and people's relations are both restricted by ethical codes, a relatively stable social order is easy to form, which is one of the important reasons why Chinese feudal society lasted for more than two thousand years.

4.4.2 Social values

Confucianism puts forward strict patriarchal ideas in order to maintain social order and stability. Supported and encouraged by successive feudal dynasties and Confucian scholars of past decades, the patriarchal system has exerted great influence on Chinese society.

Chinese society is formed on the basis of consanguinity. The worship of forebears of consanguineous clans originated in ancient times. Ancient Chinese peoples offered sacrifices and prayers to their ancestors. Ancestor worship was at the heart of the patriarchal system. The relationship of clan consanguinity was preserved from primitive society to slave society and to feudal society: ancestor worship played an important role in that development. Confucianism pushes ancestor worship to a new height.

Originally, a strict hierarchy existed inside the consanguineous clan distinguishing people according to seniority in the family or clan, lineage, collateral descendence and superiority or inferiority. Confucianism greatly strengthens this kind of hierarchy by means of theory and practice, and the Confucian idea 'Let the ruler be a ruler, the minister be a minister, and the son be a son' and the relevant regulations make the patriarchal system penetrate all aspects of ancient Chinese society.

According to Confucianism, it is 'propriety' that demonstrates and safeguards the patriarchal system and gives priority to three sorts of distinction among people: the first is between the noble and the humble, the senior and the young, the superior and the inferior; the second is between the intimate and the formal, the lineal and collateral; the third is between men and women.

In this kind of patriarchal society, a subject should be loyal to his ruler, an inferior should obey his superior, a son should be filial and obedient to his father and his seniors. As Chinese patriarchy and feudal institutions were closely combined and formed an important part of Chinese traditional culture and customs, the ingrained unity influenced people, and still plays a role today. For instance, in ancient Chinese society, 'Being loyal to his ruler' and 'Being patriotic to his country' were usually moulded into one unity. Many Chinese people with high ideals would sacrifice their lives for their country rather than serving alien peoples and rulers in times of conflict. They never betrayed their country, there were numerous patriotic heroes in Chinese history. The political psychology of being loyal to the ruler and obedient to the superior were also advantageous to the stabilization of social order and political calm at certain times.

As to family life, under the influence of the traditional patriarchal system and its ideals of style of reverence to the old and filial towards the senior had been formed in Chinese people. This kind of style is still beneficial in keeping harmonious relationships among family members and maintaining the family's stabilization.

Finally, due to the influence of Confucius' thoughts, Chinese tradition has always advised 'Respect spiritual beings but stand afar' when dealing with the relationship between human and spiritual beings, and taught that human concerns take priority over those of the deity as in the saying: 'Try your best, obey the destinies', which shows a kind of tolerant and magnanimous attitude. Confucius' propositions like 'How can you understand death if you don't understand life?' and 'How can you serve spiritual beings if you can't serve people well?' are the reflections of a similar attitude towards the unknown. People can enjoy a stable and realistic life, not abstaining completely from the unknown world if they adopt a pragmatic view. People are advised to take a respectful attitude towards the unknown and be fully aware of the limitation of human power. For these reasons the Chinese are mostly sceptical of religious beliefs.

4.4.3 Spiritual values

Confucianism emphasizes moral quality and self-cultivation. Chinese intellectuals in the past pursued the perfection of moral quality and spiritual self-cultivation, and valued the spiritual more than material life. Generations with high ideals have been brought up not to seek gain for themselves, but to sacrifice their lives to the achievement of great harmony in the universe, and the national spirit of encouraging people to struggle for truth has developed. Chinese people remembering Confucius' respect for humanity, value moral courage and high ideals, and have a strong sense of national self-esteem. For thousands of years, such sayings as 'Never hesitate to do what is right', 'Never decline to shoulder a responsibility', 'Die to achieve virtue', 'Lay down one's life for a just cause', 'Do not bend one's own will, and never disgrace one's own names', '[to be the] one whose heart cannot be dissipated by the power of wealth and honour, who cannot be influenced by poverty or a humble station, who cannot be subdued by force and might', have been practised consistently by the Chinese people. The more powerful the force of evil is, the more the Chinese people persevere against that evil. What is described as 'Devote one's life to what justice lies in without fear of difficulty and adversity, and advance wave upon wave' has become the 'national spirit' of the Chinese.

Chinese intellectuals of today are also concerned with valuing human life and with the position of current affairs in traditional Confucian culture: their patriotism is apparently stronger and more enduring than that of other countries. Those intellectuals of the late nineteenth to the early twentieth century who were urging reforms, looked to the values of Chinese traditional culture and Confucianism. Even the Three People's Principles (Nationalism, Democracy and the People's Livelihood) initiated by Sun Yat-sen (1866–1925), who led the revolution overthrowing feudal rule in China, still showed the profound influence of Chinese traditional culture. Sun used the thoughts, 'populace being fundamental' and 'valuing the common people' in Chinese traditional Confucianism, and endowed them with a concept of civil rights, to strengthen nationalism. It is said that progressive figures in modern China, no matter whether they were reformers or revolutionary pioneers, revolutionary national- ists or incipient communists, were affected by Chinese traditional culture.

Chinese people have fostered the idealistic broad-minded, and optimistic national character. Confucius once said, 'the superior man has three accomplishments which I have not achieved yet: the man with humanity does not feel worried, the wise man does not feel confused, and the brave man is fearless', '[I am] so happy that I forget my worries, and am not aware that old age is coming on', which reflected his optimistic attitude towards life. Chinese people face difficul- ties in practical life with these thoughts in mind: they think that adversity and frustration are both inevitable. However, they believe that 'Out of the depth of misfortune comes bliss', 'Failures foster success' and are full of confidence towards the future.

4.4.4 Negative influences

Confucianism also played a negative role in Chinese tradi- tional society and culture in many respects: it even hindered the process of social development to a certain degree.

Confucianism placed too much emphasis on ethical morality. It stressed individual self-cultivation while despising, even excluding, the development of thought in many areas, including science and technology. As a result, Chinese intellectuals of the past seldom considered the natural science, which was one reason why ancient Chinese technology was not studied or systematized for a long time.

The strict feudal patriarchal system under the influence of Confucianism played a much more negative role. In spite of the Confucian emphasis on man's independent will, and character, these tenets were subsumed into the patriarchal system so that feudal centralization of state power would be strengthened. In the strictly stratified feudal patriarchal system, the individual was completely divested of his democratic rights and political independence, he became only one member of society, being subjected to the ruler or his officials. The ruler, father, superior, senior could also tyrannize his subjects and inferiors in such a way that 'a subject has to die at the order of his ruler's, and a son has to die at the demand of his father', the individual's civil rights were not guaranteed, and his moral quality could not be protected by any law. Civil rights have never been advanced in China because of this acceptance.

The patriarchal system also produced political nepotism, which made it possible that 'when a man gets to the top, all his friends and relations, get there with him', and resulted in severe political corruption.

The more serious problem was that under such a political system, people had to become accustomed to acting on orders and obeying their superior's will on all matters. This kind of benighted and distorted morality affected human nature too, and resulted in many bad national characteristics, such as worshipping power, being in awe of the superior, cowering before responsibility, being sophisticated and selfish, and avoiding telling the truth.

The negative influence of patriarchal systems on families was mainly shown by the despotism existing inside the families in which everything, no matter how important or how trivial, was handled by the patriarch; all the assets were managed and distributed by him. Children could not act

87

freely without the senior's interference, and everything was decided according to the patriarch's will and sense of right or wrong. Any trip far away from home or any risky action was regarded as non-filial. The demands of the senior could not be flouted, not only when they were alive but even after their death. These ideas were incorporated within the precepts 'being loyal to rulers and being obedient to the senior', and further strengthened the concentration of power and the despotism in ancient Chinese society, thus impeding its reform and progress.

As far as state administration was concerned, Confucius praised the self-sufficient small-scale peasant economy. He valued agriculture and despised commerce. Because people were tied to the land, and their horizons limited, the further development of Chinese society was severely hindered.

4.5 Confucianism and China's modernization

Many of the doctrines and practices of Confucianism have been seen as obstacles to the progress of society, science and culture, and campaigns have been launched criticizing Confucius and his teachings. For example, the May Fourth Movement in 1919 raised the clarion call 'Down with the Confucius' school shop!' In the 1970s, a 'Condemning Lin Biao and Confucius Movement' was started on the Chinese mainland during the Cultural Revolution (1966–76) vehemently attacking Confucianism. Many Confucian ideas were wholly discarded as feudalist dross.

In recent years, with the gradual development of Chinese economic reform and the open-door policy, there have been many debates on how to treat Confucianism and the traditional culture. Many people believe that glorifying the national culture is a vital condition for inspiring the Chinese national spirit, enhancing self-esteem and self-confidence, and inspiring patriotism. Chinese political and social reforms, accompanied by the swift pace of modernization, will inevitably effect change in Chinese culture. But China cannot ignore its national characteristics, and must not lose its outstanding cultural legacy. Mao Zedong (1893–1976) often emphasized that people should not fragment history, but should see its own complexity, from Confucius to Sun Yat-sen, to inherit that precious cultural legacy. The saying, 'discard the dross and select the essential' is still valid. Many fundamental principles of Confucianism are still suitable for today's Chinese society. They can and should be accepted by today's people to serve the demands of modernization.

The kernel of Confucius' thought is 'humanity and righteousness'. Humanity means that people should be benevolent to each other, while righteousness means that there should be stability and security in a society. In China today the goal of offering people a life without hunger or cold with sufficient wealth near the level of other developing countries, belongs in the category of humanity. The hope for stability and security, with unity, belongs to the category of righteousness. The policy adopted by China of opposing hegemonies and advocating peaceful coexistence in international affairs is an example of the Confucian idea of 'Attracting people far away from your country by education and moral cultivation if they are not in favour of your administration'.

Scholars also point out that the Confucian idea of satisfying the needs of people is the same as valuing people, and this should be borne in mind at a time when China is carrying out economic reforms. The tenet 'the people are the foundation of state' should be given wide public attention: China's modernization should first improve the people's level of living.

The issue of valuing or 'esteeming' people in China becomes more important at a time of policy and economic reform. To value people is to abide by the principle that people 'are fundamental to the state'. It means changing the system in which officials decide policies, the intellectuals formulate them, and the grass-roots units carry them out. It also means reforming the decision-making mechanism, encouraging mass political participation, and preventing corruption which hinders modernization. People will become more enthusiastic about constructing a modern society with democratic reforms, and with greater regard for the value and dignity of the individual.

89

Economic reform and opportunity increase various mal-practices, such as extreme individualism and hedonism. The ethical and moral essence of Chinese traditional culture should provide a foundation for new ideas of culture and value. It has to be proven that modernization does not contradict the essence of traditional ethics and morality. On the contrary, traditional morality can harmonize the social relationships and alleviate the conflicts of living in a commodity economy.

Chinese people can still today establish a kind of egalitarian, independent and harmonious relationship according to Confucian principles of humanity, righteousness, propriety, wisdom and faithfulness. Chinese citizens should have independence of minds, they should establish new norms and principles of propriety, seek the truth, become 'the sages', abide by the principle of 'faithfulness'. This type of self-cultivation tries to minimize the conflict between the individual and society; it is one of the most complicated problems in an industrialized society.

4.6 The dissemination of Confucianism abroad: comparison between Confucianism and Western culture

Confucianism has not only had a far-reaching influence in China, it also spread into neighbouring countries.

4.6.1 Influence in Vietnam

Confucianism had spread to Vietnam in the second century AD, and was accepted as an ethical and moral system by successive Vietnamese dynasties over a long period of time. The 'Three Cardinal Guides' and the 'Five Constant Virtues' influenced the Vietnamese, while the 'Four Books,' – The Great Learning (*Da xue*), the Doctrine of the Mean (*Zhong yong*), the Analects of Confucius (*Lun yu*) and the Mencius (*Meng zi*)) and the 'Five Classics' – were the main source of the imperial examinations. Many anti-colonial and anti-imperialist revolutionaries in modern Vietnamese history came from the intellectual or official classes who were proficient in Confucian theories. Strengthened by the Confucian ethos of

90

'to die for the sake of the just cause' and 'to sacrifice oneself for righteousness', they devoted themselves to the cause of revolutionary struggles. For example, Ho Chi Minh was given the Confucian sages' works to read when he was young. Even after he became a communist, he still venerated Confucius whom he called 'the great sage Confucius' with veneration, and quoted in his works and speeches many sayings from the works of Confucius and other Confucian scholars. This gave great impetus to the Vietnamese people's struggles for national liberation. Ho paid special attention to Confucian theories about how to cultivate morality and bring peace and stability to country. He fully approved the virtues advocated by Confucianism and urged people to practice those doctrines. He spoke highly of the Confucian idea that 'people are the most important'. He valued people's support, and endeavoured to make people live a rich and happy life. Many Vietnamese scholars think that Ho's thoughts are the convergence of Confucian theory and Marxism. Due to the great influence of Ho Chi Minh, many Confucian ideas and theories appreciated by Ho still occupy an important position in Vietnam.

4.6.2 Influence in Korea

Confucianism has had a long-standing influence on Korea. As early as in 682, Korea had established its 'national school' where the main subject was Confucian theories. After the system of choosing officials by imperial examination was set up in late eighth century, people could be promoted quickly if they mastered a broad knowledge of the Five Classics, Three Historical Books, and books of the various schools of thought and their exponents. During the Chinese Yuan Dynasty (1279–1368), the Confucian theories reformed by Zhu Xi were introduced into Korea and propagated widely in the courts and among the people with the kings' encouragement. A number of famous Confucian scholars emerged after this. The Confucian concepts of the 'kingly way', and 'humane government' had a profound influence in the successive dynasties of Korea. It has also given great impetus to the swift economic development in Korea today.

91

4.6.3 Influence in Japan

Confucianism was introduced into Japan also at a very early time, in about the fourth century. In early the eighth century, Confucianism had already played an important role in Japan's politics. The Japanese kings also followed their Chinese counterparts in holding grand ceremonies to worship Confucius. During the period between the Song and Yuan dynasties of China, Zhu Xi's *li xue* (a Confucian school of idealist philosophy) was also introduced into Japan and soon spread widely. Confucian thoughts and theories had also promoted Japan's Reform Movement in the nineteenth century and the process of Japanese modernization. Some Japanese scholars believe that the fact that Japan has turned into a developed country avoiding the 'civilization illness' emerging in the West is due to the benefits of Confucianism. Some scholars even think that this should be 'the Era of Confucian culture'.

4.6.4 Some Comparisons between Confucius and Socrates

During the seventeenth to eighteenth centuries Confucianism was brought to the West by priests coming back from China. It supplied European thinkers of the Enlightenment with new theories for their challenge to the authority of the Church and the rule of feudal despots. Voltaire, the French philosopher of the Enlightenment, had praised Confucius and his theories. In the West, some scholars regarded Confucius as the Socrates of the Orient.

Confucius, born in 551 BC, was the founder of Confucianism; Socrates, born in Athens in 469 BC, was a philosopher, the son of a stonemason. The two men lived in the same era, and they both have had a great influence on oriental and occidental philosophy. It is, then, important to compare the similarities and differences in their philosophies in order to understand the cultural differences between the East and the West.

Socrates believed that the spirit and all objects are created by the gods for a certain purpose. The gods rule the world, and their powers are absolute. Socrates instead, asked people to examine the *wisdom* of the gods.

Confucius accepts the Chinese traditional thoughts about the Mandate of Heaven. He regards Heaven as the foundation of his theoretical system. Although, he attaches importance to the Ways of Heaven, he values the role of human beings more. He thinks that Heaven means no more than the process of change, the four seasons, and the unfailing process of creation and death of natural things. Although he admits the existence of spiritual beings, he avoids talking about them all the time. Sometimes, he even takes a negative attitude towards them. Confucius' thoughts on valuing the role of human affairs, studying nature while ignoring spiritual beings are not only contradictory to his own thoughts of fatalism with veneration for Heaven, but are very different from Socrates' thoughts on the universe and nature.

Socrates is mostly concerned with moral and ethical issues. He posited that virtue is cognate with good. 'Good' is the perpetual, universal, absolutely unchangeable knowledge and is also the criterion for judging whether a person has morality. He believes that moral behaviour is based on and comes from knowledge. The source of perpetually unchangeable knowledge is deity. Therefore in Socrates' eyes, 'Good' means to observe the will of the gods: to obey the gods means knowledge, knowledge means virtue, and finally religious belief is mixed up with views of morality.

According to Confucius' theory, 'humanity' is also connected with 'wisdom', Confucius think the superior man's character results from cognizance. But Confucius advocates the doctrines of the 'Human Ways', and that people should respect each other and build up a relationship full of love and trust among people, which differentiates greatly from Socrates' view of religious ethical morality.

Socrates was known for his dialectical method: the rigorous questioning of propositions. He often catches his counterpart out in contradictions and makes his counterpart admit his ignorance by heckling within the dialogue. Finally, Socrates obtains a satisfactory definition which reveals the nature of certain moral behaviour.

Confucius' thoughts about education were of great significance. He advanced the view that 'in education there should be no class distinction' for the first time, which broke the bounds of clan hierarchy. He practised the heuristic teaching method, and encouraged the combination of learning and practising. Confucius attached importance to seeking the truth: urged his students to 'study it extensively, inquire into it accurately, think it over carefully, sift it clearly and practise it earnestly.'

Some scholars compare the characteristics of oriental culture with those of occidental culture. For instance, Cai Yuanpei (1868–1940), the Chinese modern educationist, has made a comparison between such ideas as conscientiousness and altruism, humanity and benevolence, and faithfulness and righteousness in the cultural, and ethical views of the Chinese Confucian tradition and Western ideas of freedom, equality and universal fraternity. He thinks that these pairs of ideas reflect, with a few exceptions, the Western idea of freedom and the Confucian idea of righteousness, the Western idea of equality and the Confucian idea of altruism, the Western idea of universal fraternity, and the Confucian idea of humanity.

4.7 Conclusion

The thoughts and theories of Confucianism founded by the ancient Chinese thinker and educator, Confucius, has played an extremely important role in the formation and development of Chinese traditional culture. With the cultural communication between China and other countries expanding, Confucianism has also affected greatly the oriental countries, such as Vietnam, Korea and Japan. So it can be said that Confucianism forms, to a certain degree, an important part of the oriental culture, especially the culture of eastern Asia. Confucianism has had a profound influence on the Chinese people and the peoples of other Asian countries. It would benefit understanding, exchange and communication between China and the West, if the West was more aware of traditional Chinese culture and its origins in Confucian thought.

References

Chinese Academy of Sino-Japanese Relationship History, (ed), *The Oriental Culture and Modernization*, (Current Affairs Press, 1992).

Li Yingke (1989) *Confucianism and the Chinese People,* (Shanxi Teachers University Press).

Song Yanshen and Xiao Guoliang (ed) (1993) *The Studies of Confucius and Confucianism,* (Jilin Educational Press).

Song Zhongfu *et al.* (1991). *Confucianism in Modern China* (Zhongzhou Ancient Books Press).

Wu Feng and Song Yifu (ed) (1992) *The Comprehensive Dictionary of Chinese Confucianism* Nan Hai Publishing Company.

Wu Jiang (1992) *A Sketchy Study on Chinese feudal ideology: the Illustration and comments on Confucianism,* (Party School Press of the Party's Central Committee of CPC).

Zhou Yiliang (ed) (1987) *History of Cultural Communication between China and Foreign Countries,* (Henan People's Press).

Chapter 5

Islamic and European Values Similarities and Differences

Fateh Mohammad Malik

5.1 Introduction

Let me state at the outset that there is a wide gulf between the ideals of Islam and the realities of the present day Muslim world. According to Muhammad Iqbal (1877–1938), who dominates Islamic thought in the twentieth century, 'the birth of Islam is the birth of inductive intellect'. Elaborating on the idea of the end of the institution of prophethood, he declared:

> In Islam prophecy reaches its perfection in discovering the need of its own abolition. This involves the keen perception that life cannot for ever be kept in leading strings; that in order to achieve full self-consciousness man must finally be thrown back on his own resources. The abolition of priest-hood and hereditary kingship in Islam, the constant appeal to reason and experience in the Qur'an, and the emphasis that it lays on Nature and History as sources of human knowledge, are all different aspects of the same idea of finality.[1]

In spite of this affirmation of rational ways of thinking, the worst kind of fanaticism and an ugly sectarian strife is raging in various parts of the Muslim world. In spite of the total rejection of kingship and priesthood in Islam, the contemporary Muslim world is being ruled by kings and amirs, military dictators and civilian despots, and the people are helpless victims of *mullahs* and *sufis*.

96

5.2 Islam as a universal message

Islam is the youngest of the Abrahamic creeds. It is a restatement of the divine truth preached by a long series of prophets of whom Muhammad was the last. 'There is no God but Allah and Muhammad is His prophet' sums up the religion of Islam. The word Islam means peace as well as submission to the will of God, whose proper name is Allah. Islam calls other scriptures 'light and guidance' and it enjoins Muslims to revere all prophets who have preached monotheism. According to K. A. Hakim:

> The religious outlook of Islam has an Israelite background which is evident throughout the Qur'an. Islam calls itself the creed of Abraham and all other Israelite prophets. So far as the fundamentals of religion are concerned Islam claims no originality. A Muslim is asked to believe in not only what has been revealed to prophet Muhammad but to all prophets among all the peoples that have gone before him; Islam is a great believer in the continuity of human culture and the essential unity of its fundamentals.[2]

The simple, non-racial, non-sectarian, universal creed of Islam spread rapidly and created a state and society based on the concept of the brotherhood of man, in which man is free within 'the limits of God' prescribed by the Qur'an (the holy scripture) and the *Sunnah* of the prophet. 'With the dawn of Islam', observes Afzal Iqbal,

> all the familiar values of pagan Arabia were either discorded or destroyed. But did the pre-Islamic Arab completely shed his past as soon as he entered the fold of Islam? The answer is not simple. The new values of Islam gradually replaced the old without completely destroying them. The conflict between Islam and pagan Arabia was long and tortuous, and even when Islam emerged triumphantly from the ordeal it could not be said that the outlook represented by paganism had completely vanished. In fact as soon as the caliphate passed to the house of the Umayyads the old rivalries, jealousies, and feuds, which had existed in the days of ignorance returned with redoubled vigour.[3]

After the first four successors to the Prophet (the caliphs) the old pagan spirit asserted itself under the Umayyads who suppressed the egalitarian spirit of Islam and converted the nascent democratic system into Arab imperialism. The revolutionary movement of original Islam was thus assailed by counter-revolutionary forces of pre-Islamic paganism. 'But even with all these setbacks Islam remained the leader of humanity for about eight centuries. Having lit the torch of modern civilization the Muslim peoples crushed by un-Islamic priesthood and autocratic monarchies, became listless and stagnant'.[4]

5.3 The Rediscovery of the original spirit of Islam

The self-serving ruling elite, is no doubt, concerned with the exploitation of Islam for its narrow political ends, but the Muslim masses are determined to remain true to the spirit of Islam. The fact that the rulers are forced to pay lip service to Islam in order to gain a popular base is evidence that Islam is a matter of life and death for the Muslim masses. After five hundred years of slumber the Muslim intellectual has re-awakened and has attempted to recon-struct religious thought in Islam in the light of modern knowledge. In this process basic similarities between the original spirit of Islam and the spirit of the modern times have been discovered. Recognizing the Islamic origins of much Western scientific and technological accomplish-ments as well as intellectual and philosophical thoughts, Muhammad Iqbal argues:

> There was a time when European thought received inspiration from the world of Islam. The most remarkable phenomenon of modern history, however, is the enormous rapidity with which the world of Islam is spiritually moving towards the West. There is nothing wrong in this movement, for European culture, on its intellectual side, is only a further development of some of the most important phases of the culture of Islam. Our only fear is that the dazzling exterior of European culture may arrest our movement and we may fail to reach the true inwardness of that culture.[5]

98

While the Muslim ruling elite have their eyes fixed on the glittering image of the West, the Muslim intellectual is in search of the inner spirit of Western culture. The intellectual has sought to rediscover the original spirit of Islam and to bring it closer to the spirit of modern times. Original Islam is liberal, humanist and democratic. It grants freedom of consciousness to every human being, so much so that the Prophet of Islam regarded difference of opinion as a blessing; the divine scripture commands, 'no coercion in religion' (Qur'an 2:256). The Qur'an is unambiguous in its emphasis on religious liberty.

> If it had been thy Lord's will, they would all have believed all who are on earth! Will thou then compel mankind against their will, to believe!
>
> (Qur'an 10:99)

> And argue not with the people of the book unless it be in a way that is fair, save with such of them as do wrong: and say: we believe in that which hath been revealed unto us and revealed unto you; our God and your God is one, and unto Him we surrender.
>
> (Qur'an 2:46)

The Prophet not only preached but demonstrated that Islam stands for the utmost tolerance and complete liberty in matters of faith. Once a deputation of Christians waited upon him, and while he was in conversation with them in the mosque at Madinah, the time for Christian prayer approached. The Christians brought the fact to the notice of the Prophet and proposed moving out of the mosque, but the Prophet asked them, 'Why don't you pray here?' They replied: 'Our prayer is accompanied with instrumental music and it may be disapproved of.' The Prophet said, 'Pray as you like in your own way', and so the Christians held their service in their own way in the mosque of the Prophet of Islam.

Describing the democratic ideal of perfect equality, to which the Prophet had given uncompromising support, Iqbal has asserted that:

> There is no aristocracy in Islam . . . There is no privileged class, no priesthood and no caste system. Islam is a unity in which

99

there is no distinction, and this unity is secured by making men believe in the two simple propositions – the unity of God and the mission of the Prophet.[6]

Democracy, then, is regarded as the most important political ideal of Islam. This ideal survived for only thirty years and vanished with the emergence of the Umayyed dynasty. It remained dormant in the Muslim world because of the historical circumstances which led to the establishment of Arabian imperialism in the first century of Islam. Such ideals could only be realized by a return to the original purity of Islam. In order to achieve this objective, Iqbal initiated a process of rediscovery of the basic principles and values of Islam through reinterpretation and reconstruction of Islamic thought. He took up the challenge of 'emancipating the superb idealism of Islam from the medieval fancies of theologian and legists' with a rare insight. Explaining the sociopolitical implications of the central concept of *Tauhād* (oneness of God), he argued, 'It demands loyalty to God, not to thrones. And since God is the ultimate spiritual basis of all life, loyalty to God virtually amounts to man's loyalty to his own ideal nature.'[7] And again: the essence of *Tauhid* as a working idea is equality, solidarity and freedom. The state, from the Islamic standpoint, is an endeavour to transform these ideal principles into space-time forces, an aspiration to realize them in a definite human organization.[8]

5.4 Separate Muslim homelands in South Asia

In order to transform these principles of equality, solidarity and freedom into practice, Iqbal articulated the ideology of a separate Muslim nationalism as opposed to the idea of a composite Indian nationalism. Since 'all that is secular is sacred in the roots of its being and all this immensity of matter constitutes a scope for the self-realization of the spirit', there is no question of dividing spirit and matter in Islam. The rejection of the modern Western concept of the duality of church and state enabled Muslims to envisage and struggle for the creation of separate homelands in the Indian subcontinent. But this rejection has created an

unsympathetic environment for Pakistan in Western intellectual circles.

Unmindful of the facts that there is no sanction for
priesthood in Islam, the ethical ideal of Islam is organically
related to the social order which it has created and the concept
of secularism sprang from the specific historical circumstances
in Europe, the Western intellectual is anxious to see the whole
world accept secularism as an unquestionable doctrine.
Intellectuals in the West appear to have taken no time to
reflect on the arguments of the Muslim intellectual, he says:

> The protest of Luther was directed against the Church
> organization . . . If you begin with the conception of religion
> as complete otherworldliness, then what has happened to
> Christianity in Europe is perfectly natural. The universal ethics
> of Jesus is displaced by national systems of ethics and polity.
> Europe is consequently driven to the conclusion that religion is
> a private affair of the individual and has nothing to do with
> what is called man's temporal life. Islam does not bifurcate the
> unity of man into an irreconcilable duality of spirit and matter.
> In Islam, God and the Universe, spirit and matter, Church and
> State, are organic to each other. Man is not the citizen of a
> profane world to be renounced in the interest of a world of
> spirit situated elsewhere. To Islam matter is spirit realising itself
> in space and time . . . A Luther in the world of Islam, is an
> impossible phenomenon; for here there is no Church organiza-
> tion, similar to that of Christianity in the Middle Ages, inviting
> a destroyer.[9]

In spite of the fact that an Islamic state cannot accept
theocratic rule and Pakistan was created by a democratic
movement spearheaded by the most liberal leadership of the
day, its partition in December 1971 was hailed by Western
intellectuals as a victory of secularism over Islam. Needless to
say that this was an incorrect reading of the situation.
Mumtaz Ahmed has aptly remarked that the 'separation of
Bangladesh from Pakistan was not a revolt against Islam or the
theoretical foundations of the idea of Pakistan. It was a
question of fair distribution of economic resources, political
participation and much more importantly, it was a question
of human dignity.'[10]

The lack of understanding of the realities of the Muslim world reminds me of a memorable episode in my life. I congratulated a close German friend on the vanishing of the Berlin wall and the consequent reunification of Germany. Her spontaneous response was the question: When will the partition wall between India and Pakistan vanish? I was astounded at the innocence of my journalist friend, who aimed to specialise in Pakistan. She had no idea that unlike Germany, British India was not a country, it was a continent, like the Austro-Hungarian Empire. The unity of the Indian continent was imposed first by Muslim and then by British Imperial might. Division of India was not imposed by the victorious powers as a consequence of the defeat in war. India was partitioned and Pakistan was voted into existence as an expression of the unified will of Muslim India, acknowledged, and accepted among others, by Mahatma Gandhi and Jawaharlal Nehru.

Nearly one billion Muslims of the world venerate the Prophet Muhammad as the pre-eternal light, the best of creatures and the leader of mankind. Poet-philosopher Muhammad Iqbal identified him as the rallying point as well as the principal source of Unity of the Muslim World. Highlighting the love of Muhammad as the greatest value in Muslim community he declared: 'You can deny God, but you cannot deny Muhammad.' Because denial of the Prophet amounts to the denial of the distinct identity of the Muslim community which is always jealously guarded by a Muslim: 'In God the individual, in him [i.e. Muhammad] lives the Community.'[11]

The community which sprang from the religious experience of our holy prophet is a non-racial, non-sectarian universal community believing in a God who is the Lord of the world, the Lord of all persons of whatever faith, who are descendants of Adam and are, therefore, brothers worshipping the same God. As the tradition goes, before embarking upon his heavenly journey, Prophet Muhammad performed ritual prayer in Jerusalem alongside Abraham, Moses and Jesus, and the Qur'an declares:

> O, people of the Book! Come, let us join together on the 'word' (Unity of God), that is common to us all.
>
> (Qur'an 3:63)

This vision of the unity of mankind could not be translated into reality because of the crusades and the holy wars, and later, due to European imperialist aggression in its various forms. Today the 'secular dogma' of the duality of the West is among the greatest hindrance in its way: the Western mind is the product of this secular dogma.

Bernard Lewis has pointed out that 'in classical Arabic and in the other classical languages of Islam, there are no pairs of terms corresponding to 'lay' and 'ecclesiastical', 'spiritual' and 'temporal', 'secular' and 'religious' because these pairs of words express a Christian dichotomy that has no equivalent in the world of Islam.[12]

Elaborating upon the 'recurring unwillingness' of the intellectual 'to recognize the nature of Islam, or even the fact of Islam, as an independent, different phenomenon', Bernard Lewis has observed that:

> Modern western man, being unable for the most part to assign a dominant and central place to religion in his own affairs, found himself unable to conceive that any other people in any other place could have done so . . . This is reflected in the recurring inability of political, journalistic, and academic commentators alike to recognize the importance of religion in the current affairs of the Muslim world and in their consequent recourse to the language of left-wing and right-wing, progressive and conservative and the rest of the western vocabulatory of ideology and politics.[13]

The secular perspective is reminiscent of the British in India in the 1930s and 1940s where administrators together with the Indian nationalists were struggling to stem the rising tide of a separate Muslim nationhood. The rejection of the imported European concept of ethnic and territorial nationalism was their main source of anguish. Their well-articulated campaign in favour of territorial nationalism proved to be a failure; the Muslim masses listened to the inspiring voice of their poet-philosopher Muhammad Iqbal,

> The idea of Islam is, so to speak, our eternal home or country wherein we live, move and have our being. To us it is above everything else as England is above all to Englishmen and

103

Deutschland über alles to the Germans . . . The religious idea
constitutes the life principle of the Muslim Community.[14]

This proved to be true in case of the Muslim community in
India at the time of independence and it is true in the Muslim
community today.

Notes

1 Dr Sir Muhammad Iqbal *Reconstruction of Religious Thought in Islam*,
(Oxford, 1934) 126. Muhammad Iqbal, the spiritual father of Pakistan
and the poet-philosopher of Islam was educated in the Punjab, Cambridge, Heidelberg, and Munich. He composed poems of rare vitality and
sustained emotional power in Urdu and Persian and attempted to
reinterpret Islam in modern philosophical terms in his English work.
According to Aziz Ahmed he 'is the key figure in twentieth-century
modernism. Unlike that of any previous modernist, the central discipline
of his scholarship was western *Islamic Modernism in India and Pakistan*
(Oxford 1967) 149. For the nature and extent of his influence and prestige
in the contemporary world of Islam see Malik 'Role of Muhammad Iqbal
in Muslim reawakening' in Andre Wink (ed.), *Islam, Politics and Society in
South Asia*, (New Delhi, 1991). Iqbal's works are widely translated into
European languages. From among the many studies on Iqbal's life art,
and thought in English please: Annemarie Schimmel, *Gabriel's wing, a
study into the religious ideas of Sir Muhammad Iqbal*, (Brill, Leiden, 1963);
Iqbal Singh, *The Ardent Pilgrim*, (London 1954); L.C. le Maitre, *Introduction
to the thought of Iqbal* (Karachi, 1961), trans. A. Dar; Hafiz Malik: *Iqbal*,
(New York 1971); and Abdur Rauf Malik (ed.), *Soviet Scholars on Iqbal*,
(Lahore 1983).
2 Institute of Islamic Culture, *Islamic Ideology* (Lahore 1959) Intro. p. x.
3 *The Culture of Islam*, Institute of Islamic Culture, Lahore, Introduction.
4 *Islamic Ideology*, op.cit., Introduction p. xii
5 Cited by Javed Iqbal in *Ideology of Pakistan*, Lahore, 1971) 71.
6 Latif Ahmed Sherwani (ed.), *Speeches, Writings and Statements of Iqbal*, (3rd
edn.) (Lahore: Iqbal Academy, 1977) 102.
7 Muhammad, Iqbal *Reconstruction of Religious Thought in Islam*, op. cit., 87.
8 Ibid. 91.
9 Sherwani, Speeches, Writings and Statement of Iqbal, op. cit., p. 4–5.
10 *Is Bangladesh Secularist?*, The Nation, Lahore, 20 September 1995.
11 Iqbal, Muhammad, *Secrets of the Self*, translation by R.A. Nicholson,
Lahore, 1921, p. 78.
12 Bernard Lewis, *Islam and the West*, Oxford, 1993, p. 136.
13 Ibid. 133–134.
14 Latif Ahmed Sherwani, *Speeches, Writings and Statements of Iqbal*, op. cit.
pp. 105, 106.

References

Aziz Ahmed (1967) *Islamic Modernism in India and Pakistan* (Oxford).

Javed Iqbal (1971) *Ideology of Pakistan,* (Lahore).

Dr Sir Muhammad Iqbal (1934) *Reconstruction of Religious Thought in Islam,* (Oxford).

Muhammad Iqbal (1921) *Secrets of the Self,* translation by R.A. Nicholson (Lahore).

Bernard Lewis (1993) *Islam and the West* (Oxford).

L.C. le Maitre (1961) *Introduction to the thought of Iqbal* (Karachi), trans. A. Dar, Hafiz Malik: *Iqbal* (1971) (New York).

Abdur Rauf Malik (ed.) (1983) *Soviet Scholars on Iqbal,* (Lahore).

Annemarie Schimmel (1963) *Gabriel's wing, a study into the religious ideas of Sir Muhammad Iqbal* (Brill, Leiden).

Iqbal Singh (1954) *The Ardent Pilgrim,* (London).

Latif Ahmed Sherwani (ed.) (1977) *Speeches, Writings and Statements of Iqbal,* (3rd edn.) (Lahore: Iqbal Academy).

Andre Wink (ed.), *Islam, Politics and Society in South Asia,* (New Delhi, 1991).

Institute of Islamic Culture, *Islamic Ideology* (Lahore, 1959).

Is Bangladesh Secularist?, The Nation (1995) (Lahore, 20 September).

Sarajevo turns an illiberal face to the world The Guardian (1994) (London, October 15 Saturday).

Chapter 6

Hindu Values

Debabrata Sen Sharma

6.1 Introduction

Hinduism, as is well known, is one of the oldest religions in the world. It has a vast literature and great following even today. It is the most ancient religion in Asia dating back several milliennia before Christ. Ancient Hindu scriptures refer to *Sanatana–Dharma*, the religious tradition which has come down to us from time immemorial. It is believed to be eternal in this part of the globe, and lasting as long as man lives on this earth. The word 'Hindu' does not appear anywhere in our religious texts. It was coined by the Arabs in the medieval period to classify people of this country belonging to this particular faith.

The socioreligious writers in the past were not merely social thinkers and theoreticians; a large majority of them were seers who had obtained a direct vision of the Supreme Truth. They had developed an intuitive vision which enabled them to look at man as the Universal Being, not belonging to a particular country or conditioned by a particular time. Their perspective was so all-encompassing that nothing was left out which concerned man's existence on the earth. They never talked about man as belonging to one particular faith, but man as entire humanity. Our ancient thinkers looked upon man as the finest specimen of creation on the earth who possesses an innate capacity to elevate himself to the highest level of perfection. They focused their attention on him, considering his problems seeking to alleviate his suffering.

6.2 The *Sanatana-Dharma*

Early writers spoke of terms of the universal man (*manava*) and his socioreligious beliefs as the universal religion (*manava dharma*). Rabindranath Tagore explained it as the 'religion of man'. These writers discussed about the ultimate values, the goal in life which all humanity cherished, irrespective of time or place. Their motto was 'regard the entire world as one family'.[1] Every devout Hindu still utters the following prayer at the close of every religious ceremony, 'let all people be happy, let all be free from disease, let us see the well-being prevailing everywhere, let no person be subject to misery or unhappiness'.[2]

This universal outlook was the consequence of the perception that there is one spiritual principle underlying creation: the cosmos or universe, which encompasses not only all humanity, but all animate and inanimate things, is bound by a thread of one Unified Spiritual Principle, as it were. 'All exists in One, and One exists in all' – this is the supreme understanding of Hinduism's ancient seers, on which their philosophy is based.

Some of the distinguishing characteristics of Hinduism or the *Sanatana-Dharma* are its open-mindedness and its infinite capacity for assimilation from similar religious traditions. These unique qualities in the Hindu religious tradition have provided it with inner strength which has enabled the *Sanatana-Dharma* not only to survive the attacks of other religions, but also to gain strength. Hindu seers welcomed moral and social ideas from outside as they proclaimed 'Let thoughts enter into us from all sides'. The attitude of confrontation and conflict is not found in Hinduism's religious tradition: it is the 'religion of man'. For instance, the ideals of non-violence (*ahimsa*), austerity (*tapas*), complete non-attachment (*vairagya*), stress on following the middle path (*madhyama pratipada*) in spiritual discipline and the Eightfold Path (*astanga marga*) figure prominently in Jainism and Buddhism respectively, and have been accepted with some modification and given prominent place by Hinduism's religious thinkers and have enriched Hindu thinking. The Buddha was included as one of many incarnations of God.

107

One might ask why Sankaracarya and Ramanuja, the protagonists of Vedic religion in a later period were so vehement in their challenge to Jain and Buddhist teachers, refuting their religious thoughts and beliefs, while their teachings had been tolerated and assimilated before. The main reason for this attack was that the Buddhists and Jains did not accept the authority of the Vedas, the holy scriptures of the *Sanatana-Dharma*, and were branded as atheists or non-believers, worthy of condemnation by the Vedic schools. Hindu philosophers did not reject the ethical or moral and spiritual code of conduct prescribed by the Buddhists and Jains. The criticism of the Buddhists and Jains by Sankaracarya and others was based on philosophical grounds. In fact, Sankaracarya himself borrowed many philosophical ideas from the Buddhists, especially the *Madhyamika* and *Yogacara* schools and was labelled by later philosophers as pseudo-Buddhist. The main cause for the disappearance of Buddhism from India was not criticism by the orthodox Hindu teachers but lack of royal patronage which declined after the death of Emperor Asoka.

Hindu thinkers always spoke of the purpose of human life, the ultimate destiny, the revelation of man's divine nature, which every individual would eventually reach in his life.

6.3 The notion of value

The notion of value is a Western concept which attempts to shed light on what is valuable or precious to man, or important for the qualitative improvement of his life. It is a subjective notion as it attempts to define what is excellent in life and conducive to his happiness. The Hindus are practical in outlook, they do not believe mere speculation, they define values as principles of life, seeking man's improvement in ethical, spiritual, and social terms so that he may enjoy happiness in this world and attain perfection in the end.

6.3.1 Threefold values

The threefold values are the moral or ethical values, the spiritual values and the social values. These systems are not

108

mutually exclusive, they overlap and form one unified set of values. Most of the ancient Indian texts on Hindu law, and the epics, the *Puranas* and others such as Kautilyas *Arthasastra*,[3] refer to values which aim at achieving all-round improvement in the quality of life, making men happy and well contented. The two ideals in life are discussed in the texts: first is the ideal of the upliftment of man in the worldly sense, the enjoyment of material comforts and happiness; second, the ideal of the attainment of the Supreme Goal in life, the unfolding of man's true spiritual nature.

6.3.2 Moral values

The moral or ethical values advocated by the Hindu, Buddhist and Jain thinkers serve a dual purpose. The purification of the mind, culminating in the revelation of the self. Moral values emphasize excellence in social behaviour, and the removal of all causes for conflict between one individual and another. The individual striving for excellence should abstain from violence in any form, and should refrain from causing injury to anyone through deed, word, or thought. This is called non-injury (*ahimsa*). It has been asserted that the individual adopting *ahimsa* becomes completely fearless and invincible. Every individual should always stick to the truth and follow the path of righteousness. He should never deviate from the path of Truth, for Truth always triumphs (*satyam eva jayate*). Mahatma Gandhi tried to apply the ideal of truth to the politicians. Linked with this is the virtue of honesty which one should observe in one's behaviour. Hypocrisy has no place in the behaviour of a person whose goal is self-purification. No one should take by force that which does not belong to him; he should not steal. Men should observe sexual restraint and man should not allow himself to be seized by passion and lust as these desires not only disturb the tranquility of mind but also pervert his social behaviour. The exercise of self-control advocated by our religious thinkers does not imply repression and inhibition so much talked about today by Western psychologists, for these have been condemned by Lord Krishna in the *Bhagavad Gita*. The *Gita* says that 'even a mind that knows the right path can be dragged from his path when the senses are so unruly. But he who controls the senses and recollects his mind and fixes it on the God, I [Lord Krishna] call him the illumined.'[4] Direction rather than repression is the method prescribed by our holy men for achieving self-control.

A person striving to gain excellence should not amass more wealth than is essential for the maintenance of his life. Man has a natural propensity for amassing material wealth for his personal enjoyment. Little does he know that the thirst for enjoyment, for the gratification of his senses, cannot be satiated. He should purify his mind by observing cleanliness, both external and internal. One should cultivate a sense of non-attachment towards worldly goods in order to achieve contentment of mind; the mind then becomes free from tension. One of the methods for conserving energy is to observe silence. Anger, arrogance and vanity are considered vices which inhibit the achievement of purification. The *Bhagavad Gita* refers to these vices as demonic tendencies that deprave men (XIV, 1–4). Anger is considered to be the worst of all vices as it is said to delude man and he loses the power of discrimination between good and bad, useful and harmful. Hindu scriptures stress self-examination in order to develop the ability to seek perfection. Moral or ethical values, when put into practice, not only improve the personal life and behaviour of the individual, but they also contribute to a better society.

6.3.3 Spiritual values

The spiritual values advocated by the practitioners of Yoga and by Indian teachers are similar to moral values. Purification of the mind is an essential prerequisite for spiritual studies. The values which a spiritual aspirant should practise include the withdraw of the senses from the sense objects by practising austerity as enjoined in our scriptures. He should develop a renunciatory attitude in life. The *Isavasyopanisad* prescribes enjoyment through the practice of renunciation.[5] Renunciation is the beginning, the middle and the end of spiritual life. The *Bhagavad Gita* regards renunciation as inseparable from the yoga of action, the yoga of knowledge, and the yoga of devotion. However, it does not imply adopting a monastic way of life, for it can be practised by all, the monk as well as the householder who pursues the spiritual path. Other-worldliness does not mean shunning the duties and obligations of family life. The *Bhagavad Gita* teaches that the duties of life can be undertaken with a heart free from attachment and thoughts of worldly gain. It insists on the performance of one's secular duties (*sva-dharma*) in the spirit of yoga in the initial stage, but later, when following the spiritual path, all *dharmas* or worldly duties can be abandoned and refuge can be taken in the Supreme Being. Complete detachment and self-surrender are the best ways for realizing the divine consciousness, thereby attaining eternal life and infinite peace. The ultimate goal of a spiritual aspirant, in the Indian view, is to be released from the cycles of birth and death, by realizing the true nature of the self according to some schools of spiritual thought, or by realizing one's divine nature according to others. Some Hindu religious schools teach that the discovery of the presence of the Divine in themselves by spiritual aspirants is the highest ideal. The religious texts of these schools declare that every individual being is potentially divine, but he is not aware of this because he is enveloped in a thick veil of ignorance. The spark of divinity lying latent in him must be kindled by the knowledge of his real nature. The Vedic seer therefore prays to the Supreme Being – 'lead me from the untruth to the truth, from darkness to the light, from death to immortality'.[6] The cherished goal of man is to make the whole world divine, according to some of our spiritual masters. Hindu seers do not hope to see individual but collective excellence in order that the kingdom of heaven may be built on this earth.

The most refined ideal, the virtue of love, arises from the realization that one spirit permeates all creation. The sage Yajnavalkya told Gargi, his wife, 'One does not love his son because he is his offspring, but because he sees his own reflection in his children. His wife is not dear to him because she is wedded to him. He loves his wife because he sees his own image in her'. The presence of the universal self in the individual arouses the spontaneous feeling of love and this is the most ennobling and sanctifying experience that men can ever have. Our scriptures advise us to feel the presence of God, the divine Being everywhere, in every plant and creature; they advise us to see God in each other. This God is not a deity different from our inner self: until and unless we experience the presence of the universal self in all creation, we shall not break through the barrier of individuality which we have ourselves created.

6.3.4 Social values

Social values cannot be divorced from the moral and spiritual values which the individual has been encouraged to pursue by Hindu religious teachers. Social values are seen as integral to moral and spiritual values: the main aim of social values is to improve society as a whole and thus benefit the individual. This univeral outlook is undoubtedly the unique character-istic of the Hindu religious tradition which is not seen elsewhere. Hindu teachers always stressed the need for enlarging our perspective, giving up narrowness and self-ishness and developing the feeling of brotherhood among all human beings. When Swami Vivekananda addressed learned scholars and representatives of different faiths in the Parlia-ment of Religions at Chicago more than a hundred years ago using the words 'O brothers and sisters of America', it created a sensation. No one before him had addressed the gathering in that way; no one had experienced the oneness of people living together in society. The young Swami had realized the presence of the universal being, his inner self in the gathering of people, and these spontaneous words endeared him to all.

Our teachers advised us to cultivate a feeling of respect for elders and show hospitality to guests. The seer in one of the *Upanisads* gives this advice to his students who on completing their study in the house of the teacher are about to leave. 'Regard your mother as goddess and treat her accordingly. Look upon your father as God and treat him accordingly. Consider the guest as a god and show him due respect.' This exemplifies a noble ideal. One should always honour the teacher as he is responsible for the student's enlightenment. We should respect others, we should never speak dispara-gingly about anyone.

Hindu law enjoins man to keep a sizeable part of his income to be given to the poor and needy (*dana*). Charity brings people nearer to each other, it creates fellow feeling. The Hindu ancient texts advise giving charity in secret; in that way the donor cannot demonstrate his superiority, which is considered to be sinful.

The values of *maitri* (friendliness) and *karuna* (mercy) are essential in an enlightened being, and their importance has been emphasized by both Hindus and Buddhists.

The Hindu teachers were aware that it is not possible to prescribe a set of absolute values or a standard code of conduct applicable to all men on the earth. They postulated that we should follow whichever virtue leads to the attainment of the Supreme Goal in life, i.e. achievement of liberation or revelation of our real nature. We should avoid following the path of vice and refrain from sinful actions as they obstruct our realization of the Supreme Goal. Hindu teachers advise that we should observe the conduct of people who were better trained morally and better placed in society: 'perform only those actions which might be regarded as faultless by the society. When you are faced with a dilemma and are unable to decide what is good and what is not, look towards the conduct of those Brahmins [learned and wise people] who are free from blemish, follow their path'.[7] It is interesting to note that the Greek scholar Aristotle also expressed the view that the opinion of a trained character should count as the principle of moral authority when one feels bewildered and is not able to choose the way of moral action on account of ignorance.

The importance of the voice of our conscience was recognized by our ancient teachers. When we are faced with a crisis, it is conscience which puts us on the right road. We should not still the voice of conscience by arrogance and vanity, but should hear it in our inner being if our minds are pure. Tolerance of other views is another virtue which can remove the cause of conflict and discord, making our lives peaceful and happy. The advice given by Jain teachers is worthy of emulation, they said that every object of knowledge is multidimensional and we can grasp only one dimension at a time. Our knowledge is always partial and one-sided, but is

113

not totally false; it is incomplete. We should always beware of our limitations and refrain from attacking the perception of others.

6.4 The role of *Karma* in maintaining moral balance

According to the doctrine of *Karma*, accepted by all ancient faiths in India with the sole exception of the hedonist materialists, every action we perform leaves residual impressions on our minds which accumulate without our being aware of them. After a time, these impressions, called 'seeds' of action produce certain tendencies which motivate all our future actions. All our actions come under two categories: meritorious deeds and sinful deeds, producing in turn agreeable results and painful results. There is a well-known biblical proverb 'for whatsoever a man soweth, that shall he reap'.[8] Such is the law of nature. The *Bhagavad Gita* prescribes the yoga of *Karma* which enables us to escape from the bondage created by our actions. Our faith in the doctrine of *Karma* and the fear of suffering caused by sinful deeds have served as a deterrent in the past; it has helped society in maintaining its moral balance, forcing people to follow the path of virtue.

6.5 The Effect of caste on Hindu society

Modern social scientists and anthropologists blame the old Hindu laws for creating an artificial hierarchy in an otherwise homogenous society by introducing the caste system. There is no doubt that the caste system as it is prevalent now is a curse responsible for many ills. It has created divisions and raised artificial barriers between people professing one faith and one spiritual philosophy. One tragic consequence of the caste system is that it has negated the basic tenet of Hindu philosophy – namely, the oneness of the Spirit pervading all creation.

The much maligned caste system in modern Hindu society is only a degenerated form of another kind of classification made by the Vedic seers, which was based on men's different capacities and inclinations. It was called *Varna-Vyavastha* (literally, the classification based on the 'colour' of the

114

individual). The earliest reference to this unique kind of division of Hindu society is found in one of the hymns in the *Rgveda* where all human society is conceptualized as the body of the Universal Being, called *Purusa* (the primordial man), and the different classes of humans as his different limbs. It was said that the *Brahmans*, the most talented section of the society from his mouth, the *Ksatriyas*, people of the warrior class from his hands, the *Vaisyas*, experts in business and agriculture from his belly and *Sudras* or people with no talent emerged from his feet.[9] The hierarchy reflected in this metaphorical description shows that the Vedic seers did not divide society on an arbitrary basis. They noticed that men do not possess the same talent, or capacity for work, because this is against the law of nature. Variety and differentiation is inherent in the act of creation. The Vedic seers had noticed this inequality inherent in men, and devised this classification as a way of maintaining social balance. It was a sound and scientific principle for a division of labour in which the capacity and the inclination of the individual members were taken into account.

This kind of hierarchy lasted until the age of the epics as may be evident from a statement made by Lord Krishna in the *Bhagavad Gita* where he declares 'I [the Supreme Being] created this fourfold *Varna*-division on the basis of talent, qualities and inclination of individual beings for the efficient functioning of Society'.[10] There are many cases recorded in the Vedic texts of persons born in the family of inferior castes having elevated themselves to a higher caste by dint of endeavour, cultivating and developing the superior qualities generally seen in people of a higher class (*Varnas*). This situation continued till the end of the Vedic age and the beginning of the age of the Epics.

When the Hindu law makers saw that people made inter-tribal marriages, throwing all past practice to the winds, the ancient hierarchical stratification was replaced by a rigid mode of class division based on the birth of the individual in the family. The original flexible division of society based on the different talents and capacities of the individual degenerated in the course of time and was forced into a fixed order. This happened just before the appearance of Manu, the father

115

of modern Hindu law. It appears that the need for maintaining the purity of different classes (or the operation of the law of eugenics) became the prime concern for the Hindu lawmakers in the post-Vedic period, with the disastrous consequences with which we are all so familiar. Despite the attempt by Hindu social reformers like Guru Nanak, Swami Dayanand and Raja Ram Mohan Roy to do away with the caste system, this stigma of Hindu social structure persists today. Political leaders have recently wrought havoc by exploiting the caste-based division of Hindu society purely for their personal gain. The situation on this front is grave indeed.

6.6 The present situation

There is always a gap between theory and practice and this applies equally to the pursuit of values by Hindus in modern times. It is unfortunate that the country which once preached sublime spiritual ideals and exalted values should face crisis and confusion today in moral and spiritual fields. The educated youth of India today has, in the name of modernity and progress, not only abandoned the path shown by our forefathers, they have also turned blind eye to our rich and glorious past. The glamour of the modern Western way of living has blinded their vision to such an extent that they now ape Western materialistic utilitarian pursuits. The only ideal that catches their imagination today is the value of material comforts of life at all costs. The pursuit of a materialistic goal is nothing new or alien in India. The hedonist schools like Carvaka and Ajivaka in the Buddhist and post-Buddhist periods preached a materialistic philosophy of life, but they were vehemently criticized by all other schools of Indian philosophical thought. Now the old spiritual ideals have been replaced by new materialistic goals, old values have been abandoned for a new set of materialistic values. Young people have little faith in the Hindu doctrine of *Karma*.

One example of the changes in modern Hindu society is the joint family system. It was the norm in the past for one family of parents and grandparents, brothers and their families to live together. The grandchildren learnt moral values and good conduct from their grandfathers and grandmothers through stories. Men and women learnt the value of tolerance and adjustment by living together in the joint family. This joint family system has been replaced by single family units in the towns for economic reasons, depriving children of the wisdom of their grandparents. Materialistic consumerism has brought with it a form of spirtual decline as fewer and fewer people continue to follow the old ideals and cherish the age-old values of life that are perennial as well as universal.

Notes

1 Vasudhaiva Kutumbakam
2 *Sarve sukhinah santu sarve santu niramaya / sarvatra bhadrani pasya ma kascid duhkhabhag bhavet.*
3 Vedic texts on *Dharmasastra* are the *Grhyasutras*, the *Kalpasutras* etc. Later texts on Hindu law, that are popular, are the *Manusmrti*, the *Yajnavalkya smrti*, the *Parasara smrti*. The epics are the *Ramayana* and the *Mahabharata*. The *Purana* texts are eighteen in number, and the *Arthasastra* of Kautilya is a well-known ancient work on Indian policy.
4 Bhagavadgita Chap.II, verse 60 s.
5 op. cit.: *Tena tyaktena bhunjitha.* V. 1.
6 *Asato ma sad gamaya, tamaso ma jyotir gamaya, mrtyor mamrtam gamaya/ Upanisad.*
7 Taittiriya Upanisad, Siksavalli.
8 Galatian s 6:7
9 Op. cit. X, 90, 12.
10 Op. cit., IV, 13.

Chapter 7

'The Market' in Asian Values

Raul Pertierra

7.1 Asian diversity

Asia as a region is too vast and differentiated for it to constitute a meaningful unit of analysis. Nevertheless, its descriptive use is by now well established and as a consequence we must accept this term, even if we insist that its unity as a region is highly questionable. Moreover, we should note that much of Asia's putative coherence is a result of contrasting it with Europe. Asia is Europe's other, and just as this contrast obscures Asian differences, it simultaneously affirms Europe's unity. In this chapter, I shall use the Philippines as an example of the unities as well as the differences found throughout Asia.

Religion is often used to represent Asian difference. Hence, Hinduism, Buddhism and Islam are often contrasted with Christianity and seen as expressing what separates Asia from Europe. It is perhaps for this reason that Judaism has historically provoked Western animosity. While religion continues to play a significant role in contemporary Asia, it is a mistake to assume that its primary texts are the major influence in everyday life in the region. If such is the case, it would be difficult to understand the differences which characterize countries in Asia adhering to the same religion, such as Pakistan and Indonesia, Sri Lanka and Japan, or East Timor and the Philippines. At least since the beginning of Western colonialism, and probably even before, the patterns of trade and other exchanges have profoundly influenced Asian society, including its religious practices. In this context, the development of capitalism has had as significant an influence in Asia as it had in the West. The growing importance of the market under capitalism is the primary force in shaping the routines of everyday life in Asia as in Europe, even if their respective lifestyles are expressed in distinct religious and cultural idioms.

The extent to which market forces dominate everyday life in Asia is indicated by the response of governments to what they perceive as changes beyond their immediate control. Some Asian states chose to use religion as a way of modifying market forces, calling on their people to revive traditional values. Others focus on an institution such as the family, and by using it as a metaphor for society's attempt to convince their members that their interests lie in re-affirming kinship ties. The extraordinary effect of the market in Asia is indicated by the phenomena of rural women leaving their families to work overseas in order to provide for the consumption needs of their children. That these consumption needs are often themselves market generated and government approved only serve to indicate their pervasiveness.

7.2 The Philippines

The Philippines straddles a major cultural division in Asia, occupying the border between its hinduized and sinicized regions. This position explains why the country includes Indian and Chinese influences as essential elements of its original culture. The Indian influence affected basic orientations in religion (e.g. specialized and hierarchic deities, *bathala*) and social organization (such as *pinuno*, the body as political metaphor), while Chinese trade shaped attitudes relating to property (for example ceramics as an index of wealth) and the family (sibling hierarchy). In the colonial period, Spanish Catholicism and later American education permeated most aspects of Filipino life, giving its contemporary culture an impression of bricolage. Needless to say, Filipinos responded creatively to all these external influences, rejecting some and adapting others. In this continuing process of rejection, adaptation and cultural invention, the Philippines retains certain basic orientations even if, at the same time, it has undergone fundamental structural changes.

119

In order to understand contemporary Philippine society one must be as aware of these continuities as of its equally significant transformations. For this reason, while Filipinos readily identify what they consider basic values (such as persisting orientations), they often fail to indicate the contexts within which these values operate (social transformations). A value such as communal cooperation (*bayanihan*) takes one form in a small village and another in a large metropolis such as Manila. In the former, locality plays a dominant role, while in the latter, kinship or association may be more significant. This value may be operative in a range of contexts, but outside this range it may no longer be relevant. For instance, it is notoriously difficult to elicit this cooperation in a public context (environmental care) not involving specific private interests. When private interests clearly threaten the collective good, public officials are often reluctant to intervene. This was illustrated in 1995, when the floods devastating large areas of the province of Pampanga (Central Luzon) were aggravated by the building of private fishponds in the major river systems. Their owners insisted in defending their private interests even when it became clear that these threatened the public good.

7.3 Capitalism as a knowledge regime

The requirements of modern capitalism have resulted in an extraordinary expansion of the structures of knowledge. Not only does capitalism require the coordination of ever-increasing economic structures, but it must achieve this through the rational competition of consenting agents. The first condition brings together an array of distinct local economies, while the second presents formidable cultural barriers for consensus formation. Their resolution can only be achieved through an ever-expanding system of information retrieval and dissemination. Structures of communication enabling the rational basis for resource allocation had to be developed for the overall economic system to persist. Whereas early capitalism was fuelled by booty obtained through military adventures, late capitalism can only be serviced by a knowledge regime. The latter is a form of domination only possible under specific epistemic conditions exemplified in the contemporary Western state. Its most significant feature is the development of public institutions for the production and implementation of knowledge.

The conditions requiring strong public institutions ensuring the production and implementation of knowledge structures do not presently exist in the Philippines. This partly explains the low levels of competence expected of most public officials. Such officials generally treat their public duties as an extension of their private interests, which are determined by concrete and idiosyncratic obligations rather than formal agreements. In this context, the acquisition of abstract and professional skills is seldom necessary. In their place, Filipinos cultivate a highly developed personal network whose members exchange a wide range of services and resources. Outside a solid core of dependent kin and close friends, the main rationale for such a network is primarily strategic and instrumental; hence their members may hold distinct and sometimes conflicting interests, even if they share common values. Under such conditions, the requirement for the acquisition of abstract skills is limited since their possession, in the absence of appropriate public structures, is insufficient for success. Instead of a regime of knowledge, Philippine society is based on a form of personal and collective prowess ensuring protection for allies, friends, or kin and marked by a predatory orientation towards others. Strangers are fair prey until they are converted into consociates, often through a mechanism of obligatory hospitality. Foreigners are often puzzled and charmed by such expressions of hospitality, a rarity in the West, until they realize that these represent attempts at incorporation into a personal network. While such displays of hospitality may be strategic, they are not necessarily duplicitous but simply ways of transforming a stranger into a consociate. Such a transformation is necessary if interaction is to proceed amicably rather than predatorily.

7.4 Strategies of prowess

Filipino society is largely maintained by the astute manipulation of strategic ties on the basis of kinship, locality, or personal connection. In the context of often conflicting aims and in the absence of a strong state with impersonal structures of domination, Filipinos are required to resort to social strategies favouring personal prowess. While no longer primarily a warrior society, contemporary Philippine life still requires its members to test their abilities against competitors in individual contests. Success in subduing competitors attracts followers who can then be used as a basis for further contests. The political arena is the clearest manifestation of these contests, seen as *mano-a-mano* duels rather than ideological or even collective conflicts. This results in extraordinary coalitions often involving people holding opposing ideological positions who combine as individuals against other similarly placed competitors. Outside observers are often at a loss to explain these extraordinary political coalitions, mistaking them for collective agreements rather than personal strategies. *Tunay na lalake (pudno nga malalake)* are men who astutely succeed in these contests by either subduing their competitors or outsmarting their superiors. While knowledge and information are often important ingredients of success, courage, valour and personal skill are ultimately more essential. Since these contests are basically personal strategies; they mostly involve concrete operational skills rather than abstract and formal rules. It is not that the latter are unknown but only that they are less likely to achieve success. The contemplative monk, the introspective scholar, or even the disinterested scientist are replaced by individuals skilled in dissimulating strategies aimed at practical success.

This emphasis on individual actors rather than on collective categories means that women can also play this game since success is its only goal. A common joke during the Marcos dictatorship was that the only man in the higher judiciary was a woman. Women entering the public domain generally have to adopt the same strategies as their male competitors and, interestingly, women of prowess are not perceived as being less feminine. An indication that public interaction often requires the expression of prowess is provided by men (*bakla*) who take on female mannerisms, often including personal subordination to male lovers, but whose public behaviour is no less aggressive than that of most men. In other words, *bakla* take on female characteristics as part of their sense of private self, which does not prevent them from asserting their prowess in public encounters. The converse appears in the case of men noted for their violent public behaviour but who also display a tenderness towards children. Unlike in the West, where macho men are expected to conform their private lives to their public roles, Filipino men are allowed to switch affected styles when dealing with friends and close kin. Women displaying male mannerisms (*tomboy*) are also expected to act aggressively in public while reverting to non-aggressive interactions in their private roles. As these examples indicate, it is not gender orientation but the division between private and public conduct which determines strategies of placation or prowess.

7.5 Personal vs. individual

The personalistic nature of Philippine society must be distinguished from the Western notion of individualism. Filipinos consider themselves as the centre of a personal network of alliances based on ascribed elements such as family and locality. To this they add whatever personal ties become available as they progress through life. This world consists largely of consociates (including enemies) with whom the individual shares personal experiences and moral orientations, outside which are found strangers with varying potential for assistance or hostility. In this world, and in the absence of trust in appropriate public institutions, strangers can only be assimilated by their conversion into consociates.

By contrast, the Western individual exists in a world of contemporaries who share common projects but who, nevertheless, maintain their anonymity from one another. Whereas Filipinos personalize their world in order to achieve their ends, Westerners ensure that society applies its laws and rules equally and impersonally. Only in the latter context can individuals act rationally and predictably without fear of arbitrary impositions arising from personal advantage. This condition is only possible through the presence of a strong and intervening Western state. Its absence in the Philippines encourages a strategy of personal prowess where success

123

ensures the stability and loyalty of followers at the same time as cowing potential competitors. By asserting self-interest, Filipinos ensure the protection of their dependants, whereas a Westerner must first concede the autonomy of structure before pursuing individual goals. The Filipino operates in a world inhabited by other persons (including supernaturals) whose cooperation or opposition must be considered. The Western individual faces an impersonal structure serviced by functionaries ideally detached from personal obligations. The first encourages a personal morality backed by the possibilities of mollification or the threat of retribution. The second requires a rigid acceptance of rules and an understanding of their consequences. The former often validates immediate experience, while the latter is predisposed to abstract analysis. For this reason, Filipinos have an extraordinary capacity to adjust to a wide range of social situations but rarely formalize this ability in an abstract way. Outsiders have often mis-interpreted this personalism as a form of irresponsible egoism due to a 'damaged culture'. In an increasingly globalized world, Filipino culture is no more damaged then any other; indeed it has shown an extraordinary capacity to resist the impositions of colonial masters by representing assent as consent. However, the Filipino emphasis on personal strategy, while successful in its context, is less appropriate in a world requiring collective and structural responses.

7.6 Private vs. public spheres

The difference between these systems of acting is illustrated in the orientation towards the public and private spheres. Filipinos personalize the public sphere and when possible use its resources to pursue private gain. Such an expropriation does not necessarily indicate selfish motives, since true leaders redistribute these gains among their followers. Thus the heirs of Marcos' fortune regularly attempt to win public opinion by claiming that his estate has been left to the Filipino people. For the same reason (that is to protect their private interests), members of the family continue to run for public office and are supported by a band of followers. The public domain is seen as potentially exploitable by enterprising individuals keen to expand their circle of opportunities. This domain is inhabited by strangers whose loyalties and alliances are available for incorporation into personal networks. For a Westerner, the public domain consists of impersonal rules which must be kept distinct from private interests. Moreover, this public sphere guarantees the integrity of society which is frequently threatened by the upsurge of personal ambitions. In the absence of a common morality brought about by a secular consciousness, the public domain in the West is upheld by a complex set of rules and laws implemented by disinterested functionaries.

In contrast, Filipinos act within a moral universe embedded in the private sphere, which ensures that actors conform to the norms and expectations of society. In politics, this has produced the slogan Pro-God, Pro-family and Pro-life; clichés which indicate that public life arises out of a personal and common morality. This morality, arising directly from a religious base, discourages a secular orientation towards life which assumes that moral differences can be politically rather than theologically resolved. A nominally modern and secular state such as the Philippines is unable to deal politically with moral disputes rooted in the private sphere because public norms for their resolution are weakly developed. This inability of the political order to resolve moral disputes is often associated with a weak Philippine state but it is also a consequence of a theory of society which sees the collective as resulting from the sum of personal interests.

In an unequal society such as the Philippines, this view results in the imposition of strong private interests over the public good. It is for this reason that the public sphere is used to conceal private interests. The market itself may provide opportunities to substitute private interests for ostensibly public goals. The banking system in the Philippines and other large business enterprises are illustrations of private interests using the market to masquerade as serving the public good.

7.7 Mythologies of politics and education

Most Filipinos proudly point to their democratic political institutions and their high levels of schooling as the major

125

accomplishments of their society. Together with the refrain that the Philippines is the only Christian nation in Asia, this trinitarian litany constitutes the mythology of national identification, reflecting the country's colonial past as well as its post-colonial present.

By Asian and other standards, the Philippines has exhibited an extraordinary commitment to electoral politics, even during the decade of the Marcos dictatorship. This concern with the basis of legitimacy may be traced to the Spanish colonial period and marks an unbroken line of Filipino political tradition to which the Americans added the notion of universal suffrage. Throughout the period of Spanish colonization which emphasized hierarchy and preaching, to the American notions of literacy and democracy – including the present practices resulting in the candidacies of movie stars, basketball players, and socialites as well as traditional politicians – the Filipino elite's grip on its constituents has barely weakened, even if the discourse of domination has changed. Underlying these different discourses of legitimation is a persisting social structure which favours personal prowess over collective or abstract skills. This prowess is primarily developed around the private sphere, as part of a network which ensures its members' viability. The practice of elections and the promises of education have to be located within this persisting structure to explain why things remain the same in the face of apparent change.

In the absence of structural transformation, the diversions of an electoral politics and the rhetoric of schooling provide the main ideological props for the status quo, occasionally allowing poor but competent aspirants to achieve high office, thereby confirming the system's democratic claims. Meanwhile, public officials consider their offices as extensions of their private interests, defending them against outside incursions. Politics is mostly perceived as the pursuit of partisan interest rather than an acknowledgement of a common good. Consequently, government funds and projects are allocated on the basis of reward rather than entitlement.

Besides a passion for politics, Filipinos quickly learnt the opportunities made available by American introduced schools. Education had always been a mark of the Filipino elite and barely a generation after the Pontifical University of Santo Tomas (UST) accepted its first Malay students in the middle of the nineteenth century, the Philippines had the most Westernized and cosmopolitan native elite in South-East Asia. During the 1860s, Jose Burgos and his generation of locally trained scholars had published ethnological studies of tribal Filipinos. The next generation comprised *ilustrados* such as Jose Rizal and Juan Luna who complemented their local education with overseas training. They were followed by, among others, Pardo de Tavera and Rafael Palma both of whom, while still Hispanophile and humanistic scholars, had begun to re-orient themselves to American and increasingly secular education. The venerable University of Santo Tomas (older than Harvard as Filipinos proudly point out), the bastion of conservative Spanish Dominican learning, was quickly overtaken by American-run religious and secular institutions. The University of the Philippines (UP), the Ateneo de Manila Jesuit College and Silliman (Episcopalian) University became the forerunners of what would quickly become an educational boom.

Democratic politics as well as an oversubscribed system of education became the hallmarks of Philippine society which, up to the mid-1960s, pointed the way for other newly independent and modernizing nations in the region. During this period the Philippines achieved rates of schooling which placed it firmly among the developed nations. In terms of gender participation, it surpassed even these nations by having more women than men in tertiary institutions.

What followed is by now well documented. From being a regional leader in education, the Philippines presently lags behind its neighbours in both expenditure and quality of schooling. This is particularly obvious in the tertiary sector, where the market and the search for quick profits have resulted in oversubscribed as well as poorly resourced universities. This has produced peculiar anomalies. Thus, while the country has an excess of nurses, hospital services are generally substandard, particularly since the best practitioners often choose to practise their profession overseas. In addition, poor rural communities often lack basic nursing care. This imbalance results from the pursuit of individual strategies by

127

students on the one hand, and on the other, the quest for profits by nursing schools. Attempts to balance these interests for the public good are rarely suggested. In the absence of strong public institutions, a discourse of collective needs is weakly developed.

I am not claiming that electoral politics and impractically high rates of schooling in themselves prevent development, but only that under certain conditions they combine to allow the reproduction of conservative structures. In other words, the processes of development cannot exists only in the presence of certain key institutions such as electoral politics and mass education but rather in the overall relationship these have with other aspects of domination. In the case of the Philippines, these institutions have reinforced conservative power structures and prevented the rise of a progressive and emancipated middle class. Large numbers of Filipinos who would otherwise constitute such a middle class have to seek work abroad instead, increasingly in the Middle East and Europe, or stand in the queue at the American and Australian embassies waiting for permanent resident visas.

7.8 The middle class

One of the major questions facing sociologists in the Philippines is the extent and significance of the middle class, particularly in determining economic, political and social issues. Most theorists of modernity point out the crucial role of the middle class not only in providing society with its professional skills, but also in instilling the value of paid work and the rewards of achievement. People born to wealth or those trapped in a cycle of poverty tend to view the world as constitutively determining their future. They do not see life as requiring a long period of apprenticeship during which one obtains formal professional qualifications entitling the holder to dispense appropriate services. For this reason, people born to wealth or to the cycle of poverty naturally depend on kin and other personal networks, rather than on achieved and often impersonal criteria of competence.

If life in the palace or the village is characterized by the intimacy of relatives, friends and neighbours, modern middle-class life consists of interactions with strangers. Such strangers exchange services on the basis of formal rules and criteria of competence, as part of normal urban life. To facilitate such exchanges, in the context of anonymity, members of the middle class resort to a conscious strategy of politeness. For those used to a more personalized world, such strategies are seen – from the respective viewpoints of the elite or the peasantry – either as pretentious displays or as forms of insincerity. In a world of contemporaries rather than con-sociates, a formal propriety ensures that one is well disposed to a continuing and possibly more intimate interaction. Much of middle-class life consists of learning complex codes of behaviour (linguistic, cultural and social) appropriate to such public interactions. Alternatively, one can characterize public interactions by their emphasis on complex and often reflexive rules. The middle-class, both in its formation as well as orientation, is more rule conscious than are other classes. A traditional aristocracy or elite makes up or breaks rules with impunity, while members of the peasantry cultivate complex strategems for avoiding their consequences. In both cases, the private sphere takes priority and determines the response to public structures. In contrast, the middle class is a product of the public sphere and defines itself in its terms. For members of this class, the world is not constitutively given but must be created through rule-governed actions. While their members naturally have private interests, these are ideally separated from their public duties and expectations. For this reason, middle-class life revolves around the distinction between domestic and private concerns, and publicly appropriate behaviour. Such a distinction becomes crucial in the context of urban life where most interactions occur between strangers rather than among a palace coterie or co-villagers. In contrast, the private interests of the elite and the peasantry extend into the public realm. More correctly, for these two groups the concept of personhood transcends the private–public dichot-omy, whereas for the middle class such a dichotomy defines their notion of the person. It is for this reason that modernity and its adaptability intimately associated with the middle class.

In the political sphere, the middle class is supposed to instill the respect of the law and for individual rights, these being the foundations of a democratic polity. Theoretically such a polity is formed by consensus where each party formally establishes its legitimate claims through processes of public debate. That is through processes which involve abstract and general rules implemented by unknown functionaries rather than private decisions reached on the basis of hereditary rights. The middle class is also responsible for ensuring the independence of the public sphere with its guarantee of universal rights for all individuals irrespective of birth or status (strangers have equal rights). Finally, the interstitial position of the middle class allows it to serve the needs of capital in the provision and management of labour. Most of the qualities of the middle class are associated with its strong emphasis on formal schooling as the determining factor for allocating social roles and for inculcating cognitive structures favouring abstract modes of thinking.

What is less often associated with the middle class is its crucial role in popularizing high culture. This cultural role has a political function since popularization is often the basis for the constitution of a national culture. Such a culture must be representative of the entire nation rather than a section or region. Moreover, such representations tend to be exemplary and serve as normative models for the public sphere. In fact, much of the public sphere is constituted by such exemplary and general representations (that is they are often counter-factuals). While the way of life of a traditional elite or peasant community generate corresponding representations, these tend to be organically linked to the conditions which produce them. Representations in the public sphere (law, art and science) under the conditions of modernity often exercise a transformative force not generally present in organically produced ones. For the reasons discussed above, the middle class is ideally placed to express a national imagination and its members are best able to practise a way of life based on a conscious appreciation of culture as 'artifactual'. Accustomed to view behaviour as a set of abstract rules, the middle class is ideally poised to respond to the creative challenges of high culture and to reproduce it for socially transformative ends. This neglected aspect of the middle class as cultural entrepreneurs and innovators, as well as its better known

130

influences in the economic and political orders, plays an important function in implementing values within the public sphere.

The Philippines provides a good example for Bourdieu's notion of the convertibility of capital from its economic or political mode into its social and cultural equivalent. One can see daily evidence of this in newspapers which offer their readers countless descriptions of important weddings, parties and other social gatherings of the elite. While these activities deal mainly, if not exclusively, with Manila high society, their readership includes a wider base whose main constituents belong to the English-reading middle class. As Bourdieu has pointed out, linguistic competence is a major way of displaying cultural capital, in this case a proficiency with English or increasingly even with Filipino. What is odd, is that these accounts of social gatherings seldom involve typical members of the reading public and instead describe the private lives of the rich and famous. Even columnists who are not themselves members of the country's elite mimic this tendency to translate personal affairs into matters of public concern.

The strongest voice of the emerging Philippine middle class is found among intellectuals whose members have mostly replaced the earlier generation of *ilustrado*-capitalists and scholar-dilettantes. Teaching in universities, practising as journalists and writers, or surviving as performing artists, a whole generation of mainly middle-class cultural brokers have entered the national scene. Characterized by a largely secular discourse, their orientation differs considerably from other perspectives which unselfconsciously invoke divine intervention or other manifestations of supernatural powers. However, despite their influence, Filipino intellectuals lead an economically precarious existence. Since their natural domain is the public sphere, often drawing their salaries from the state or other non-profit institutions, they are easily persuaded to mute their social criticisms. The general weakness of public institutions in the Philippines, in particular those concerned with the generation or dissemination of knowledge, disempowers intellectuals as well as other members of the middle class. To survive, their members often have to serve private interests or adopt the strategies of exclusion characteristic of the elite. Much of what is problematic about Philippine society is related to the undeveloped role of the middle class. The low wages of professionals, including nurses, teachers, civil servants and even junior managers in private enterprise prevents them from exercising a sobering and constraining influence in public life which, through their training and aptitude, they are ideally placed to exercise.

7.9 Philippine values

In a recent (1988) study submitted to the Philippine senate, a committee composed of academics and politicians identified what they perceived as the leading values of Filipinos. Interestingly, none of the identified values are explicitly related to Catholicism, the country's major religion (approximately 85 per cent), presumably to avoid a sectarian orientation in an otherwise secular document, but also to satisfy nationalist demands to define society in pre-colonial terms. The first set of values were identified as positively contributing to the nation's welfare. These are:

● *Pagkikipagkapua-tao* – the strong feeling of empathy for others which Filipinos readily concede. These range from *bayanihan* (cooperation), *pakikiramay* (to console others for their misfortune) to *pagtitiwala* (trust). These values are related to notions of sensitivity (not necessarily expressed or articulated explicitly) which relate individuals to their reference group. While the family and extended kin group is the main referent, this may be extended to associations and other secondary groups. Many of these values are related to religio-moral obligations in a context where supernatural events are often seen as aspects of everyday life.

Another set of values are seen as hindering societal bonds and hence weakening national obligations. These are:

● *Kanya-kanya* – an extreme personalism which neglects public duties in favour of personal or family obligations. Another manifestation of this idiosyncratic attitude is *pasulot* or skirting proper rules to favour friends and supporters. Related attitudes such as *ningas cogon* refer to a lack of consistency to ensure that tasks are properly completed. Filipinos are seen as being too patient or long-suffering (*matiisin*), a consequence of a colonial mentality. They also lack self-reflexivity which is responsible for the use of rhetoric and the frequent substitution of form (*porma*) for substance.

● The senate report believes that the proper balance of these positive and negative values must be achieved before the country attains its full potential. These values are frequently encompassed under the general rubric of: *maka-Dios* (God-fearing), *maka-tao* (orientation to the needs of others) and *maka-bayan* (community or national consciousness).

● Apart from the values discussed above, Filipinos also observe certain behavioural norms such as *utang-na-loob* (balanced reciprocity), *delicadeza* (avoiding shaming others), and *hiya* (loss of face). Anthropologists have argued that these norms lead to a form of social interaction-smooth interpersonal relations (SIR), which avoids open conflict in preference for a nuanced and unexpressed hostility. While identification of these values and norms is relatively unproblematic, their expressions and consequences in everyday as well as formal behaviour are far from clear.

The personalistic orientation of Filipinos, with its emphasis on private interests rather than public duties, affects the way in which these values are enacted. This explains why many Filipinos persevere in working under difficult conditions overseas in order to assist their families. When, in unusual conditions, this family orientation is extended to a much broader unit, as in the overthrow of the Marcos regime (EDSA, 1986), Filipinos are capable of an extreme and convivial communalism (*makiramay*). However, in other circumstances, Filipinos can also show an extraordinary neglect of a public conscience. The lack of contrition of government officials, even in the case of having clearly breached public trust, is a common example of the latter.

The lack of self-reflexivity mentioned in the senate report is also a consequence of a view of the self which is unable to assimilate strangers other than as potential consociates. This inability prevents the rise of a secular consciousness which connects *ego* to *alter* as strangers to one another but who are nevertheless willing to engage in common projects as contemporaries, not through presumed moral bonds, but through a sharing of legal norms within a publicly redeemable discourse. Furthermore, this inability to incorporate strangers in a common project also inhibits the pursuit of 'disinterested' knowledge, particularly in the public spheres such as science and technology. Hence the relatively low regard for these competencies in favour of immediate strategic gain. Under these conditions attempts to resolve problems through scientific-technological means is problematic. During the Marcos regime reports circulated about the discovery of a stone-age people in the jungles of Mindanao. The Tasaday were hailed as the anthropological discovery of the century only to be declared a hoax after the fall of Marcos. Subsequent attempts to verify the true nature of the Tasaday have proved impossible in the Philippines, where the disputants, including scientists, consistently fail to agree on common criteria for reaching a judgement. This was finally achieved in an anthropological convention in the USA. Even more tragic is the failure among officials and technical personnel to agree on the most effective way of containing the volcanic lava presently devastating large areas of central Luzon. What is undoubtedly a difficult technical problem is compounded by the inability to distinguish instrumental from strategic criteria. In attempting to maximize gains, people are willing to loose common resources.

The earlier discussion of aspects of Philippine society was intended to situate values in their social context. This context must acknowledge the predominantly Catholic adherence of Filipinos and explains why practices such as abortion and divorce are generally disapproved. Moreover, the emphasis on the private sphere and its moral underpinnings arise out of the strong influence of the Catholic Church and its related institutions in areas such as education, health, social welfare and politics. One can almost consider the institutionalized church as acting in parallel with the state, providing the latter's basis of legitimation through religion's more intrusive penetration of aspects of everyday life. While Catholicism has a very significant influence in Philippine society, it would be a mistake not to consider the indigenizing transformation that this religion has undergone. It would probably be fair to say that Catholicism has had a greater influence in public than in private behaviour. This is a consequence of its strong association with an often resisted colonial power, and the successful attempts to indigenize many of its interior orientations. An example of the latter is the common attitude among rural Filipinos not to consider sexual practice as coterminous with moral probity. The long list of sexual prescriptions associated with Catholicism are as often breached as observed. While the public behaviour of Filipinos conforms to Catholic norms, their private behaviour often contradicts them. Rather than seeing this inconsistency as an instance of uneven socialization (split-level Christianity), it simply expresses the fact that universal norms linking the private–public spheres are undeveloped. Moves for such a development, especially in the moral domain are conspicuously initiated by middle-class Filipinos. Couples for Christ is a middle-class organization whose aim is to practise Catholic norms in public and private spheres. Its appeal in rural areas and among the urban poor is negligible.

7.10 Philippine values in an Asian context

An interesting consequence of a new Asian consciousness is the closer relations which countries in the region presently seek. New economic, cultural and political structures are emerging which ensure a growing cooperation across Asia. However, this emerging globalism and regionalism also increases competition and with it the possibilities of conflict. At times these conflicts may be exacerbated by the different ways in which values are publicly expressed. These expressions often reflect the relationship between private and public structures. States with a strong tradition of civil society such as the Philippines articulate values differently from states with more dominant political institutions such as Singapore.

In February 1995 a major dispute erupted between Singapore and the Philippines. Flor Contemplacion, a domestic helper, had been accused of murdering another Filipino worker and the latter's ward. Her death sentence resulted in an enormous swell of support from Filipinos from all walks of life who sympathized with this unfortunate woman, forced to work abroad to support her family. The public's response required strong action from government officials, prompting President Ramos to make a personal appeal for clemency, or at least the postponement of her execution, pending the assessment of reputedly new evidence. The Singaporean authorities did not heed any of these appeals and carried out the sentence as prescribed. Pictures showing Contemplacion's children, who had flown to Singapore to be with their mother, on opposite sides of a glass partition outraged scores of Filipinos. The offence to Filipino notions of propriety and decency was perceived at several levels. The Singaporean rejection of President Ramos' personal plea was seen as insulting to national dignity. The perceived callousness in separating the children from their mother during their last moments together convinced many Filipinos that Singaporean officials lacked compassion. Rallies were organized throughout the Philippines to support Contemplacion, rousing speeches against Singapore were delivered, and local journalists wrote inflamed denunciations of the island state's authoritarian regime. As expected, Singaporean officials were both surprised and offended by the response of the Filipinos, particularly as the former are unaccustomed to such strong public expressions of dissent. The Filipino tendency to overstate their case in order to maximize strategic gain was misinterpreted by Singaporean authorities as government encouragement and collusion to inflame anti-Singapore feelings. Where Filipinos allow their private emotions to colour their public response, the Singaporeans insisted on a very formal exchange of views, more adequate in a system where private interests are strongly excluded from the public domain. In the end both sides learnt from the incident. Filipinos now appreciate better the implacability of the law and Singaporeans realize that their public posture is not always appropriate in dealing with inter-regional issues.

A few months later a dispute regarding the conditions of entry for Filipinos working in Malaysia threatened to disrupt the normally good relations between these countries. These good relations have been maintained despite a serious territorial disagreement (*Sabah*), largely because both parties are acutely sensitive about not giving offence. Both the Philippines and Malaysia share a common Malay preference for settling disputes through private consensus rather than through public channels. In the above case, Filipino officials reacted cautiously, expressing some disquiet but acknowledging the reasons given by their Malaysian counterparts. A delegation travelled to Malaysia which resulted in a change of entry conditions for Filipinos, but only after the delegates expressed the appropriate gratitude to their Malaysian hosts. In this case what could have been a serious public dispute was resolved by minimizing public postures in favour of private negotiations. It was the public refusal of Singaporean authorities to concede to Filipino sensibilities that resulted in the latter's outrage. On their side Singaporeans presumably wanted to make it clear that their laws proceeded independently of private sensibilities. This difference is as much concerned with the proper relationship between the public and private spheres as it is with specific values. Another illustration of the complex ways in which public–private political interactions reflect national styles involved a conference on East Timor held in 1994 in the Philippines. As expected, such a conference upset the Indonesians and they made their position clear, including the possibility of economic sanctions. Publicly the Ramos government acceded to Indonesian requests, including barring of foreign participants, but the conference was nevertheless allowed to be held and in private Filipino officials sympathized with the local organizers.

These examples show that while Asia has some overarching values resulting from common cultural and colonial experiences, there are equally significant differences. Moreover, the value system for each country has to be located within existing structures, including the relationship between the private and public spheres. This relationship determines how individual strategies are linked to collective results.

Chinese, Indian and Japanese expatriate communities are extensive throughout Asia, not only in the contemporary

137

period but dating back to a distant past. They have influenced attitudes in culture, religion, politics and trade. However profound this influence has been, it has also changed according to the fortunes of the originating societies. Recipient societies, in turn, have creatively adapted foreign influences to suit their own needs better.

Chapter 8

Asian Values and Their Impact on Business Practices

Karin Bogart

8.1 Introduction

Culture and the sociocultural environment provides the context for business. All too often there is little knowledge of the underlying sociocultural variables which have shaped the character, personality, value system and attitudes of the businessman.

Yet sociocultural environment dictates how business will be done in a certain country or region. An understanding of the cultural, religious, historical, and political influences will prepare the potential businessman for a successful encounter with the region.

In this chapter we will examine Asian values, especially as they affect the way business is done. Do Asian business values exist? *The Far Eastern Economic Review* in a survey (10.10.95; vol. 158, no. 32, p. 37) on 'Managing in Asia' looked at Asian business values, and cited what people in the region think these values are:

> Asians place community rights over individual rights; Asians believe more strongly in the family; Asians let their governments dictate their community's moral stance; Asian communities are hostile to permissive values; Asians are not indulgent parents; Asians have a knack for capitalism; Asians don't expect welfare; Asians place a higher value on education; Asians save more of their earnings.

The term 'Asia', however, is vast and encompasses countries very different from each other. Asia as a concept was first used by the Greeks in the fifth century BC. We will concentrate mainly on three areas within the Asian region: Japan, the Chinese and South-East Asia.

These three offer a good representation for a general understanding of business practices and values in Asia. Following decades of isolation and being an insular country, the Japanese have developed certain societal traits and business practices which differ greatly from other countries in the region. Their business presence in Asia cannot be underestimated. In many countries in the region business is in the hands of persons of Chinese descent. The Confucian value system underlies business, politics and culture in most of East Asia. To understand business in Asia it is vital to have an understanding of business practices of the Chinese. Lastly, we will look at South-East Asia and specifically at the newly industrializing economies of Malaysia and Thailand. Malaysia is a multi-racial society, encompassing Malays, Chinese and Indians. I will outline some traits underlying Indian business practices.

In my research into business practices in the region, I have found that there are a number of similarities, even if the history, geography, or schools of philosophy or religion differ. Section 2 will look at traits and values which are common to the whole region.

Section 3 will look at culture and value systems and how they affect the way business is done in each of the three regions, reviewing specific business practices. An example will be given of one European company operating in Japan, looking at how it modified its business practices in order to be successful.

8.2 General comparison

8.2.1 Roots of a collective culture

A widely accepted theory is that countries in East Asia – China, Japan, Korea, Indonesia – for example, are to be understood predominately as rice-cultivating cultures. The temperate climate and the rainy season favoured the development of a rice-growing, village society. Collectivism and inter-group responsibility are two main characteristics of such a society. Rural communities formed along rivers and delta regions and were relatively isolated from each other by mountains and distance. It was only natural that they formed their own close-knit groups, dependent on each other within the community for survival. Rice farming tended to be labour-intensive, requiring much time and care. All-out cooperation by everyone alike was not a matter of choice, but of necessity. Work in many communities was not seen as an obligation, but as a community or religious duty, in contrast to the Christian concept which sees work as a kind of punishment imposed on man by God for his violation of the covenant between them.

Noboyoshi Namiki, who was chief economist of the Japan Economic Research Centre, adds that in the case of Japan the shortage of water also played a role in shaping the character of the Japanese. Water for irrigation was a precious commodity that had to be evenly distributed among the rice paddies. This sharing of water led to the emergence of local leaders whose control over the distribution of water imparted a sense of communal obligation and discipline through the ranks of society. From this stems the 'soft, compliant and cooperative nature of the Japanese society'.[1] In a rice-cultivating society, the importance of the individual to the group was unconsciously bred into the way of thinking. There was a sense of obligation towards the community: they had to cultivate together or starve.

8.2.2 Influence of Confucianism

The importance of the group over the individual was further reinforced and extended upon by Confucius and his disciples. Confucianism has permeated and influenced Chinese society and the Chinese way of doing business for centuries. Kung Fu-Tze, whom we know as Confucius, lived c551–479 BC. Confucianism is not a religion, but a code of ethical and moral conduct. 'In the first millennium AD the Confucian world view, associated with the Chinese written language and principles concerning government and social relations, spread through the region; Korea and then Japan borrowed extensively from the preeminent civilization of China.'[2]

141

Confucius started with the assumption that human nature is good and that a good leader (endowed with certain values) can produce moral and diligent behaviour in others. He based his teachings on absolute respect for tradition, and laid down the principles for the correct observance of social relationships within a hierarchical society. All these relationships were defined by a strict code of conduct or etiquette and, underlying this, sincerity and righteousness. In Confucian terms the ideal man was described as a gentleman, meaning one who was upright and moral in all things, showed altruism and benevolence, and observed the proper rituals of etiquette in his behaviour.

Confucianism placed a high value on education, harmony, the importance of social order (hierarchy) and the family as the corner stone of social organization. According to Min Chen, the Confucian ethic cultivates a different kind of capitalism emphasizing:

- the self as centre of relationships,
- the sense of personal discipline,
- personal cultivation, and
- a consensus formation and cooperation.

Accordingly, a high priority and value is placed on education, rituals, fiduciary and governmental leadership.[3] As Chen notes: 'The managerial ethos comprises a ritual of learning a set of patterns for doing things and packaged know-how.' Chen continues, 'in the Confucian ethic there is also a transformative potential'. Asians have a collective strength in business; they can mobilize relatives, trusted friends and business contacts.[4]

The Confucian value system still underlies the way business is done in much of East Asia. The main values prevalent in Chinese societies and in the way the Chinese conduct business include (in no particular order): filial piety, humility, benevolent authority, patience, harmony, loyalty, importance of education and learning, self-cultivation, sincerity, courtesy, trust, respect for tradition.

8.2.3 Values and traits common to the region

The concepts of hierarchy and collectivism are two traits which have strongly influenced the sociocultural environment in Asia. There are a number of values and traits which are common to all the countries covered in this report and to most of East Asia, even if the cultural source (Confucianism, Buddhism, etc.) of these countries is different. These all linked to the historical and sociocultural environment, elements of which have been described earlier in this chapter. All of these have an impact on the way business is done. In the countries with a strong colonial legacy some values and traits have become diluted. Certain Western values have been grafted onto the society.

Even so one can put together a list of values and elements which are similar, in varying degrees, to all Asian countries:

- The Eastern mind is more holistic and dialectical; things are not either black or white but can be shades in between or can be both (*yin/yang*).
- The continuing existence of cohesive and strong family ties in a basically paternalistic structure. The family is seen as basic unit of society, the head figure is male. Obligations to the family are not only financial but also ritual.
- Filial piety and respect for age and seniority. Respect and status increase with age in the workplace. The older members of society are the teachers and advisors of the younger members.
- Importance of cultivating and developing personal contacts and networks (*ningen kankei* in Japanese, *guanxi* in Chinese).
- The first meetings with a new business partner are 'getting-to-know you' sessions. It is important to see if there is the basis of a successful relationship based on trust; business comes later.
- The importance of building trust in relationships.

Francis Fukuyama distinguishes between two types of trust: low trust and high trust. The Chinese have low trust; they are very family oriented and trust does not extend beyond the family. This is why businesses tend to remain as small family-owned entities: skilled or educated strangers are not trusted to work. The Japanese, on the other hand, have high trust. Traditionally trust is extended not just to family members but also to others who enter one's circle. This allows them to create large corporations more readily.[5]

143

- *Importance of 'face'.* The concept of face (*mianzi*) is of great importance in China. It could be understood as dignity, self-respect, prestige and status. Face is a fragile commodity; it can be given, earned, lost, saved, or taken away. The importance of face to relations is that one must have face to develop one's personal connections. Within the network of business relations, the more face one has and gives to others, the stronger and more durable the network of interlocking relationships, and in turn the more success at business.
- *Conflict avoidance societies.* Emphasis on consensus inked into this: the importance of maintaining harmony; im-plicit/indirect language (and avoidance of saying things outright); importance of patience. In collective cultures maintaining harmony is primordial. Direct confrontation of another person is undesirable – even saying no is unacceptable as it could create disharmony, so other ways are found to say no.
- *Physical contact is avoided,* public displays of affection frowned upon.
- *Smiling* in many Asian cultures is used to cover up embarrassment or nervousness. The emphasis here is on maintaining harmony in all situations.
- *Education is important* as it prepares the individual for his place in society. In collective societies it is assumed that one continues learning throughout one's life, it is a continuing process. Parallel to this is the high priority given to information and preparation for formal business meetings. The former is a legacy of the stress on education, the latter has its roots in the importance accorded to protocol and seniority.
- *Importance of protocol,* rank and status. For example, the exchange of business cards at one's first meeting helps to establish rank and protocol.
- *Sanctity of contract.* The sanctity of contract is not understood in the same way as it is in the West. In the United States and in Europe a contract is seen as binding and stable in a changing world; here it is expected that if conditions change the contract must be renegotiated. Many agreements are

144

verbal or gentlemen's agreements. The main exception to this practice is Malaysia, but to some extent Hong Kong and Singapore have also been influenced by this. Because of their strong colonial ties and the British legacy, in certain aspects of their business dealings Hong Kong and Singapore have become more 'Western'.

8.3 The Japanese

8.3.1 Japanese values and culture

Collectivism in Japan

The concepts of groupism and inter-responsibility in Japan were further enforced during its two centuries of feudalism. There was a rigid class system in place and villagers rarely moved around. Following the Meiji restoration, which did away with feudalism, the government took measures to establish a modern centralized state. They used the villagers' strong sense of conformity and solidarity as a means of promoting conformity on a national scale. The family–state idea was established, which considered the imperial family as the 'parents of the nation' (one might say at the top of the pyramid), and the relationship between them and their subjects was one of family. Japan's strong homogeneity played an important role in creating a national identity. This strong sense of national identity and homogeneity has created a reinforced, exclusionary society.

A key to understanding Japanese behaviour and the structure of Japanese society lies in the word *amae*. *Amae* describes the passive love and dependency that exists in the mother-child relationship. The child desires to be enveloped in an indulgent love and fears separation from its mother. This behaviour has extended itself into Japanese adult behaviour, implying a dependency on others and a desire for group acceptance. It plays an important role in inter-personal relationships. The Japanese believe that the individual exists because of the group; a concept absent in other Asian nations. The individual's welfare depends on his group, in which he finds security, warmth, protection, dependability

145

and stability. Japan's long isolationism and relative lack of foreign influence helped to preserve *amae* and root it deep in Japanese society.

Amae is important in human relationships. Takeo Doi, a leading Japanese psychiatrist, has written a book on the subject. He divides human relations into three forms: inner, outer and strangers. The inner circle includes one's relatives; the outer circle includes the groups to which one belongs, for example one's colleagues at work. In reality, these circles often overlap each other, often making the boundaries rather vague. The presence or absence of *enryo* decides what form human relations take. *Enryo* is a state of mind based on *amae*. It can be roughly translated as restraint or holding back. This means that one holds back rather than presumes too much on the other's good will. In one's inner circle there is no *enryo* because *amae* is present, so the individual feels accepted and protected no matter what he does. In the stranger circle there is no *enryo* because the barriers are not considered. The individual feels no *enryo* towards strangers. He does not have to control himself in a place where he is not known, he has no emotional ties with people he does not know. *Enryo* is the yardstick that measures human relationships in the outer circle. One must observe *enryo* to keep harmony within the group.[6]

Influence of Confucianism

Since the introduction of Confucianism into Japan in the seventh century from China via Korea, it has had a great impact on the society and on the business practices of the Japanese.

As Edwin Reischauer comments:

> Behind the wholehearted Japanese acceptance of modern science, modern concepts of progress and growth, universalist principles of ethics and democratic ideals and values, strong Confucian traits still lurk beneath the surface, such as the belief in the moral basis of government, the emphasis on inter-personal relations and loyalties, and the faith in education and hard work. Almost no one considers himself a Confucianist today, but in a sense almost all Japanese are.[7]

146

Implicit communication

Implicit communication is the product of a collective, conflict-avoiding society. It plays a major role in all inter-personal relationships and in all facets of business.

A Westerner tends to think logically and likes everything to be clear-cut, well defined and well structured, while the Japanese use more emotional sensitivity. Due to the homo-geneous nature of their society, they have established an effective non-verbal communication system. They use intui-tion rather than rational analysis in a given situation. Their language is allusive and non-specific; it is vague and opaque; there is less concern with the meaning of the words than with the tone of the voice, the implications, the hidden feeling. Preference is given to non-verbal communication and to the language of silence. It is a graphic language; it is easier to understand by its ideograms than by the spoken word. It does not always lend itself easily to translation. What is non-verbal and intuitive in a Japanese context may be very difficult to explain in a logical, rational way in another language. The Japanese businessmen prefer intuition and gut feeling to cold, calculated decisions. Another aspect of indirect com-munication, and one which ties into the values of 'face' and of keeping harmony in society, is the concept of *honne/tatemae*. *Tatemae* could be translated to mean the face one shows to the outside, saying and doing what is expected. *Honne* could be translated to mean one's real intentions, thoughts or feelings. Japanese and Chinese are what Edward Hall calls 'high context cultures'.[8] One of the characteristics of such a culture is the fact that relationships are cultivated over time.

8.3.2 Japanese business practices

The managerial family[9]

The structure of a company in Japan is based on cultural values. A Japanese firm can be compared to the rural rice villages of old: it provides for all the needs of its members – economic, social, educational and recreational. As Ruth

147

Taplin writes, 'it mirrors the Japanese family with its ranked order, its understanding of place, obligation and loyalty. The Japanese family is an essential site of emotional acceptance (*amae*), security and understanding'.[10] Each member accepts his obligations rather than insisting on his rights. This is still one of the legacies left by Confucianism and feudalism.

Companies conduct their main hiring procedures once a year when new graduates are hired into a company. The number of employees hired by the firm does not represent the firm's present need, but what the firm expects it will need in the long term. The employee is not hired for a specific job or position, but rather accepted into the 'company fold'. They prefer to take a new graduate fresh out of college, with no experience and 'form him according to the corporate culture and needs'. The new recruit does not sign a contract nor does he have an explicit job description.

The idea of a corporate family is backed up by such policies as life-time employment, generous personal benefits such as personal loans for education, training, housing and comprehensive health care arrangements'.[11] In Japan the employee identifies with his firm, it is a total emotional participation with his group. An employee identifies first with his company: he will say he is a Mitsubishi or Toyota employee rather than 'I am an electrical engineer' or 'I am an economist'. The employee–employer relationship requires total commitment. It is not a contractual relationship based on conditions and terms. The employee places his company's interest before his own, and regards the company's growth and performance to be equal to the improvement of his own life. As in a family, he will share in the company's ups and downs, profits and losses. In return, the company shows concern for the total person, his public as well as his private life.

The employee stays with the firm until he retires. With the downturn in the Japanese economy companies are reluctant to lay off workers. Ruth Taplin observes that 'firing of an employee is not usually a viable option and to be fired would be similar to the intolerable shame and dishonour of being disowned by one's family'.[12] Instead firms prefer to retire workers early or farm them out to other departments or sister companies. The concern for the welfare of employees in today's Japan is not as great as it once was, but it is still present. The above descriptions hold true, especially for big to medium-sized companies.

Although the firm looks to the outside world as a single unit, inside can be found a collection of small groups. Competition in Japan is not only inter-firm but also inter-department. 'To rise in a society composed of groups and factions, you must attach yourself to a group. If you betray one group or faction without making sure you have another group to fall back on, you will be left out in the cold and despised by all.'[13] Mark Zimmerman goes on to add that 'Since the source of Japanese ideas about morality does not lie in an absolute code of values, it should come as no surprise that the Japanese have no compunctions about indulging in what we would think of as unethical practices, if such practices will promote the interests of the company/group.'[14]

Seniority and rank play a role in both language and in the way business is conducted. The form of speech used when speaking to another is determined by the other's age, rank and the level of intimacy you have with him. In Japanese this linguistic style is called *keigo*, it has three levels: honorific, humble and polite. When addressing someone, one must determine the relationship with this person and choose one's language accordingly. This is also the main reason why business cards are exchanged at the first encounter, in order to establish the other person's place in the hierarchy. The name card is given and accepted with two hands, a sign of both humility and respect. Rank and status are portrayed by implicit and indirect means: seating in an office or at a banquet, language, level of the bow one makes, and so on.

Ningen Kankei – human relations

To be successful in Japan it is vital to develop *ningen kankei*. This has its roots in Confucianism, which is concerned 'with the question of how to establish a harmonious hierarchical social order in the human-centered world; the individual is not born as an isolated entity. Man can therefore be defined as a social being who should interact with others under the

149

guidance of *ren* (benevolence and humaneness)'.[15] Confucius laid down the five main relationships, four of which are hierarchical, the last one equal: father–son, master–servant, husband–wife, older brother–younger brother and friend–friend. Each of these relationships carries with it duties and obligations which are reciprocal in nature, all designed to maintain peace and harmony within a hierarchial system (known as *on/giri* in Japanese). Failure to keep these could lead to a loss of face.

Mark Zimmerman sums up *ningen kankei* best when he says that 'if Japanese society is seen as a network of interlocking relationships, hierarchically arranged, the strands of the net are formed by *ningen kankei*'. He continues, 'It is a measure of the amount of closeness and cooperation there is in a relationship. It is the expression used to describe the overall state of one person's relationship to another'.[16] The building of *ningen kankei* is started by finding a common base: coming from the same school, locality, company, neighbourhood, and so on. The cultivating and developing of *ningen kankei* requires patience and perseverance.

Decision-making and negotiation

Decision-making in large to medium-sized companies tends to be bottom-up. Proposals are made at every level and all are encouraged to submit ideas or proposals. When a decision must be made on an issue it tends to be a long process. All official decision-making is preceded by informal discussion and all those taking part in the decision are consulted. This is called *nemawashi*. *Nemawashi* refers to the groundwork that is done behind the scenes and informally to secure support and consent from the people affected by the decision prior to a formal decision being taken.

In the negotiation process, the emphasis is on maintaining harmony in the relationship. It is imperative to create an atmosphere of trust from the beginning. As Japanese do not like a hard sell technique, it is best to adopt a humble role while at the same time being quietly assertive. Seniority is important, so the negotiating team should include senior people.

Doing business in Japan – the example of Oxford Instruments

Let me give an example of one foreign company which is successful in Japan, and what it did to ensure its success in a market many say is impenetrable. Oxford Instruments realized it had to adapt its business practices to be successful in Japan. It realized that if it wanted to grow it would have to take a long-term view and that in the initial stages the venture would not be very profitable. Oxford Instruments started selling superconducting magnets and dilution refrigerators in Japan through a Japanese distributor in the late 1960s. In the late 1980s they realized that 'selling through distributors was putting a barrier between the company and its customers', and the only way forward was to set up their own company.[17] For some companies wanting a foothold in the market, using distributors may be the best solution. There can be drawbacks, however. The distributor's aim is to maximize his profits; he will charge high prices which prevents the market from growing to its full potential. The distributor's main interest is to promote his own name and not his client. Distributors do not want the client's company to be too successful or the client may decide to take over the selling for himself. According to Paul Brankin, 'the best technique they have developed is simply to prevent the principal from getting to know about the market and his customers'.

Oxford Instruments took the time to study the market, to cultivate relations and to show commitment. It sent one of its senior executives to Japan for four months to 'explore the potential market for the company's products in Japan and develop specific plans for establishing a Japanese subsidiary company'. During his four months he spoke not only to their own customers and distributors, but also to government agencies and other companies established in Japan.

The key to success is a well-recognized and well-known brand name and having a niche or unique product. Oxford Instruments realized this and set out to create a positive company image. 'To survive in the market in the long term,' Brankin points out, 'a Western company has to adopt Japanese standards and provide Japanese levels of delivery, reliability, and after-sales service.' One other vital key to a

151

successful business venture is personal relations. As Brankin comments, 'The different social relationships find many expressions: a willingness to put the company's needs before those of the individual, longer working hours, long-term business relationships, greater emphasis on customer service, etc.'

In 1991, Oxford Instruments KK, a fully owned subsidiary company, was established. In order to maximize business potential, a Japanese was appointed president of the new company and about half the staff were Japanese, half foreign.

As continuity, seniority and business relationships are very important, Martin Wood, who established the company's first links with Japan in the late 1960s continues to visit Japan regularly on behalf of the company and maintain the business and customer contacts.[18]

8.4 The Chinese

The term 'the Chinese' is used here to refer to both the Chinese in China and ethnic Chinese who are citizens of other countries. In terms of culture and value system these are the same for both groups. The groups differ when working in the business environment. The Chinese in China work within a socialist system with a command economy. The Chinese living in Taiwan, Hong Kong, Singapore and the ASEAN countries operate in a system which is more 'capitalistic' in nature.

8.4.1 Chinese culture and values

Collectivism in China

Collectivism in China, as in Japan, is based on a rice-cultivating culture. The family is the most important social unit. As Edward Hinkelman comments, for the Chinese, 'the family is the source of identity, protection, and strength. In times of hardship, war, or social chaos, the Chinese family structure was a bastion against the brutal outside world, in which no one and nothing could be trusted. As a result, trust and cooperation were reserved for family members and extremely close friends.'[19] The Japanese identify themselves with like groups, but the Chinese take the concept further to include the clan, those coming from the same locality or those with the same last name. They will work and cooperate with those within the clan, those outside are either inconsequential or seen as potential threats. This behaviour has its roots in history. The Chinese from certain coastal provinces emigrated to other countries in search of a better future or as indentured labourers. The Chinese diaspora is committed and loyal to Chinese civilization and Chinese roots. Chinese try to trace their ancestors back to Huang Ti, the Yellow Emperor. Chinese are in general very proud of their cultural heritage and their civilization of 5000 years.

It is interesting to note that a Taiwanese author contends that the virtues of diligence and self-reliance, which are values especially of the Chinese overseas, are not really Confucian values. He notes that 'the values of diligence and self-reliance arose far more as a response to a strong sense of insecurity than as a reflection of traditional values'.[20]

Implicit communication

The Chinese, like the Japanese try to keep harmony at all costs; language is implicit and indirect so they avoid of saying no. One must watch body language, subtle remarks and patterns of conduct. There are terms for addressing others, which indicate respect for age or status.

8.4.2 Chinese business practices

Organization of the firm

Anyone who is familiar with Japanese business practices will be well prepared for China. There is a difference in social systems between mainland China and ethnic Chinese living overseas. The system of government in the People's Republic of China is a socialist one with a command economy. At the Chinese Communist Party's National Congress in October 1992, Deng announced a new socialist market economy. Since then China has been trying to transform itself into a market-

153

based economy. The system before 1992 was an inflexible labour system, in which everything was guaranteed through one's *dan wei* or work unit. The work unit maintained social control over people's lives. Now, for many, the 'iron rice bowl' is broken and people must secure their own jobs. Economic reform has allowed free enterprise while in the past the economy was dominated by state enterprises.[21] The quick development of the Chinese economy has transformed the lives of the population, either for better or worse. It is still essentially a planned economy and change takes time. Cooperation between the provinces is poor and there is great competition between them for foreign investment. One cannot treat China as a homogeneous whole; to do business in China means doing business with a province or main city. Experts writing on business in mainland China warn of the difficulties, 'any businessman entering China today should be aware that a lot can still go wrong in the country'.[22] There is uncertainty about the economic climate in the post-Deng era.

Due to the political climate it is easier to deal with the Chinese overseas. Taiwan, Hong Kong, Macao and Singapore are countries where a large part of the population is Chinese. In the rest of ASEAN a large proportion of business is in the hands of the Chinese. The economies of these countries are dominated by small family-owned businesses, with the exception of Hong Kong where there are a number of British *hongs*.

The Chinese depend on global family and business links for both information and investment. The firm is based on the family and business is done first with members of the extended family, then one's own clan or ethnic group. This fits in with Fukuyama's analysis that China bases its relationships on low trust. Chinese have a clan mentality, and those outside the clan are seen either as strangers or potential threats. Chinese management style is based on Confucian values. Another element is the importance of information, the possession of which is seen as power. The main differences between the mainland Chinese and other Chinese stem more from politics than from culture.

The foundation on which business is built in China, as in Japan, is based more on intuition, indirectness, conflict

154

avoidance, sensitivity, superstition. The Chinese have a number of superstitions concerning colours and numbers. In business there is always an element of *joss* or good luck. Jade is also good luck and most Chinese wear jade or have jade objects present in their home or work place. The practice of Feng Shui (wind and water divination) is vital before building and decorating. These tokens or auguries have a bearing on whether good or evil spirits will affect the premises.

Guanxi

Guanxi, like *ningen kankei*, is a concept of vital importance to conducting business with the Chinese. The Chinese seek to develop a long-term relationship based on trust. As in Japan, it is the cultivation of personal connections with reciprocal obligations, with roots in the traditional concept of family and in Confucianism. Business is done or not done due to *guanxi*. Min Chen says, 'As most of the Chinese family businesses are small and managed by core family members, they are heavily dependent on business opportunities and credit lines provided by their *guanxi* network. No company in the Chinese family business world can go far unless it has good and extensive guanxi network.' '*Guanxi* binds millions of small Chinese firms into a big web, within which they excel in competing with Western firms.'[23]

Decision-making and negotiations

Status, protocol and seniority are important. In business, the Chinese are known to be tough negotiators. Before negotiations start there is usually the ritual 'getting-to-know-you' session. Foreign businessmen should prepare thoroughly for the meeting and take detailed notes during it. Patience is an important virtue. According to Hinkelman in his book *China Business*, the Chinese are shrewd negotiators and use a number of tactics, such as showing calculated anger to put pressure on the opposite side, looking for inconsistencies in the others, position, using friendship as a way of gaining concessions. If they know the date of their counterpart's

155

planned departure they may delay negotiations in order to put pressure on at the last minute.[24]

8.5 South-East Asia

8.5.1 Culture and values

Background

The underlying culture of most of South-East Asia comes first from India. Hinduism and Buddhism were carried by Indian traders and travellers to South-East Asia. Their influence on the great civilizations of Cambodia and Java can still be seen in the remains of Angkor Wat and Borobudur, and in the importance of the Ramayana epic in the cultural lives of the Javanese or the Thai. A number of words used in the region come from Sanskrit, for example 'Singapore', from the words *singa* meaning lion and *pura* or city/port. Hinduism is the majority religion of the Indian community of Malaysia and Singapore, and in its indigenous form is also that of most of the inhabitants of certain islands around Bali. The main religion of Thailand, Theravada Buddhism, comes from India. Singapore has a Buddhist-Confucianist majority.

It was the Indian and Arab travellers who brought Islam to Indonesia and Malaysia around the thirteenth and fourteenth centuries. They did not insist that the Hindu/Buddhist cultural heritage be abandoned: on the contrary, Islam was grafted on to the existing Hindu/Buddhist foundations in these countries. A large majority of Indonesians and Malays are Muslim.[25]

In addition to this, there is the influence of Chinese civilization. The Chinese came as traders from the southern coastal regions of China or were brought in by the British and Dutch as labourers. Elements of all these cultures remain in South East Asia.

Influence of the Chinese

The ethnic Chinese control business in almost every South-East Asian nation and some of the concepts of Chinese culture and value system have been discussed above.

156

Malaysia: background

In order to understand how business is done in Malaysia, it is important to give some historical background. Malaysia is a multiracial society: it is divided into about 60 per cent ethnic Malays, 30 per cent Chinese and 10 per cent Indian. Business is mainly in the hands of the Chinese and the political power in the hands of the Malays. Following the 1969 ethnic riots, the government tried to redress the imbalance of wealth between the Chinese and the Malays by drawing up the New Economic Policy (NEP) in 1970–71. Its purpose was to increase the share of business owned by the ethnic Malays or indigenous peoples of Malaysia (*Bumiputras*) to 30 per cent in 1990 (it was only about 20 per cent in 1990). The Indians are mainly labourers or professionals, although there are a small number of family-owned Indian firms.

In terms of the integration of the three ethnic groups, there is a low inter-marriage rate. Generally, government policy and social attitudes of the majority Malays have inhibited Chinese assimilation into the community. Bahasa Malaysia is the official language, although English is widely used in business. Each group tends to speak its own native tongue at home.

Malay society, values and business practices

The underlying ethnicity of Malaysia, Indonesia and the Philippines is 'Malay'. Malays are also found in Singapore (14 per cent of the population is of Malay origin). The close-knit village is the basic social unit. The foundation of Malay life is Islam and in general Malays are Sunni Muslims and not the more fundamentalist Shiite. When Islam came to the Malayan archipelago it merged with existing Buddhist/Hindu belief systems. The resulting Islam differs from Arab Islam. It was influenced by the different historical backgrounds, customs, cultures. languages, and ethnic and tribal identities. The core of belief remains the same: for example, Muslims are expected to pray five times a day, and the Koran sets down strict rules for behaviour, including rules for social interaction between the sexes, and also dietary rules. However, the extent and manner to which Islam manifests itself in public life differs.

157

The Malay people have a strong sense of community spirit. They adhere to a moral system of behaviour called *budi*, which is concerned with both outward social relations and internal personal ethics. Some of the basic values under Budi include: respect; courtesy; filial piety and respect for elders; harmonious relations within the family, the village and society as a whole.

Malays emphasize that responsibility and clean living are superior to the pursuit of material gain. Diligence and hard work are important, but individual greed should not be placed above group harmony. These values mirror the values we have seen in societies influenced by Confucian ideology. The Malays tend to be more easy-going than the Indians and Chinese, and in business place a high importance on personal relations trust, loyalty and sincerity. They are also more status conscious.

Ever since the colonial era, Western influences on management in this multicultural environment have had a significant impact. Generally, the large- to medium-sized businesses that are not family-owned adopt management practices which are predominantly Western oriented, whereas family-owned concerns incorporate management practices which are more local (Chinese, Indian, Malaysian). The Malays prefer to do business with trusted partners – again, interpersonal relations are a vital component. Introduction through a trusted intermediary is the best way to make contact: the intermediary assumes the informal role of the guarantor of the asking party.

Indian society, values and business practices

Indians were mainly brought to Malaysia by the British, to provide plantation labour for their colony. Indians in Malaysia are Tamil, the rest are Malayalis, Punjabis, Gujeratis and Bengalis. The largest religious group are Hindu, although there are also Sikhs, Buddhists, Muslims, Christians and others. Each observe different customs and traditions and it is difficult to generalize. In India, due to its geographical size, different regions have different business practices. Even for negotiations to succeed one should know the state from which an Indian comes and the nuances of character and values. Indians in Malaysia today tend to be either labourers or in the professions such as doctors or lawyers. The number of Indians in business is growing and many of the businesses are small and family owned.

The family is the basic social unit and business tends to be done within their own social group and through personal contacts. The Indian diaspora, like the Chinese, exists and is the centre of business. Indians tend to associate with Indians of the same background. The social system is hierarchical, especially for the Hindus for whom the caste system is important (see Chapter 6). Indians place great importance on trust, loyalty and sincerity in business. As with the rest of Asia, building up personal relationships is important, and business discussions are not started until after the preliminary discussions are finished. In terms of communication, Indians also prefer to avoid saying no. An understanding of what silence means is important, as with the other societies in Asia. (Chinese society, in this respect has been covered in Chapter 4.)

Thailand: background

Thailand has never fallen under colonial rule and the Thai are proud to have maintained their freedom. Buddhism is the main religion, practised by both Thais and the Sino-Thais. Buddhism's main virtue is tolerance (see Chapter 3). The Chinese are integrated into society; this integration has been attributed to religious and cultural tolerance in Thailand and the high rate of inter-marriage. The Sino-Thai business community dominates business. Status and rank are very important in Thailand. For example, if one passes someone of higher rank, one should tread softly and when passing, the person bows slightly to show respect. The monarchy stands at the apex of society. The current King, King Bhumibol has reigned over his people for fifty years. Thai society has a set of unwritten but widely understood and rather rigid rules by which interpersonal behaviour is regulated. There are clearly defined roles one must play and language one must use when meeting a person who is superior or subordinate.

159

The concept *kreng chai* is important in social etiquette. It is evoked in personal relationships and carries with it the feeling that one may put someone under an obligation. There would then be a reluctance to act, for fear of causing inconvenience to the other person.

Thais do not show anger or annoyance at an inconvenience. They say *mai pen rai* – never mind, it doesn't matter. The emphasis is on maintaining harmony and showing tolerance. If one is late for a meeting, the other, even if inconvenienced, would say *mai pen rai*.

Thai business practices

Most businesses in Thailand are small family-owned firms, although there are a few Sino-Thai conglomerates in the private sector. Many women go to university and become executives in companies in small family-run entities. A woman with a university degree who works hard will be recognized and promoted in the business world. In the public sector, however, there is a glass ceiling above which it is difficult to rise.

Thai society is essentially a conflict-avoidance society. Everything is done to maintain harmony. Avoidance of conflict is the governing principle of every aspect of life, including business negotiations. In the face of frustration or anger it is better to stay calm. Thais applaud the quality of *jai yen*, which means keeping calm. Calm, coupled with respect and politeness, is appropriate behaviour.

Generally, Thais prefer to do business face-to-face rather than over the phone. The cultivation of personal relations, courtesy, humility, face, status and seniority are the main business values.

8.6 Conclusion

Asian business values differ from Western ones; they are a product of an Asian sociocultural environment. Understanding of the environment which shaped these values is vital to successful business relationships within the region.

The values and culture of a country provide the framework of business practices. First and most important in a collective society is the building of a relationship with your potential partner or client. A long-time resident and Asian specialist gave the following advice:

> A successful business relationship in Asia is based on trust and perseverance. These are the two key elements. The initial domain of trust is the family core and the so-called relatives. It then extends to the business associates. Asian people have a sixth sense and feel straight away whether they can do business with someone or not. A prospective Asian business associate will in the initial stages test his overseas contacts, for instance when they come over for a visit. Can he trust him? Can he build a durable long-term relationship with this person? He will also see how they act with others. For example, how do they behave in the restaurant or Karaoke lounge when they meet up with their friends. Do they give face to them?[26]

In a collective culture silence is more valued than words. In general, face-to-face meetings are preferred to letters (impersonal) or even telephone – although this varies from country to country. The fast pace of business in Singapore and Hong Kong means that a lot of business is done over the phone. With trust in a relationship contracts are only 'instruments to reiterate what was said and understood and not so much the foundation blocks for future relationship. Like in a marriage everything remains open for discussion'.[27]

Since starting a business relationship in Asia is a long and costly affair, 'it is necessary for European businesses to carefully select a market and not to shoot in all directions at the same time. General entry conditions of a market, tariffs, non-tariff barriers, purchasing power and local and overseas presence must be weighed before making the big step.'[28] It is best to do your homework beforehand, as Oxford Instruments did before setting up a company in Japan. It will take time, patience and resources before one starts to see results.

Some of the Asian values we have examined are under pressure. As societies develop and become wealthy, this affluence has a bearing on its values. Urbanization weakens family bonds; women have greater opportunities for higher education and for jobs. It is because values are under pressure

161

that governments are endorsing a return to old traditions and ways.

The young generation in Asia is more affluent and has had more exposure to Western ways. Singapore, Hong Kong and China have become quite materialistic. In the People's Republic of China, with the absence of a state philosophy, Xinhua reports that 'the disappearance of social norms, the death of morals and the disintegration of traditional values has brought about a moral crisis'.[29] In Taiwan also, the Confucian virtues of 'diligence are becoming noticeable through absence among Taiwan's younger generation.'[30]

Notes

1 Conversation between Mr Namiki and the author in 1985.
2 Gilbert Rozman, ed. *The East Asian Region-Confucian Heritage and its Modern Adaptation*, (Princeton University Press, 1991) 8.
3 Min Chen *Asian Management Systems*. (Routledge London 1995) 30.
4 Min Chen. *Asian Management Systems*. (Routledge London 1995) 30.
5 Francis Fukuyama. *Trust. The Social Virtues and the Creation of Prosperity.* (London Hamish Hamilton 1995).
6 Takeo Doi . *The Anatomy of Dependence,* (Kodansha International 1971).
7 Edwin Reischauer. *The Japanese.* (Cambridge, Mass: Belknap Press 1977). 214.
8 Edward Hall. *The Dance of Life.* (New York:Anchor Press/Doubleday 1983).
9 Small medium enterprises form the base of the Japanese economy. Only about 30% of companies fall into the category of 'large enterprises'. The characteristics referred to in this chapter, such as lifetime employment or seniority based wages are true for the large enterprises, less so for the SMEs.
10 Ruth Taplin, *Understanding the Family,* The Times Higher Education Supplement, 25 May 1990.
11 Ruth Taplin, *Decision-Making in Japan and Japan a Study of Corporate Japanese Decision-Making and its Relevance to Western Companies.* (Japan Library 1995).
12 Ibid.
13 Mark Zimmerman, *How to do Business with the Japanese.* (Tokyo: Charles Tuttle Company).
14 Ibid.
15 Min Chen, *Asian Management Systems.* (London: Routledge 1995).
16 Ibid. 75.
17 Paul Brankin, 'Establishing a sales operation in Japan,' in *Engineering Management Journal.* (August 1993).
18 Ibid.
19 Edward Hinkelman, (ed). *China Business – The Portable Encyclopedia for Doing Business with China.* (World Trade Press:1994). 158.

162

20 Dennis Engbarth, 'Pioneer Spirit at Heart of Island's Growth' in the *South China Morning Post International Weekly.* (10 June 1995).
21 Although China is increasingly open to foreign trade, it is still difficult for foreign companies, as much is still controlled by the state. There is a complex system of administrative controls which regulates foreign investors' access. Private firms are not allowed to conduct direct business.
22 Geoffrey Murray, *Doing Business in China.* (Curzon Press China Library: 1994). 9.
23 Min Chen, op. cit. 59.
24 Edward Hinkelman, op. cit.
25 D. R. Sar Desai, *Southeast Asia Past and Present.* (Westview Press,1994).
26 Oscar Cousy, Flemish Economic Commissioner, Embassy of Belgium, in Singapore, personal communication.
27 Ibid.
28 Ibid.
29 Jasper Becker, 'Confucius pays price' in the *South China Morning Post International Weekly.* (10 June 1995).
30 Dennis Engbarth, 'Pioneer Spirit at Heart of Island's Growth', in the *South China Morning Post International Weekly.* (10 June 1995).

Reference

Becker, Jasper (10 June 1995) 'Confucius pays the price' *South China Morning Post International Weekly.*
Brankin, Paul (August 1993) 'Establishing a sales operation in Japan' *Engineering Management Journal.*
Chen, Min *Asian Management Systems.* (Routledge London 1995).
Doi, Takeo (1971) *The Anatomy of Dependence* (Kodansha International).
Engbarth, Dennis (10 June 1995) 'Pioneer Spirit at Heart of Island's Growth' *South China Morning Post International Weekly.*
Fukuyama, Francis. *Trust. The Social Virtues and the Creation of Prosperity.* (London Hamish Hamilton 1995).
Hall, Edward (1983) *The Dance of Life* (New York: Anchor Press: Doubleday).
Hinkelman, Edward (ed) (1994) *China Business – The Portable Encylopedia for Doing Business with China.* (World Trade Press).
Murray, Geoffrey (1994) *Doing Business in China* (Curzon Press China Library).
Reischauer, Edwin (1977) *The Japanese* (Cambridge, Mass: Belknap Press).
Rozman, Gilbert (ed) (1991). *The East Asian Region-Confucian Heritage and its Modern Adaptation,* (Princeton University Press).
Sardesai, D.R.(1994) *Southeast Asia Past and Present.*(Westview Press).
Taplin, Ruth (25 May 1990). 'Understanding the Family' *The Times Higher Education Supplement.*
—— (1995) *Decision-Making in Japan and Japan a Study of Corporate Japanese Decision-Making and its Relevance to Western Companies.* (Japan Library).
Zimmerman, Mark *How to do Business with the Japanese.* (Tokyo: Charles Tuttle Company).

Chapter 9

The Encounter Between Europe and Asia in Pre-colonial Times

Willy Vande Walle

> I think that, if we are to feel at home in the world after the present war, we shall have to admit Asia to equality in our thoughts, not only politically, but also culturally. What changes this will bring about, I do not know, but I am convinced that they will be profound and of the greatest importance.
>
> Bertrand Russell, *History of Western Philosophy*, 2nd edn, London: George Allen & Unwin Ltd, 1961, p. 395

9.1 In search of prefigurations

The relationship between Europe and Asia may be approached from two different angles. On the one hand, it may be described in terms of the intercourse, exchange and mutual influence which from hindsight may be said to have proven beneficial to either side. On the other hand, one could equally rightfully stress the conflict, the competition, and the clash of civilizations that have marked the history of that encounter. The first approach is nowadays by far the more popular of the two, including in the scholarly community. This is easily explained against the backdrop of the generally good relations established between Europe and the major nations of Asia after the Second World War, both on a political and institutional as well as on an individual level, nurtured by the broadly-based commitment on either continent to improve relations further. The historian is lured or compelled, consciously or unconsciously, to stress the positive elements, and his research will often tend to a selective quest for events, contacts and cases of intercourse that prefigure today's

164

situation. In this chapter I will attempt to avoid the pitfalls of such exalted prejudice and try to draw an objective picture of some aspects of this vast subject.

We have come a long way from the Hegelian assessment of Asian history.[1] Since the end of the Second World War, together with the rapid decolonization process, historiography has veered towards a resolutely self-conscious Asian viewpoint. By studying Asian languages, historians of Asia have penetrated the sources available in those languages, thus letting Asia speak for itself. Furthermore, historians of Europe have reassessed the Asian impact on European culture. While most present-day historians explicitly or implicitly reflect a resolutely positive appraisal of Asian history, it may suffice to mention the work of only two scholars whose works are eminent testimonies to this approach. The first is Joseph Needham who started work on his monumental *Science and Civilization in China* in 1954,[2] and in collaboration with a number of specialists in various fields, has until his recent death been pouring out volume after volume documenting the material civilization of China. These scholars have demonstrated that China had an impressive scientific tradition of its own before the advent of Western scientific knowledge. Needham and his colleagues have shown to what extent modern Western civilization – which prides itself on its scientific achievements, is indebted to the Asian heritage. The second is Donald F. Lach, who, since 1965, has been working on his multi-volume study *Asia in the Making of Europe*,[3] charting the many and varied channels through which Asia contributed to the shaping of Europe. It is especially in histories with a comprehensive or synthetic claim, such as the two mentioned above, that the authors' view on history is most clearly articulated, but a similar view is expressed, though less conspicuously, in more limited and detailed monographs by scores of Asia specialists.

Our search for prefigurations must not prevent us from investigating the history of Asian-European relations with a critical eye. The true historian is beholden, compelled him to admit that, generally speaking, in pre-colonial times neither Europe nor Asia believed they had much to learn from each other. Both sides showed a general lack of genuine interest.

165

The Asians wanted to be left alone, and the Westerners tried to convert Asians to their own beliefs, or to lure them into commercial dealings that were beneficial to themselves. Concepts like brotherhood of men, or even less far-flung notions like 'mutual cultural enrichment', 'exchange of ideas', or 'communication' evidently did not feature in the vocabulary of those days. If we confront historical reality without fear or prejudice, we have to admit that the encounter was hampered by cultural myopia, often violent and bloody. It would be dishonest if we were to project the present-day values and patterns of intercourse on to the events of the past. Our past acts cannot stand the test of our modern standards. We have to understand the history of the encounter in its contemporaneous context, and assess it in the light of modern values and achievements only in as much as we want to determine the relative merits of the actors of those days.

Therefore, in general, the relationship between Europe and Asia in pre-colonial times can only be described in terms of power, competition and conflict. From this perspective, there is no qualitative caesura with the colonial period, but what makes the difference is the fact that until about the beginning of the nineteenth century both sides held each other in balance. This provided for conditions that made it possible to avoid major clashes, and created opportunities for expanding knowledge of each other another, if not always understanding. Although Europe was clearly the more mobile of the two partners, Asia seems to have had a deeper imprint on Europe than the other way round, although it is hard to quantify exchange and influence. During the colonial period that pattern was to be reversed. During the period from 1600 to 1800, knowledge about Asia in Europe made considerable strides forward. The period of colonialism, though certainly not the happiest of encounters, meant yet another tremendous leap forward in knowledge, if not understanding, of each other's culture. However, in view of the nearness of the events, and the sensitivity of collective memories related to them, treatment of the colonial period seems to provide a less adequate basis for building bridges between the two continents. The fact that in pre-colonial times both sides held one

166

another in balance, makes this phase of the Asian–European encounter much more attractive as a framework for finding prefigurations of the present-day relationship.

9.2 The image of Asia before the age of discovery

Contacts between Asia and Europe go back to antiquity. To the ancient Greeks and Romans, Asia was basically Persia and India. In the wake of Alexander the Great's campaigns through these regions, Greek generals, explorers or ambassadors, such as Nearchus, Onesicritus and Megasthenes, wrote down accounts of what they had seen or heard in these regions. Their records served many subsequent geographers, who usually also perpetuated the mixture of facts, errors, and fables presented in the originals. Due to the increasing trade between the Roman world and India, the subcontinent and Ceylon were featured in considerable detail in Roman geographical writings. Asia beyond India however existed only as a shadowy image, probably best epitomized in the word *seres*, derived from the Chinese word *si* (silk) and vaguely denoting the silk-producing Chinese and the peoples along the silk route. In the first century AD, the Roman geographer Pomponius Mela gave the first description of the homeland of the Seres.[4] During the same century, Pliny the Elder, basing his account on the testimony of a Sinhalese envoy to Rome, detailed more knowledge about the Seres in his *Natural History*. Ptolemy, greatest of the ancient geographers, who lived during the second century AD, endeavoured to be comprehensive in his treatment of Asia, which did not guarantee any greater accuracy in practice. He had not travelled to any of the areas he described. Even for his physical description of India he relied on hearsay gathered from sailors. He described the lands beyond the Ganges, and was the first to write of the Malay archipelago. He mentions Indo-China, which he calls *Sinai* or *Thinae*, to the north of which lies *Serica* (China).[5] The *Christian Topography* written by Cosmas Indicopleustes in 518 AD was the last important account of Asia to have any impact in Europe before the Crusades.[6] During the third century AD the Sassanids had come to power in Persia, while the Roman empire was

167

slipping into decay. What international trade remained between the Mediterranean and Asia was gradually being controlled by Persian middlemen.[7] The cessation of direct trade was followed by the rise of Islam in the seventh and eighth centuries. Europe's horizons shrank and no new elements were added to the store of factual knowledge. A deformed and fantastic East became frozen in the minds of the Europeans. The Bible instead became the main source of geographical knowledge and would remain so for the rest of the first millennium.

It would take quite a few centuries before India and China took on the clear contours of distinguished civilizations. Practically all accounts were limited to descriptions of the physical properties of humans, fauna and flora. References to social and cultural features were usually highly imaginative. During the eleventh and twelfth centuries Asia receded further back into the distance and was virtually transmuted into a mythical continent, transfused with the legends of Alexander the Great, St Thomas the Apostle of India and Prester John.[8] The Mongol empire, established across the expanse of most of the Asian continent by Ghenghis Khan in the beginning of the thirteenth century, destroyed the barrier erected by the Muslims and created a freer flow of travellers and information between Europe and the Far East. For the first time on record, Europeans travelled across the Eurasiatic land-mass to the Pacific. The Franciscan John of Plano Carpini journeyed as an emissary of Pope Innocent IV to the court of the Great Khan Kuyuk in 1245.[9] For its factual description – by the standards of the day – his *History of the Mongols* marked a turning point in medieval literature on Asia. Another milestone was the report by William de Rubruquis (Willem van Rubrouck), a Flemish Franciscan dispatched by the French King Louis IX to the court of the Möngke Khan in 1253.[10] He gave the first description of Far Eastern housing and of Chinese ideographic writing.[11] The most influential account of the Mongolian empire is, needless to say, Marco Polo's *Description of the World*, written in 1298. All three travellers recognized the strict moral codes by which the Mongols were ruled, their efficient military and social organization and the law and order that prevailed in the empire. Marco Polo described the religious toleration and coexistence of beliefs in the domains of Kublai Khan. Nevertheless, all three took it for granted that eventually the Khan should embrace Christianity, and, true to the example set by Constantine and Clovis, led his flock into the bosom of the Church.[12] Incidentally, the Venetian traveller also visited parts of South-East Asia: his voyage took him to the Indonesian archipelago, the Malay peninsula, Ceylon and the Malabar coast of India.[13] He was also the first to inform Europe of the existence of Japan (*Cipangu*). John da Marignolli, the last of the Franciscan Friars to be sent on an apostolic mission to the Mongol empire, arrived in the Chinese capital Cambaluc in 1342. For his return voyage, he set sail from Zayton (*Quanzhou*), visiting the Coromandel coast of India and Ceylon.[14]

Although these accounts certainly had their impact on contemporary scholarship in Europe, it took a long time for the information to percolate to a wider audience. An exception has to be made for Marco Polo's description, which gained wide circulation even during his life time. Ironically enough and to Polo's distress, his account was treated as a collection of fantastic stories rather than as a record of facts. Apparently the readership was more intent on a tall story that confirmed the received vision of the East, than on facts that challenged it, an observation illustrated by the fact that the highly imaginative account of the *Travels of Sir John de Mandeville* was a kind of bestseller during much of the Renaissance.

9.3 The Age of Discovery

We have to wait for the Age of Discovery before contacts were made on a totally different level. We must note that at the outset the principal aim of the explorations was India, because of the variety of goods Western traders sought on the subcontinent. During the sixteenth century the image of Asia was dramatically drawn into focus by the new discoveries made by the Portuguese, while still retaining some shadings from the past. The accounts of Galeote Pereira,[15] Gaspar da Cruz and Martin de Rada formed the basis for Juan Gonzalez de Mendoza's *Historia de las cosas mas notables, ritos y*

169

costumbres del gran Reyno de la China, published in Rome in 1585 and subsequently translated in all major languages of Europe. The Ptolemaic and medieval geography of Asia had divided the continent as follows: India before and beyond the Ganges, further India, and Cathay. This scheme was slowly being replaced by a division that corresponded better to reality: India, South-East Asia, Japan and China – still more or less the regional division we use with regard to Asia today. Europeans awakened to the diversity of Asian cultures and languages, and became aware of the differences among the Asian peoples, which were no less marked than the differences between the European peoples.[16]

The pattern of interaction between Asia and Europe ran along three lines: missionary activity, trade and secular administration.[17] These lines are interconnected to a greater or lesser degree depending on which of the European nations was involved. In the case of the Iberian powers the interconnection was particularly strong, much less so in that of the later colonial powers, Great Britain and France, and probably least of all in that of the Netherlands. No sea-faring nation had dissociated the evangelization so radically from its trading venture as the Republic of the United Provinces.

The royal house of Portugal created a unique form of state capitalism, investing the state's resources to create a trade monopoly in its Asian terrritories.[18] This enterprise had a decidedly religious thrust as a result of the *Padroado Real*, the Royal Patronage, which implied that the Portuguese crown was entrusted by the Pope with the conversion of heathen lands. Nevertheless, the profits of the spice trade ultimately dictated the policy of the Portuguese in Asia. In contrast, economics was subordinated to cultural-religious imperatives in the Spanish possessions. Imperial Spanish policy put high priority on promoting the Spanish language and culture and the Catholic religion in the pagan lands of Asia.[19] This difference among the Iberian powers is probably due to the fact that Portugal, with its limited demographic resources, could not wield the same military power as Spain and had to seek compromise and accommodation. Moreover, the Spanish enterprise in Asia was confined to the Philippines, so they had less pressure on their resources. From the outset, the

170

Christianization of the natives took indisputable precedence in the colonization of the archipelago.[20]

Evangelization, trade and territorial administration represented three strands of one and the same enterprise. In its pursuit of the huge interests involved, Europe was confronted with cultures that had totally different social structures, political organizations, world views and customs. The evangelizing effort was to clash with deeply rooted native religious traditions and feelings of superiority. While there was still a strong control on trade in Europe, it was under even stricter control in Asia, so that securing privileges to trade from local potentates or kings was an arduous enterprise involving much conflict. The possession and administration of territory, necessary to protect the trade were evidently often a cause of great friction.

South-East Asia's principal attraction to foreigners, Asians of other nations and Europeans alike, had always been the trade in spices and other exotic products. In the period between 1500 and 1800, additional motives of a higher order, such as conversion and the ambition to expand territorial control increased the drive towards these regions. Concerns of security and survival evidently played a major role in seeking safe havens for trade and settlement. These aspirations were accommodated by the relative openness of local rulers in South-East Asia to outsiders. A few cities served as the main interface between Europe and Asia. These cities were Goa in India, Macao in China (established in 1555), Nagasaki in Japan, Melaka, Batavia and Manila. In China, and even more so in Japan, these cities were under strict control of the indigenous authorities which limited the impact of foreign traders. In South and South-East Asia, however, foreigners enjoyed a far greater freedom from interference by the local rulers and developed into European-controlled centres which provided a source of novel ideas to South-East Asian society, and were even powerful enough to challenge local power bases. They created a unique mixture of foreign and indigenous elements in the architecture, the city administration, economic affairs and population. Three cities attained great prominence: Portuguese (later Dutch) Melaka, Dutch Batavia and Spanish Manila. Although they served different purposes,

171

they provided South-East Asians with a window on new ideas and practices.[21] The European involvement on the continent was far more limited than it was in South-East Asia. The main purpose for European enterprise in Asia was control of the spice trade, therefore island Asia constituted the main arena of their interest. At the same time, the population and economic resources of the empires and kingdoms on the mainland far outweighed the Portuguese or Spanish presence in Asia.[22]

9.4 Asian schemes of international order

The European presence was not strong enough to affect the overall direction of political developments in mainland Asia, but its impact on island South-East Asia was more considerable. The European conception of a state was alien to this region, yet we unmistakably see a movement towards a greater centralization of authority in the island states.[23] Before the advent of the Europeans, there was no international order governing interstate relations to which all states or political entities in the region subscribed. China imposed on all its contacts with the outside world its scheme of tributary relationship. This was largely a legal fiction, to which the Chinese adhered scrupulously. They considered all non-Chinese races as inferior in civilization. Objects from the outside world were considered as tribute, while Chinese goods in exchange were given as gifts from the emperor. According to this state philosophy, the real aim of these contacts was to dispense Chinese beneficence to other nations in the form of knowledge and material goods.[24] The so-called tributary states were not much concerned about this legal fiction. Theirs was a more pragmatic attitude, attracted as they were by the material gains that were to be derived from this official trade. In some cases, there was a political motive behind the tributary missions, in that a ruler would use the so-called investiture from the Chinese emperor for domestic purposes, in an effort to strengthen legitimacy at home.

The first time that China departed from its traditional interstate ideology was the Treaty of Nerchinsk, concluded in 1689 between the Kangxi emperor and the government of the Russian csar.

172

There was an alternative to the Chinese concept of tributary states paying homage to the Chinese emperor: the idea of a Universal Monarch, a notion enshrined in Buddhism. Theravada Buddhist rulers inherited the politico-religious notion of *cakkavatti* or Universal Monarch who would prepare the world for the advent of the next Buddha. The nineteenth-century Burmese text *The Glass Palace Chronicle* depicts the kings of Burma as the direct descendants of Buddha.[25] The *cakkavatti* obtained his position because of the great merit he has accumulated in previous lives and the charismatic glory he is blessed with in this one. Other states readily acknowledge him as king. He possesses certain sacred objects that symbolize his exalted status, such as white elephants, magical horses and women of supernatural power. Precious objects had a wide-ranging value as sources of intense spiritual power. In the Indianized areas of mainland Asia, including Burma and Thailand, several kings aspired to be *cakkavatti*, a rivalry that often led to intense conflict.[26] Perhaps the Burmese king Bayinnaung (1551–81) came closest to realizing this ideal. He sent missions to Bengal, Sri Lanka, Goa and China. He ruled 'the most powerful monarchy in Asia, except that of China'. His territory encompassed the 'great arc of Thai-speaking peoples' and his overlordship extended hundreds of kilometres from his capital at Pegu.[27] While the claim to universal overlordship was enshrined in the position of the Chinese emperor *per se* ever since the ascent of Qin Shihuangdi (third century BC), the status of *cakkavatti* had to be attained by every individual ruler, and as a result was seldom achieved. This suited the South-East Asian environment much better, because of its inherent tendency to fragmentation.

Islam offered another axis of reference to an exemplary centre of power.[28] From the fifteenth century on island South-East Asia gradually converted to Islam. The rulers of the coastal kingdoms were attracted to the idea of becoming part of a commercial network stretching from Europe to Maluku, and dominated by Muslim traders. This was an important incentive for the kings of Melaka to convert to Islam. Their conversion marked a milestone in the spread of Islam into South-East Asia. But Persian notions of kingship associated with Islam and exemplified in the Great Moghuls and the

173

Ottoman rulers, offered a potent justification for more exalted claims of suzerainty. Rum (Rome, i.e. Byzantium) as the Ottoman empire was called, was accorded the same veneration as the emperors of China.[29]

This ideology of statecraft must be seen against the backdrop of the developments during the late sixteenth and seventeenth centuries, which were marked by growing centralization and efforts to enhance the status and the power of the king.[30] The practice of the royal audience and the presentation of tribute was not a typical Chinese device. It was practised widely throughout the area. It was an occasion to confirm the ruler's superior position, and to consolidate the ties between overlord and vassal.[31] The eighteenth century witnessed the break up of the great centres of political authority, both on the mainland and in the archipelago. This fragmentation paved the way for colonial infringements that were to come in the latter half of the eighteenth and the nineteenth centuries. The impact of the European presence on these political developments must not be overrated, for the number of Europeans remained very modest. The fragmentation was rather the result of internal dynamics.[32]

9.5 The study of Asian languages and cultures

Important as understanding values is, and must be, in the last analysis encounters between cultures hinge on the prerequisite of communication and therefore language. Even as values change through time, the linguistic factor remains a core element. In the following paragraphs we want to address that core element, which lies on this side of the value system, but is just as relevant now as it was in historical times. Nowhere did the elements of language and value meet at a more complex and challenging level than in the arena of the Christian mission. Values are embedded in religious and philosophical concepts and therefore need to be understood in the religious and philosophical systems of Asia and Europe. Not only is language a prerequisite for explaining values, but it determines and is being determined by these same concepts and systems. Our time frame will be mainly limited to the pre-colonial period and seventeenth centuries, because this

174

bracket coincides with a unique phase in the history of the interaction between Europe and Asia.

Starting in the second half of the sixteenth century the Catholic missionaries, especially the Jesuits, spurred on by the fervour of the Counter-Reformation, made remarkable strides forward in the penetration of Asian cultures, especially in Japan, India and China, and to a lesser extent in South-East Asia. Although their motives were admittedly evangelical, and one can contest whether they had any genuine interest in the cultures *per se*, it seems that as time went by and they acquired a better grasp of the Asian culture they were studying, they developed a considerable degree of admiration and tolerance for these foreign cultures. Although there are no cases reported of any of them 'going native', it seems nevertheless true that by dint of long exposure to the high cultures of Asia, they were prepared to accommodate themselves as much as they could to the indigenous cultures. This is at least true of the Jesuit Congregation, who went too far for the taste of the contemporary Church.

Here again, there may be an inverse correlation between accommodation and the presence of military strength. That is at least what is suggested by the significant difference between Spain and Portugal in their missionary behaviour. The Spanish missionaries of the Four Orders kept much closer to and were more dependent on the secular powers in Manila. In contrast, the Jesuits even under the system of the *Padroado Real* were more independent and had a proper sense of direction. Although they associated themselves with Portugal's trading empire and followed the routes the merchants had taken before them, they kept themselves at some distance, had a strong spirit of independence, and were often far ahead of the secular arm. In many cases they left the trading centres to evangelize on their own. At the end of the sixteenth century for example, they were far ahead of the Portuguese traders in the penetration of inland China. Leaving the protection of the coastal settlements meant they could not rely on the support of the secular arm, and when faced with superior native strength, they opted for harmony to avoid conflict rather than reverting to their usual practice of direct action.[33]

175

The Italian Alessandro Valignano (1539–1606) was the engineer of this novel approach. After first accommodating themselves to the native culture, they would then attempt to impress on the people the superiority of their message by reasoning and explaining in their own language and within the premises of their culture. This technique was first tried out in Japan and not without success. However, after initial successes this innovative approach was rebuked by the Church and the Jesuit enterprise suffered a lasting frustration, only to be vindicated in the twentieth century. In India, success was longer lasting, but it was more spectacular in China, probably thanks to the talent of Matteo Ricci (1552–1610).[34] The Jesuit enterprise in Asia started in 1542 with the arrival of Francis Xavier in Goa. Although the Franciscans had preceded him there, and were already firmly established by that time, they were soon upstaged by the Jesuits. The Franciscans concentrated on the poor and although their work no less noble than that of the Jesuits, because the latter directed their efforts to converting the rich and famous, they loom much larger in the historical records. That is why this chapter too is heavily tilted towards the Jesuit odyssey.

9.6 The Jesuits in India during the sixteenth century

From the outset the epicentre of Jesuit activities in Goa was the College of St Paul. Here the congregation were taught a range of subjects, from elementary Latin to advanced theology. The student body was cosmopolitan: Hindus, Sinhalese, Moluccans, Chinese, Japanese, Kaffirs and Ethiopians.[35] In 1546 there were eleven different nations enrolled in the school. A decade later the proportion of Portuguese and mestizos rose, as did the number of recruits from different parts of India. The youths studied the elements of Christian doctrine, Latin, Portuguese, music and mathematics.[36] Allegedly, the Japanese and Chinese excelled in academic subjects, the East Indians in singing and interpreting, while the Indians seemed to excel in memorization, debate and dramatics.[37] The best students were allowed to go on studying philosophy and theology. If they completed their studies they were deemed fit to be ordained and were sent to their homelands as priests.[38]

176

As already mentioned, one of the most characteristic features of Jesuit evangelization is its focus on the ruler and the social elite. Worth mentioning in this respect were the three missions they sent from Goa to Akbar, the Great Moghul ruler who reigned from 1556 to 1606. Akbar's first contacts with the Portuguese dated from 1573, at the time of his conquest of Gujarat. Four years later, Pedro Tavares, commander of the Portuguese garrison at Satgâon, and Julian Pereira travelled to Akbar's court at Fatehpur Sikhri. The Moghul ruler was surrounded by thinkers of various religions and beliefs such as Brahmans, Muslims of various sects, Parsees and Jews. As his reign continued he became increasingly preoccupied with the search for an eclectic religion that would subsume all valuable elements of the other religions. Apart from a genuine philosophical interest, he was no doubt motivated by the ambition of blunting the religious division that ran through his empire and that posed a great potential threat of fragmentation.[39] Pereira talked to the monarch about the Christian religion and the Jesuits in Goa. Perhaps Akbar felt that Christianity might have something to contribute to the religion he was trying to formulate. In 1579 he sent out two emissaries to Goa requesting the Portuguese to dispatch to his court 'two learned priests who should bring with them the chief books of the Law and the Gospel'.[40]

In November 1579 the first mission left Goa under the leadership of Rudolf Aquaviva. In his company travelled the two emissaries sent by Akbar and the Jesuit Fathers Antonio Monserrate and Francisco Henriques. The latter was a Persian from Ormuz, who had been converted from Islam and was to act as an interpreter. They arrived at Fatehpur in February 1580. The fathers, detecting a high degree of sensibility to religious problems in the great monarch, tried to convert him. He was cordial to his guests and showed a keen interest in their expositions of the Christian doctrine, but he found it hard to accept some of their tenets and social customs, notably monogamy. Nevertheless, the Fathers enjoyed a great deal of freedom and were allowed to preach and make conversions among the populace, but they preferred to stay with the ruler. They taught Portuguese to his son, and took to studying Persian. In all they stayed over three years at Akbar's court.

In 1590 Akbar sent to Goa a new request for teachers of the Christian faith to engage in disputations with the representatives of the other religions at his court. In 1591 Father Duarte Leitão and Christoval de Vega were sent to Lahore where Akbar now held court. Although the monarch was less inclined to Islam than before, he was still unwilling to embrace Christianity. He allowed the Jesuits to set up a school for the training of aristocratic youth, but in the face of the fierce resistance from the Muslims at court, they thought it wiser to return to Goa. In spite of the disappointing result, the Jesuit Provincial at Goa, yielding to pressure from the Viceroy and Akbar, decided to send another mission, headed this time by Jerome Xavier, grand-nephew of Francis Xavier. Other important members were Father Manuel Pinheiro and Brother Benedict de Goes, a Portugese painter and Domingo Pires, an interpreter. They reached Lahore in May 1595. Xavier was to stay at Akbar's side for most of the last decade of the monarch's life. He learned Persian to converse with Akbar and his entourage, but in the end he failed to win the monarch over to the Christian faith, although Akbar did openly abandon Islam and gave permission for his subjects to embrace Christianity. He persisted in his search for an eclectic religion and refused to accept the divinity of Christ. The missionaries made presents to Akbar of Western books, Christian paintings and engravings, as well as prints made in Japan. His court painters copied Christian paintings or borrowed subjects from them, and also depicted European subjects from life. [41] Through their study of Persian, the Jesuits gained some understanding of the great Persian literature. Jerome Xavier studied Persian for twenty years, wrote several works in that language on Christian topics, and compiled a Persian grammar.

The first major Asian culture the Portuguese missionaries encountered in the sixteenth century was India, but they were rather slow in taking to the study of its languages. They must have been baffled by the great variety of cultures and languages the subcontinent presented. The Franciscans, the earliest to start evangelizing on a significant scale, were particularly reluctant to embark upon the language study. They communicated through lay interpreters and only a few mastered an Indian language, a situation that persisted until about the end of the sixteenth century. The Jesuits took the linguistic problem head-on. It was official policy in the Society to stimulate linguistic study and those proficient in an Asian language could often look forward to a promotion. Although this may seem obvious to us living in the twentieth century, it was not in those days. It was usually not the leading figures in the Society who invested time and energy in the study of languages, but rather lay brothers and younger priests working in remote places. In 1560 Quadros, the Provincial of Goa, encouraged some younger members of the Society to study Konkani, and by releasing them from their other duties he created the adequate conditions for rapid progress. This was a practice continued by Valignano. Most, however, studied the local dialect only, which enable them to preach. Very few acquired a sufficient knowledge of the literary languages of India. But even in the local vernacular none became proficient enough to translate the Holy Scripture into any of the local tongues.[42] In spite of all the handicaps they faced, they managed to print a catechism in Tamil in 1578–79, while by the end of the century Jerome Xavier was composing Christian works in Persian. Copies of translations of European works into Asian languages were sent to Europe to impress the home constituency.

With no proficiency in any of the literary languages, especially Sanskrit, the missionaries had only a very superficial understanding of the central tradition of Hindu culture, a fact certainly not helped by the Brahmans' practice of keeping Sanskrit literature secret. Given these adverse conditions, it is quite understandable that we have to wait until the seventeenth century before a European, Robert de Nobili, mastered the holy language of India. Nevertheless, already during the sixteenth century an Indian convert learned in Brahmanical literature had stolen a number of manuscripts of a former friend, and brought them to Goa where he translated some of them into Portuguese. Thus, the Jesuits, albeit through devious means learned about the ten Avatars of Vishnu, and the literature in Marathi. A sizeable part of the

179

Bhagavadgîtâ was rendered in Portuguese, as was the Yogarâj Tilaka, a Marathi dialogue between a teacher and a pupil about philosophical questions. Manuscript copies of these translations were sent to Europe and have been preserved at Evora and Rome to the present day.[43]

However, the Jesuits showed little inclination to try to understand the thinking enshrined in these writings. They considered it rather irrational and derisory to attempt to do so. Even Valignano, who had such admiration for many elements in Japanese traditional culture, failed to perceive the intrinsic quality of Hindu thought and practice.[44] The complicated nature of Hindu thought, the Hindu pantheon populated by a countless variety of 'idols' and the numerous magical practices were all abomination to him. In Japan he found a more secularized culture and a more unified and regimented society. In general, Jesuits had a great predilection for unity, uniformity, and unified empires. This was understandable, since they wanted to evangelize through the ruler and the elite.[45]

9.7 The Jesuits in China at the end of the sixteenth century

The Portuguese established themselves in Macao in 1557. This port-city was the gateway through which the Jesuits sought entry into China, but they had to wait until 1583 before the first fathers could travel inland. The Italian Jesuit Ruggieri was sent to Macao in 1579 where he devoted himself to the study of Chinese. In the Jesuit Catalogue of 1581, Pedro Gomez makes a reference to him, saying that he is living in the Jesuit house at Macao where he has been exempted of all duties so that he can devote his time to the study of Chinese letters and language. He has been making much progress and, according to what he had been told, he had already mastered 12,000 Chinese characters of which there were in total about 80,000.[46] Ricci joined Ruggieri in Macao in 1582.[47] The next year both missionaries succeeded in gaining entry into China and established themselves in Zhaoqing. Ruggieri was sent back to Italy in 1588 and died in his home country, but Ricci was to spend the rest of his life in China. He studied Chinese, both the vernacular and the literary language, with singular ardour. Repeatedly we come across testimonies of his language proficiency, several from his own account. Even allowing for a measure of exaggeration, to all intents and purposes, his mastery of the language must have been extraordinary and exceptional. This is borne out by the fact that even quite a few Chinese literati whom he befriended or knew him concur with his own testimony. After one year of study, Ricci and Ruggieri, helped by their Chinese teachers, were able to publish the *Tianzhu shilu* (True Account of the Lord of Heaven), and to translate the Ten Commandments, Our Father and Hail Mary into Chinese. His progress was remarkable, for in a letter of 1584 addressed to his Superior in Rome, he claims to be able to hear confession and to preach in Chinese. The next year he reports to his Superior that he can speak to all Chinese without an interpreter and is able to read books fairly well. He made great strides in the study of the literary language as well. In 1591 he started a project of translating the Confucian *Four Books* into Latin and in a letter of 1593, ten years after his entry into China, he reported to his Superior that he had already completed the first three books, and that the fourth was in progress. The translation was finished in 1594 and he sent a copy to General Acquaviva in 1595. This was the first translation of Confucian texts into a European language.

Now he was ready to take a new step: writing his own compositions in Chinese. In a letter of 1594 to a fellow Jesuit, Girolamo Costa, in Siena, he writes: 'I wanted to see if I could begin to compose something [in Chinese], and I succeeded quite well. Every day, I have two lessons with my teacher and write something all by myself. I am encouraged that starting from now I will be able to write a book presenting our faith according to natural reason. It is to be distributed throughout China when printed.' The book he is referring to is *Tianzhu shiyi*, which he started work on in 1593 and, after a long interruption, finally saw through the press in 1603.[48]

Ten years after he had started his language training, Ricci was embarking upon a compilation of his own. This seemingly unimpeded and rapid progress is in stark contrast with the lament caused by the frustration the Jesuits were facing in the mastery of Japanese. The likely truth is that Ricci

181

was exceptional; he had an uncanny power of memory. After reading four or five hundred characters only once, he could recite them both forward and backwards without any difficulty. Sometimes he would give a demonstration of his unusual power of memory to the Chinese mandarins and literati in order to impress them, which he did not fail to do. All Chinese who witnessed his feat of memory were eager to acquire his uncanny skill. It could be of particular help to those aspiring to an official career, for the daunting hurdle of provincial and national examinations had to be taken to reach that goal, and in order to pass those examinations they had to commit whole volumes to memory. In his memoirs Ricci mentions his demonstration of mnemonics. He also states that by request he taught a few Chinese the art of memory 'but not without considerable difficulty'. He even explained it in a book he wrote in Chinese entitled *Xiguo jifa* (*The Art of Memory in the West*).[49] Apart from the occasional feat of prodigious memory, Ricci also left two works specifically on the Chinese language. The first one is entitled *Xizi qiji* (*The Miracle of Western Letters*), which he published in Beijing in 1605. It is a booklet of six folios, containing three short Biblical stories handwritten in Chinese characters by Ricci and accompanied by romanization.[50] He is also credited with the compilation of a Portuguese–Chinese dictionary. Already in the beginning of the Ming dynasty glossaries had been compiled such as the *Huayi yiyü* (Chinese Foreign Translated Words), a Chinese–Mongolian bilingual glossary completed in 1388. This and other bilingual glossaries that appeared during the Ming dynasty were arranged according to a limited number of semantic categories. Ricci's dictionary, however, was the first to feature an alphabetical arrangement. The manuscript was discovered in 1934: it contains besides the dictionary proper a number of shorter texts of a miscellaneous nature. One of them is a nine-page booklet containing a dialogue in romanization. It furthermore contains a list of Chinese characters representing Chinese initials and finals, a list of disyllabic antonymous words, a list of disyllabic synonymous words, a list of measure words or classifiers, a list of Portuguese words arranged alphabetically with Chinese equivalents, and so on. Some of these lists provided in all likelihood, part of the materials he used in his Chinese–Portuguese dictionary compiled in 1598.

The Portuguese–Chinese dictionary which bears no name of an author, title, nor date, is attributed to Ricci and Ruggieri, and must have been compiled when the two stayed in Zhaoqing, that is between 1583 and 1588. The body of the dictionary consists of three columns. The first column is the Portuguese entry written by a European hand, Ruggieri or Ricci. The words are arranged alphabetically. The second column is the romanization or phonetic transcription of Chinese characters, purportedly written by Ricci. The third column lists the Chinese character entries written by a Chinese hand, probably the teacher of Ricci. The Chinese entries contain words, phrases and short sentences, for the major part taken from the vernacular. This is a departure from the lexicographical practice of the day, since Chinese dictionaries carried only single character entries, taken from literary or classical Chinese. Ricci was also the author of a Chinese–Portuguese dictionary compiled in 1598, but it has not yet been located.[51]

The romanization system Ricci used in his Portuguese–Chinese dictionary is the first attempt made by him to transcribe Chinese monosyllables into roman letters. Ricci's final romanization system was later adopted with some modifications by Trigault in his romanized Chinese character dictionary *Xiru er-mu ci* (An Audio-visual aid for Western Scholars), published in Hangzhou in 1626.[52] It was intended as a study aid to learn pronunciation of individual characters.

Ricci succeeded in transforming himself into a Chinese literate. He was thus able to befriend many Chinese in high places, which laid the foundation for accommodation. The fruits of his efforts would be reaped in the seventeenth century. For now, his approach proved to be effective. The problem of accommodation continued to elicit strong resistance from the mendicant orders and would eventually erupt at the end of the seventeenth century. The Jesuits kept pressing for official vindication of their strategy by Rome, but never secured it. The problem continued to crop up: in 1667, for example, at a time when the Jesuits had fallen out of favour at the Chinese court and were languishing in their residence in Beijing under house-arrest, they discussed the matter of accommodation. Fr de Rougemont, who at that time was consultor to the vice-provincial, formulated an answer to a few of the questions his *confrères* in Beijing had put to him. He was very much in favour of using the Chinese language instead of Latin for several reasons. The Chinese authorities were suspicous of foreigners using a language that they could not understand. If the Chinese clergy were to use Latin, it might make them suspect in the eyes of the Chinese authorities who might think they were spies. Also, the mastery of Latin might lead the Chinese to reading heretical books although de Rougemont considered it next to impossible to teach Latin to the literati of mature age. The Chinese language lacks certain sounds that are used in Latin, making it hard for the Chinese to pronounce words correctly, and this also affects the validity of the sacraments.[53] Moreover, there were good social reasons for choosing Chinese rather than Latin because of the low esteem of anything foreign in the eyes of the literate classes. The fact that this is still being hotly debated proves that although Ricci had pushed accommodation as far as he possibly could, implementation remained hard, due to the lack of linguistic proficiency among the fathers.

China arguably presented the greatest challenge for the Christian gospel. If in India and Japan, the Catholic missionaries had been confronted with highly developed native religious traditions,[54] in China they had to vanquish another formidable obstacle. The Chinese prided themselves upon being the supreme civilization of the world and scorned all foreign learning and knowledge. Ethnocentrism was at the heart of Chinese civilization, and the Chinese were unable to see intercourse with foreigners in any other terms than that of the barbarian seeking to be imbued with the beneficent influence of Chinese civilization. In contrast to Indian culture where the transcendental dimension was pre-eminent, China's leading ideology, Confucianism put its top priority on the relationship between men, enjoining all humans to be social beings. With the ethical dimension having overriding importance, the Jesuits realized that the battle for the soul of the Chinese would be won or lost in the cultural field, rather than

184

in the purely religious one. Ricci's strategy was therefore first to become a literatus, and to beat the Chinese at their own game. He focused on arousing their interest in Western science, philosophy and technology. The strategy was designed to avoid questioning the central tenets of the Chinese cultural system, and proving the superiority of Western knowledge in peripheral areas such as technique, which were not held in high esteem by the learned elite. However, this exercise had a centripetal momentum, and sooner or later, they would have to address the central tenets and defy the very heart of Chinese culture.

China under the Ming was largely isolationist, in marked contrast with the preceding Mongol rulers, who had been very international for the standard of the times, if only by the sheer scope of their conquest. After a remarkable bout of sea expeditions under the command of the eunuch Zheng He, China had cut itself off the outside world. The empire did maintain official intercourse with the outside world in as much as neigbouring countries would from time to time send them tribute missions. Yet in spite of the Chinese feeling of superiority, there was a willingness on the Chinese side to be exposed to Western technical knowledge. This was especially true in the case of the science of the calendar, an essential part of Chinese statecraft. In China astronomers have also been under suspicion of plotting the overthrow of the dynasty. The Chinese calendar had to contain all kinds of symbolic figures; the calendar of a new dynasty had to be drawn up on the basis of certain figures that represented magical powers capable of influencing the fate of that dynasty. Well into modern times the idea prevailed that to elaborate a new calendar amounted to nothing less than an act of revolution, committed by someone who had his mind set on overthrowing the dynasty.[55] It was therefore a central activity of any emperor, and after some nativist backlashes, the calculation of the calendar was eventually entrusted to foreigners.

9.8 The Jesuits in Japan at the end of the sixteenth century

The mission in Japan started in 1549 with the arrival of Francis Xavier in Kagoshima. He thought highly of the

185

Japanese and considered them the best suited of all Asian peoples for conversion. Japan was to be the testing ground for the strategy of accommodation. Alessandro Valignano, the energetic and entrepreneurial Visitor, was keenly aware of the need to master the Japanese language if the mission were ever to succeed. After his initial optimism about the chances of doing so, he grew despondent: 'however much we learn of the language, and with however much effort, we still sound like children compared to them, and we never reach the stage of knowing all about their writing, and being able to write books ourselves'.[56]

Proficiency in reading and writing was a rare commodity. Luis Frois was undoubtedly one of the best informed about Japan. He was over thirty years old when he came to Japan in 1563. He had been in Asia since 1548. He claims to have conducted a theological dispute with the monk Nichijô in front of Oda Nobunaga in 1569.[57] Frois apparently made steady progress in his study of the language, for he acted as Valignano's interpreter when the latter met Oda Nobunaga in 1581.

The Visitor Francisco Vieira who visited Japan in 1618 considered Rodrigues one of the most able linguists the Jesuits ever produced.[58] He was only sixteen when he came to Japan, and had spent more than three years in the country before he became a Jesuit novice on Christmas eve of 1580.[59] In a letter of 1598 addressed to the General Aquaviva, Rodrigues claims to have been brought up amongst the Japanese from child-hood.[60] In addition, he was fortunate enough to receive be tutored by the brother Yôhô Paulo.[61] One report says he knew Japanese very well, another noted that he preached and wrote in Japanese.[62] When Valignano met Hideyoshi in 1591, Rodrigues was his interpreter. In November 1599 when Tokugawa Ieyasu wanted to send an embassy to the Philippines, Rodrigues was called upon to translate the official letters, composed in Chinese, into Spanish a few days before their sailing from Nagasaki.

More than once Valignano deplored the poor level of linguistic achievement of the European Jesuits. He therefore urged that Japanese should become members of the Jesuit Order. The Japanese were indispensable to bridging the linguistic gap, and 'all that has been done, has been done by some Japanese brothers that we have in the Society'.[63] Even the European fathers who were able to preach to the Christians in Japanese were reduced to silence when a Japanese brother, 'even an ignoramus' was present.[64] Japanese interpreters, recruited from among the *dôjuku* (novices) and brothers, assisted the fathers in many ways, including preaching and hearing confession. The fact was that, for all the efforts made, the Society was extremely dependent on a handful of Japanese brothers. The Japanese brother Yôhô Paulo was credited by Frois to have contributed a great deal to 'the making of the Japanese grammar and the comprehensive dictionary'.[65] He was a scholar of considerable standing and is said to have translated many lives of saints and 'other things from our authors' and to have been the author of the 'monogatari'.[66]

The best translator–interpreter of all may have been Hara Martinho, also known as Martinho del Campo.[67] He was one of the four Christian boys from noble Kyûshû families who were sent on a mission to Rome in 1582. When the embassy reached Goa in 1587 on its return voyage, Hara delivered a Latin eulogy of Valignano at the local Jesuit college. He was ordained a priest in 1608 and left Japan in 1614, exiled to Macao, where he died in 1629. In Macao he lived as a member of the Jesuit community, preaching and hearing confession.[68] In 1596 two Spanish Franciscan friars, newly arrived in Japan, met Jonishi Yukinaga, who had just returned from Korea with a Chinese embassy to Hideyoshi. At the meeting Hara acted as interpreter, and the language of communication was presumably Latin.[69] Hara was, however, a notable exception. In spite of the initial optimism of Valignano, only very few seem to have progressed very far. In 1592 Valignano writes that none of the Japanese Jesuits has an acceptable level of Latin, and that situation had not altered in 1601, the year when the first two Japanese–Catholic priests were ordained.[70] The study of Latin proved to be a formidable obstacle for the Japanese, and Bishop Pedro Martins as well as Valignano were struck by the reluctance with which they learned it. This impression stands in sharp contrast with some of the more optimistic assessments by Valignano made in earlier days when he was confident that the Japanese seminarians would make excellent students. He was so carried away that he wrote that 'the children learn to read and write in our language much more easily and in less time than our children in Europe'. Some other ecclesiastics too seem to have had spells of optimism, such as Pedro Gomez for example, who reports in his annual letter of 1593–94, that the students are now studying Latin much harder than before, and he ascribes this improvement to better teachers, the availability of printed books, and the prospect of ordination. Later on, Valignano repeatedly deplores the slow progress the Japanese made in the study of Latin.[71]

Not everyone embraced Valignano's strategy. Some were squarely opposed to Europeans studying a native language, considered it next to impossible anyway, and advocated the establishment of a school for Japanese interpreters. Valignano, however, urged that all newly arrived missionaries follow a two-year training in the Japanese language. By the end of 1581 the Funai college had compiled a Japanese grammar (*arte*), dictionary and catechism, presumably in manuscript form, for the Portuguese students. The grammar was compiled by Prenestino, on the pattern of a Latin grammar, although the compiler himself was not fluent in Japanese.[72]

This was not the first effort to compile a grammar and dictionary. Frois relates that as early as 1563–4 Brother João Fernandez had for seven or eight months worked on the compilation of a grammar of Japanese and Japanese–Portuguese and Portuguese–Japanese vocabularies which subsequently served as a basis for the published grammar and vocabulary.[73] Mexia relates that a grammar was made in 1580, while Coelho in the annual letter of 1582 informed the General that 'the grammar of the Japanese language has been finished this year, and a vocabulary and some treatises in the Japanese language have also been made'. The first linguistic text that was printed on the Jesuit press in Japan was Emmanuelis Alvari e Societate Iesu *De Institutione Grammatica Libri Tres*, a Latin grammar with some explanations in Japanese, printed at Amakusa in 1594.[74] The *Dictionarium Latino Lusitanicum ac Iaponicum*, Ex Ambrosii Calepini Volumine Depromptum, a Latin–Portuguese–Japanese dictionary was published in 1595 at Amakusa. It contained 908 pages and more than 20,000 entries. *Rakuyôshû* is a dictionary of *kanji*, printed on the mission press with metal type in 1598.[75] The *Vocabulario da Lingoa de Iapam* (Nagasaki, 1603) and its supplement (Nagasaki, 1604) is an impressive piece of scholarship. It contains about 32,798 entries from a very wide range of fields,[76] differentiates between Miyako area language and Kyûshû language, pays much attention to stylistic problems and to *Kun* and *On* yomi of the characters, and has many examples taken from literature and *mai*.[77]

Arte da Lingoa de Iapam took four years to be printed: it was started in 1604 and completed in 1608. The Arte consists of three parts, called 'livros', which deal respectively with conjugation, syntax and stylistic problems. It lists numerous examples from literature, in particular from the Jesuit editions of *Taiheiki*, *Heike Monogatari*, and quotations from *Kôwakamai* plays and religious texts by the Japanese brothers.[78] The author also displays a keen awareness of social stratification in Japanese society. He clearly distinguishes the performing arts that are enacted by outcasts (*hinin, kawaramono*) from the arts that enjoyed the patronage of the martial nobility. The great care for stylistics may be gathered from the chapter he devotes to modes of address, epistolary formulas and written requests. His explanation of the term *orikami* is the letter which is folded twice breadthwise. He notes that such a letter, when addressed to actors of *sarugaku*, *dengaku* or *maimai* dancers, only contains one leaf.[79] His linguistic analysis too is astute for his time and for someone who had not been specially trained as a linguist.[80]

During the period of national isolation policy, the Dutch were the only people who were theoretically in a position to learn Japanese, but only a small percentage actually did so. For one thing, the Bakufu made every effort to discourage them from learning the language. Carl Peter Thunberg (1743–1828), who stayed in Japan during the years 1775–76, deplored the lack of interest of the Dutch in the study of Japanese and compared them unfavourably with the Portuguese.[81] However, there were notable exceptions, such as, for instance, Hendrik Doeff, who could read and write Japanese,[82] but, if he could, it was largely due to coincidence. The Napoleonic Wars in Europe kept him a virtual prisoner for several years on the tiny island of Deshima. Since in principle the Dutch were not supposed to learn Japanese, it was incumbent upon the Japanese to make the effort. The memoirs and reports of the Dutch residents in Deshima give us an idea about the proficiency of the professional interpreters (*tsûji*). During the seventeenth century at least, they concentrated mainly on the spoken language, and had a very limited range of vocabulary. It was not until the eighteenth century that members of the intellectual and social elite started the study of Dutch as an academic pursuit. Aoki Konyô and Noro Genjô began studying the language at the behest of Shogun Yoshimune. It is not clear how well Konyô knew Dutch: purportedly about 700 words, according to other sources 400 words. Yoshimune's interest in Dutch started when he browsed through a few books (or one book) that were in the Bakufu library. He was surprised by the accuracy of the illustrations. Shogunal interest at once put the study of Dutch on another social footing. However, Aoki and Norô had no books and no teacher. The only possibility for them to learn the language was to seek contact with the Dutch when they were in Edo for their yearly audience with the Shogun. On these occasions they had to rely on the tsûji who accompanied the Dutch. Because the intellectual Rangakusha wrote their own history, they have tended to downplay the scholastic merits of the professional interpreters, and, overrated their own learning and knowledge. While in many instances their general assessment may have been correct, there are notable exceptions. A few have distinguished themselves, such as Imamura Gen'emon, the assistant of Engelbert Kaempfer.

The three kinds of encounter we have mentioned in the beginning of this chapter had by now been completely dissociated. Paradoxically enough, the severe constraints under which the intercourse was now put, did not prevent a considerable amount of knowledge from flowing into Japan, and this would serve the country well, when after more than two centuries it would open its gates again to the outside world.

9.9 The Age of Enlightenment

Thanks to their linguistic achievements, the Jesuits became privileged transmitters of European culture to Asia and vice versa. During the seventeenth and eighteenth centuries, European readers were treated to a stream of books on Asia. The *Lettres édifiantes et curieuses écrites des missions étrangères par quelques missionaires de la Compagnie de Jésus*, published in France in many editions, is one of the most popular and most representative of this kind of writing. The favourite topic in the Jesuit publications was China. Japan was closed to the outside world, while in the subcontinent and South-East Asia, Christianity was preceded by a firmly established Islam. Therefore they set all their hopes on China. Since these writings were meant to gain European support for the Jesuit cause in China, they tended to idealize their subject matter. These writings enhanced knowledge about Asia among European intellectuals. No doubt due to the rosy picture they drew of China, the Jesuits became the indirect cause of a fad for things Chinese that swept across Europe, most apparent in the field of the visual arts, giving rise to *chinoiserie*. The China boom had no less affect on European intellectual life. In their criticism of absolutism, the thinkers of the Enlightenment discovered ready ammunition in the descriptions of the statecraft and institutions of China, found in Jesuit writings, such as Du Halde's *Description géographique, historique, chronologique, politique et physique de la Chine et de la Tartarie chinoise* (Paris, 1735). As one author has rightly observed, *'Le renouvellement de la pensée à la lumière d'un esprit critique de plus en plus conscient et formé à l'analyse se serait fait, bien entendu sans la Chine. Mais on peut dire sans exagérer que la Chine a servi de pierre angulaire dans la bataille du modernisme et de la libre pensée.*[83] China was allegedly administered by philosophers in the light of moral principles. To the thinkers of the Enlightenment nothing came closer to the embodiment of their own ideal. Thus the Church as well as the enlightened thinkers found elements in China that fed and reinforced their own ideas. Moreover, with Japan being closed to the outside world, and South-East Asia divided in a mosaic of states, China also corresponded best to European

191

preconceptions about the unified state. At a time when Europe was in the process of forming unified states itself and saw the unification of the state as a sign of progress, China held special attractions.

Confrontation with Chinese historiography and its consistency forced Europe to question its own Bible-based chronology and vision of world-history. As Voltaire (1694–1778) put it: *'presque tous les terms, mais surtout ceux de l'Asie, comptent une suite de siècles qui nous effraie'*.[84] Europe had to accept that Asia was the cradle of civilizations that were older than its own. Enthusiasm among the Jesuits and those who adopted their cause led them to believe that Chinese Confucianism was a kind of profane version of Christianity. Chinese religion allegedly showed traces of a forgotten Christianity. Enlightened thinkers saw in it an example of a natural religion without dogmas, rites, or revelation, a pure expression of deism. In the exalted virtues of Confucianism, they found an argument that ethics could be dissociated from revealed religious truth, an idea particularly appealing to Voltaire.

In the eyes of the Europeans China was a unified, prosperous and culturally sophisticated society and they naturally sought for the reasons and causes of this success. Not unlike present-day commentators who try to explain Japan's economic success by reference to societal values and cultural traits, they sought the explanation in the spiritual and moral characteristics of Chinese society. The travellers' accounts of the sixteenth century usually stopped at outside appearances and wrote lavishly about the prosperity of China, but the Jesuit missionaries in their accounts endeavoured to probe into the causes of the prosperity and good administration which they perceived, and they concluded that these had to be attributed to Chinese statecraft which was based on the ethical tenets of Confucianism.[85] The empire was ruled by a virtuous monarch, assisted by a class of philosophers. Voltaire construed the class of philosophers as the embodiment of participatory government. In the Jesuits' image of China, politics was reduced to a question of morals. Although for motives that differed from those of the Jesuits, this idea was taken over by the deists and the *philosophes*. It became an example of religious toleration for those who criticized intolerance and autocratic rule, as it did for the physiocrats, who advocated the freedom of labour, freedom of the peasantry from feudal obligations and tax reforms. In his book *Voyages d'un philosophe ou observationssur les moeurs et les arts des peuples de l'Asie* (1768), Pierre Poivre described China as a prosperous agrarian nation, the paradigm of rational governance, the best governed country in the world, ruled by laws that were based on nature and the heart of man.[86] These ideas were taken over and popularized by the renowned physiocrat François Quesnay (1694–1774), who also praised the Chinese educational system. In England sinophiles advocated the adoption of the Chinese examination system.[87] In our view, the positive image China projected among the intellectuals of the seventeenth and eighteenth centuries may best be summarized in the attitude of one of the first sinophiles, Gottfried Wilhelm Leibniz (1646–1716). He proposed that Europe and China become each other's teacher and pupil. Just as Europe sends its missionaries to teach them the veritable theology, it seemed appropriate that China send to Europe 'political sages, who would teach us the art of governing and all that natural theology that they have brought to such high level of perfection'.[88]

There were, however, more critical voices to be heard, and they grew more influential as the eighteenth century drew to its close. But even during the heydays of sinology, some publicists had made sceptical statements about China. Eusèbe Renaudot and Fénélon (1651–1715) were less than impressed. The well-informed Montesquieu (1689–1755) discredited the Jesuits's portrayal of the Chinese emperor as an enlightened despot. In his view China was a despotic state based on terror, he believed that this was necessitated by the nature and the geography of the country. He commended the practice of the distribution of taxes to suffering provinces and admired the ceremony of the emperor drawing the first furrow I spring.[89] Even less mitigated were the judgements of Denis Diderot (1713–1784) and Jean-Jacques Rousseau (1712–18). For Diderot, China is the country where virtue is best known but least practised, where lies and fraud abound, and where the spirit is mean and selfish.[90] Rousseau believed civilization

193

to be the source of moral corruption. Since China was depicted as a highly civilized country governed by learned and wise men and regulated by laws and etiquette, it ought to be a free and honest nation. However, the truth was just the contrary. For all their wisdom and science the Chinese had been unable to avert the invasion and consequent subjugation of their country by the Tartars, while their civility did not prevent them from being hypocritical and devious. For him China proved only how advanced civilization corrupted the morals of man.[91]

Even though Rousseau scorned Chinese society and morals, he at least accepted that it had an advanced level of civilization. The industrial, social and political revolutions that changed the European societies, planted in the minds of the Europeans the concept of progress. In this view civilization was viewed as a unilinear scale running from the primitive to the advanced. It was used as a universal yardstick to gauge the level of development of each society and culture. Europe had progressed much farther on this scale than any other civilization. Asian cultures were no longer seen as having an excellence of their own, but as reflections of more primitive stages of development.[92] This idea gained wide acceptance and became the underlying assumption of authoritative analyses of history such as those made by Hegel, Comte and Spencer. But this is another story.

Notes

1 There is a vast literature on this topic alone. See e.g. Ernst Schulin, *Die weltgeschichtliche Erfassung des Orients bei Hegel und Ranke*, Veröffentlichungen des Max Planck Instituts für Geschichte 2 (Göttingen: Vandenhoeck und Ruprecht, 1958).

2 Joseph Needham *Science and Civilization in China* (Cambridge: Cambridge University Press, 1994).

3 Donald F. Lach, *Asia in the Making of Europe*. 5 vols. (Chicago and London: University of Chicago Press, 1977).

4 Henry Myers (ed.), *Western Views of China and the Far East*, Vol. 1, *Ancient to Early Modern Times*, Asian Studies Monograph Series (Hong Kong: Asian Research Service, 1982), 61.

5 Ibid. 69.

6 Lach, op. cit. i. 1, 22.

7 Myers (ed), op cit. i. 78.

8 Lach, op. cit. i. 24.; Myers (ed), op. cit. i. 25.
9 Lach, op.cit. i. 1. 32; Myers op. cit. i. 91–2.
10 See e.g. Christopher Dawson (ed)., *The Mongol Mission: Narratives and Letters of the Franciscan Missionaries in Mongolia and China in the Thirteenth and Fourteenth Centuries* (New York: Sheed and Ward, 1955).
11 Myers (ed).op. cit. i. 93.
12 Ibid. 98.
13 Nicholas Tarling (ed). *The Cambridge History of Southeast Asia,* Vol. 1, From Early Times to c.1800 (Cambridge: Cambridge University Press, 1992), 10; Lach, op. cit. i. 1. 37.
14 Lach, op. cit. i. 1. 42.
15 Ibid. i. 2. 748.
16 Ibid. i. 1. 335.
17 Ibid., 90 distinguishes three major channels that brought information about Asia to Europe: the spice trade, the printed word, and the Christian mission. However, since we are considering the encounter, use of the printed word as a separate category seems less useful.
18 Leonard Y. Andaya, 'Interactions with the Outside World and Adaptation in South-East Asian Society, 1500–1800', in *the Cambridge History of South-East Asia,* (ed).Tarling, vol. 1, *From Early Times to c.1800* (Cambridge: Cambridge University Press, 1992), 355.
19 Ibid. 361–2.
20 A.J. Stockwell, 'South-East Asia in War and Peace' in: Nicholas Tarling (ed). *The Cambridge History of South-East Asia,* Vol. 2, *The nineteenth and twentieth centuries* (Cambridge: Cambridge University Press, 1992), 356–7.
21 Leonard Y. Andaya, op. cit. 362.
22 Barbara ,Watson Andaya, 'Political Development between the Sixteenth and Eighteenth Centuries,' in The Cambridge History of South-East Asia, ed. Tarling, vol. 1, *From Early Times to c.1800* (Cambridge: Cambridge University Press, 1992), 414.
23 Ibid. 417.
24 Leonard Y. Andaya, op. cit. 346.
25 Barbara Watson Andaya, 'Religious Developments in South-East Asia, c. 1500–1800', in The Cambridge History of South-East Asia, ed. Nicholas Tarling, vol. 1, *From Early Times to c.1800* (Cambridge: Cambridge University Press, 1992), 547.
26 Barbara Watson Andaya, ibid. 412–13.
27 Victor Lieberman, *Burmese Administrative Cycles. Anarchy and Conquest, c. 1580–1760* (Princeton: Princeton University Press, 1984), 32–3.
28 Barbara Watson Andaya, ibid. 520.
29 Ibid. 517.
30 Barbara Watson Andaya, ibid. 433.
31 Ibid. 435.
32 Ibid. 445, 448.
33 Lach op. cit. i. 1.329.
34 Ibid. 314.
35 A known example is Wan Qiyuan (1635–1700) who travelled to Goa in the company of Prospero Intorcetta in 1669. He was known as Paulo Banhes

or Vanhes. He intended to travel to Europe to join the Society, but for some unknown reason he stayed in Goa. He later returned to China and was admitted into the Order in 1671. He was one of the three Chinese Jesuits ordained by Luo Wenzao in 1688. See Albert Chan, 'Towards a Chinese Church: the Contribution of Philippe Couplet S.J. (1622–1693)', in: *Philippe Couplet, S.J. The Man who Brought China to Europe*, (ed). J. Heyndrickx C.I.C.M., Monumenta Serica Monograph Series 22 (St. Augustin-Nettetal: Institut Monumenta Serica and Ferdinand Verbiest Foundation, 1990). 66.

36 Lach, op. cit. i. 1. 263.
37 Ibid.
38 Ibid. 263–4.
39 Ibid. 275.
40 Edward Maclagan, *The Jesuits and the Great Mogul* (London: Burns Oates & Washbourne, 1932) 24.
41 Lach op. cit. 276–8.
42 Ibid. 278–9.
43 Ibid. 280.
44 Ibid.
45 This explains Xavier's disappointment when he arrives in Miyako, the imperial capital of Japan, found anarchy, a powerless emperor and a Shogunate on the verge of collapse there. See Lach, op. cit. 284.
46 Josef F. Schütte S.J., (ed). *Monumenta Historica Japoniae I: Textus Catalogorum Japoniae, Monumenta Missionum Societatis Iesu* Vol. XXXIV, (Roma: Monumenta Historica Soc. Iesu, 1975), 116.
47 Jonathan Spence, The Memory Palace of Matteo Ricci, (London: Faber and Faber, 1985), 173.
48 See Paul Fu-mien Yang, SJ, 'The Portuguese–Chinese Dictionary of Matteo Ricci: A Historical and Linguistic Introduction,' in *The Proceedings of the Second International Conference on Sinology*. Section on Linguistics and Paleography (Taipei: Academia Sinica, 1989), 193–4.
49 Ibid. 196.
50 A copy of the original edition was discovered in 1983 in the Vatican Library. See Ibid. 202.
51 Ibid. 206–8.
52 Ibid. p. 202.
53 See Chan, op. cit. 65.
54 Lach, op. cit. i. 1. 302.
55 Irene Pih, Le Père G. de Magalhães. *Un Jesuite portugais en Chine au XVIIe siècle*, Cultura Medieval e Moderna 14, (Paris: Fundacão Calouste Gulbenkian, Centro cultural portugues, 1979), 181. Also Wolfram Eberhard, 'The Political Function of Astronomy and Astronomers in Han China', in: *Chinese Thought and Institutions*, (ed). John K. Fairbank (Chicago: University of Chicago Press, 1957), 65–6.
56 J.F. Moran, The Japanese and the Jesuits: Alessandro Valignano in sixteenth-century Japan (London and New York: Routledge, 1993), 179.
57 Matsuda Kiichi, Nanban shiryo no hakken, Chûkô shinsho 51 (Tokyo: Chûô kôronsha, 1964), 52, 67.

58 Michael Cooper, *Rodrigues the Interpreter* (New York and Tokyo: Weatherhill, 1974) 68.
59 Moran, op. cit. 181.
60 Ibid. 170.
61 Cooper op. cit. 68.
62 Ibid.
63 Alessandro Valignano, *Sumario de las Cosas de Japon* (1583) *Adiciones del Sumario de Japon* (1592) (1583), (ed). José L. Alvarez-Taladriz, Monumenta Nipponica Monographs 9 (Tokyo: Sophia University, 1954), 183.
64 Ibid. 199–200.
65 Luis Frois, *Historia de Japam*, 5 vols., ed. por José Wicki (Lisboa: Presidencia do Conselho de Ministros, Secretaria de Estado da Cultura, Direccao-Geral do Patrimonio Cultural, Biblioteca Nacional de Lisboa, 1976–1984), vol. 1, p. 172; Moran dismisses Wicki's assumption that Frois is referring to the printed Latin grammar of 1594 and the Latin–Portuguese–Japanese Dictionary of 1595, pointing out that for one thing, Frois is referring to a Japanese grammar, not a Latin one, and he further surmises that the dictionary he is referring to is the Vocabulario da Lingoa de Japam; neither of these works had been printed in Frois' or Yôhô Paulo's time; see Moran, op. cit. 223, n. 40.
66 Moran, op. cit. 86.
67 Matsuda Kiichi, op. cit. 74.
68 Moran op. cit. 19.
69 Ibid. 93, 187.
70 Ibid. 92, quoting Alessandro Valignano SJ, *Adiciones del Sumario de Japon* (1592), and id. *Libro primero del principio y progresso de la religion* (1601), ch. 7.
71 Moran, op. cit. 151, 162, 168.
72 Cooper, op. cit. 53, 59, 68.
73 Luis Frois, op. cit. I 357; 357; see also Moran, op. cit. 156.
74 Johannes Laures, Kirishitan Bunko: *A Manual of Books and Documents on the Early Christian Mission in Japan*, (3rd rev. and enl. edn). (Tokyo: Sophia University, 1985), 16 and 50; see also Cooper, op. cit. 221, 226.
75 Ibid. 58–60.
76 Cooper, op. cit. 222.
77 Thomas F. Leims, *Die Entstehung des Kabuki: Transkulturation Europa-Japan im 16. und 17. Jahrhundert*, Brill's Japanese Studies Library vol. 2 (Leiden E.J. brill, 1990). 20.
78 Ibid. 211.
79 Ibid. 213.
80 Engelbert Jorissen, '16–17 seiki ni okeru yôroppa-jin to nihongo', Biburia 102 (October 1994), 169.
81 Frits Vos, 'Mihatenu yume-An Unfinished Dream: Japanese Studies until 1940,' In Leiden Oriental Connections 1850–1940, (ed) Willem Otterspeer (Leiden, New York, Kobenhavn, Köln, E.J. Brill, 1989) 359.
82 Ibid. 360–1.
83 Danielle Elisseeff-Poisle, Nicolas Fréret, reflexions du'un humaniste du XVIII e siècle sur la Chine, (Paris, 1978), 21.

84 In the Introduction to his Essai sur les moeurs et l'esprit des nations. See Oeuvres complètes de Voltaire (Paris: Bacquenois, 1835). iii. 5.
85 Raymond Dawson, *The Chinese Chameleon. An Analysis of European Conceptions of Chinese Civilization* (Oxford University Press, 1967) 35.
86 Ibid. 55.
87 Ibid. p. 61.
88 My translation from the text in: Virgile Pinot, *La Chine et la formation de l'esprit philosophique en France (1640–1740)* (1932; reprint, Geneva: Slatkine Reprints, 1971) 335–6.
89 Montesquieu, Charles de Secondat, baron de, *L'Esprit des lois, avec les notes de l'auteur et un choix des observations de Dupin, Crevier, Voltaire, Mably, La Harpe, Servan*, etc. (Paris: Firmin Didot Frères, 1862), 106.
90 Basil Guy, *The French Image of China before and after Voltaire, Studies on Voltaire and the eighteenth century* 21 (Geneva: Publications de l'Institut et Musée Voltaire, 1964) 333.
91 Jean-Jacques Rousseau, *Julie ou la Nouvelle Héloise* (Paris: 1967), 309; also Myers ed., op. cit. i.
92 Dawson op. cit. 74.

References

Andaya, Leonard Y. (1992) 'Interactions with the Outside World and Adaptation in South-East Asian Society, 1500–1800 *The Cambridge History of South-East Asia* (ed) Tarling, Vol 1. (Cambridge University Press).

Cooper, (Michael 1974) *Rodrigues the Interpreter* (New York and Tokyo: Weatherhill).

Dawson, Christopher (ed). (1955) *The Mongol Mission: Narratives and Letters of the Francisvan Missionaries in Mongolia and China in the Thirteenth and Fourteenth Centuries* (New York: Sheed and Ward).

Dawson, Raymond (1967) *The Chinese Chameleon. An Analysis of European Conceptions of Chinese Civilization* (Oxford University Press).

Eberhard, Wolfram (1957) 'The Political Function of Astronomy and Astronomers in Han China, in: *Chinese Thought and Institutions*, (ed). John K. Fairbank (Chicago: University of Chicago Press).

Elisseeff-Poisle, Danielle/Fréret (1978) Nicolas reflexions d'un humaniste du XVIII e siècle sur la Chine, (Paris).

Frois, Luis *Historia de Japam*, (ed) (1976–1984). 5 vols por José Wicki (Lisboa: Presidencia do Conselho de Ministros, Secretaria de Estado da Cultura, Direccao-Geral do Patrimonio Cultural, Biblioteca Nacional de Lisboa).

Guy, Basil (1963) *The French Image of China before and after Voltaire, Studies on Voltaire and the eighteenth century* 21 (Geneva: Publications de l'Institut et Musée Voltaire).

Jorissen, Engelbert (October 1994) '16–17 Seiki ni okeru yôroppa-jin to nihongo', Biburia 102.

Lach, Donald F. (1977) *Asia in the Making of Europe*, 5 vols. (Chicago and London: University of Chicago Press).

Laures, Johannes/Bunko, Kirishitan (1985): *A Manual of Books and Documents on the Early Christian Mission in Japan* (Tokyo: Sophia University).

Leims, Thomas F. (1990) *Die Entstehung des Kabuki: Transkulturation Europa-Japan im 16. und 17. Jahrhundert*, Brill's Japanese Studies Library vol. 2 (Leiden: E.J. Brill).

Le Père G. de Magalhães, Irene Pih. (1079) *Un Jesuite portugais en Chine au XVIIe siècle*, Cultura Medieval e Moderna 14, (Paris: Fundacão Calouste Gulbenkian, Centro cultural portugues).

Lieberman, Victor (1984) *Burmese Administrative Cycles, Anarchy and Conquest. c. 1580–1760.* (Princeton University Press).

Maclagen, Edward (1932) *The Jesuits and the Great Mogul* (London; Burns Oates & Washbourne).

Moran, J.F. (1993) The Japanese and the Jesuits: Alessandro Valignano in sixteenth-century Japan (London and New York: Routledge).

Montesquieu, Charles de Secondat, baron de (1862) *L'Esprit des lois, avec les notes de l'auteur et un choix des observations de Dupin, Crevier, Voltaire, Mably, La Harpe, Servan, etc.* (Paris: Firmin Didot frères).

Myers, Henry (ed) (1982) *Western Views of China and the Far East, vol. 1* Asian Studies Monograph Series (Hong Kong: Asian Research Service).

—— *Ancient to Early Modern Times* (1982) *Western Views of Chine and the Far East, vol. 1* Asian Studies Monograph Series (Hong Kong: Asian Research Service).

Needham, Joseph (1994) *Science and Civilisation in China* (Cambridge: Cambridge University Press).

Pinot, Virgile (1971) *La Chine et la formation de l'esprit philosophique en France (1640–1740)* (1932; reprint, Geneva: Slatkine Reprints).

Rousseau, Jean-Jacques (1967) *Julie ou la Nouvelle Héloise* (Paris:).

Schulin, Ernst (1958) *Die weltgeschichtlicheErfassung des Orients bei Hegel und Ranke* (Göttingen: Vandenhoeck und Ruprecht).

Schütte, Josef. F (ed) (1975) *Monumenta Historica Japoniae I: Textus Catalogorum Japoniae, Monumenta Missionum Societatis Iesu Vol. XXXIV* (Roma: Monmenta Historica Soc. Iesu).

Spence, Jonathan (1989) *The memory Palace of Matteo Ricci* (London: Faber and Faber).

Stockwell, A.J. (1992) 'South-East Asia, Vol. 2 *The Cambridge History of South-East Asia* (ed) Tarling. Vol. 2. (Cambridge University Press).

Tarling, Nicholas (ed) (1992) *The Cambridge History of Southeast Asia* Vol. 1 Early Times to c. 1800 (Cambridge University Press).

Watson Andaya, Barbara 'Political Development between the Sixteenth and Eighteenth Centuries' *The Cambridge History of South-East Asia* (ed) Tarling, Vol. 1. (Cambridge University Press).

—— 'Religious developments in South-East Asia c. 1500–1800. Centuries' *The Cambridge History of South-East Asia* (ed) Tarling, Vol. 1. (Cambridge University Press).

Valignano, Alessandro (1954) *Sumario de las Cosas de Japon* (1583) *Adiciones del Sumario de Japon* (1592) (1583), (ed). José L. Alvarez-Taladriz, Monumenta Nipponica Monographs 9 (Tokyo: Sophia University).

Vos, Frits 'Mihatenu yume-An Unfinished Dream: Japanese Studies until 1940,' Leiden Oriental Connections 1850–1940, (ed) Willem Otterspeer (Leiden, New York, Kobenhavn, Köln: E.J. Brill, 1989).

Yang, Paul Fu-mien (1989) 'The Portuguese-Chinese Dictionary of Matteo Ricci: A Historical and Linguistic Introduction' *The Proceeding of the Second International Conference on Sinology*. (Taipei: Academia Sinica).

200

Index

For Product Safety Concerns and Information please contact our EU
representative GPSR@taylorandfrancis.com
Taylor & Francis Verlag GmbH, Kaufingerstraße 24, 80331 München, Germany